Real and Imagined Readers

Real and Imagined Readers
Censorship, Publishing and Reading under Apartheid

Rachel Matteau Matsha

UNIVERSITY OF KWAZULU-NATAL PRESS

Published in 2018 by University of KwaZulu-Natal Press
Private Bag X01
Scottsville, 3209
Pietermaritzburg
South Africa
Email: books@ukzn.ac.za
Website: www.ukznpress.co.za

© 2018 Rachel Matteau Matsha

All rights reserved. No part of this publication may be reproduced or transmitted in any form or by any means, electronic or mechanical, including photocopying, recording, or any information storage and retrieval system, without prior permission in writing from University of KwaZulu-Natal Press.

ISBN: 978 1 86914 402 9
e-ISBN: 978 1 86914 403 6

Managing editor: Sally Hines
Editor: Alison Lockhart
Layout: Patricia Comrie
Indexer: Christopher Merrett
Cover design: Marise Bauer, MDesign
Cover images: Various covers of banned literature during apartheid

Print administration by DJE Flexible Print Solutions

This book is dedicated to the memory of my father,
Marcel Matteau.

Contents

Images appear between pages 95 and 96

Foreword by Isabel Hofmeyr	ix
Acknowledgements	xiii
Abbreviations	xv
1 Introduction	1
2 Censorship in Apartheid South Africa	9
3 Censorship versus Publishers, Librarians and Booksellers	53
4 Readers' Roles in the World of Books	96
5 Imagined Readers in the Censors' Reports	146
6 Conclusion	207
Select Bibliography	212
Index	219

Foreword

The question of readers and reading has always carried a political charge in South Africa. One does not have to go far to find accusations that the country lacks a reading culture and that South Africans do not read. This colonial chestnut has been around for a long time and has its roots in imperial ideas of the book as a symbol of English authority, but also a 'gift' to help 'civilise' colonised subjects. These subjects could supposedly never possess the book in the same way as those who had brought it and to whom it apparently 'belonged'.

These ideas persist into the present, apparent among those who can only understand a reading culture as what white middle-class folks do. Any other modes of book consumption do not seem to count as reading. Over the last few years, a range of scholars have started to revise this picture.

Archie Dick's *The Hidden History of South Africa's Book and Reading Cultures* (2013) documents common readers excluded by racist structures, actively or passively prevented from reading, but managing to read nonetheless. It presents a rich cast of characters – slaves, soldiers, political prisoners, township activists, political exiles – and the various ingenious ways in which they managed to read against the odds.

More recently, Caroline Davis and David Johnson's *The Book in Africa: Critical Debates* (2015) decolonises the older colonially shaped accounts of books and reading in Africa, which focus mainly on Christian mission presses and overlook the pre-colonial Muslim traditions of manuscript book production.

There is, in addition, a rich and growing tradition of work on southern African book history that examines the varied ways in which people have produced, disseminated and read various forms of print culture, whether newspapers, pamphlets, novels or manifestos (Sandwith 2014; Van der Vlies 2012).

Rachel Matteau Matsha's work makes an exciting intervention into this field. By examining questions of reading and readers under apartheid, she opens up new vistas, providing insight into the vibrant and inventive ways in which people under apartheid read against the odds.

Matteau Matsha examines different dimensions of the literary systems under apartheid: censors, publishers, librarians, readers. She outlines the workings of the censorship machine and the notions of readers and reading that animated its officials and bureaucrats. She describes the official publishing and library system in South Africa, committed to creating and extending racial segregation.

Yet, however powerful these institutions, they could not succeed in keeping inventive readers away from banned books. Matteau Matsha outlines the workings of an alternative literary circuit created by anti-apartheid writers, small independent publishers and devoted readers.

Together, these people created inventive means of publishing, distribution and reading. Publishers printed contentious books and then rushed them out to subscribers before they were banned. A few dissident librarians made banned books available to trusted associates. Banned material was photocopied and passed among comrades and was also debated in small reading and discussion groups. As Matteau Matsha notes: 'Relations of trust and connivance grew between the various spheres of the alternative literary circuit, as oppositional writers, readers, publishers, booksellers and librarians worked in close collaboration to get books read and shared by the largest possible number of readers. However, they did not always meet in person.'

Matteau Matsha's work draws on interviews with readers and so we get a graphic sense of what people read, how they acquired banned books and where they hid them: 'Banned books could also be hidden in yards and ceilings or even burned once read . . . Another hiding place cited was a box hidden in a dog's kennel.'

These encounters with banned books made powerful impressions on readers. Matteau Matsha quotes Njabulo Ndebele's recollection of discovering a box of banned books in his parents' garage:

> On top of [the box] was a heavy layer of unused floor tiles; old copies of *Huisgenoot*, *Zonk*, and *Drum* magazines [. . .] Once I had removed everything from the top of the box, I opened it. Inside, were many books on music, art, and poetry, and others that I thought my father must have used for his degree studies at the University of the Witwatersrand. But as I got closer to the bottom of the box, my heart leaped with disbelief! Here was *Down Second Avenue* by Ezekiel Mphahlele; and *Road to Ghana* by Alfred Hutchinson; and *Blame me on History* by Bloke Modisane; and *Naught for your Comfort* by Trevor Huddleston; and *Tell Freedom* by Peter Abrahams; and *Splendid Sunday* by James Ambrose Brown; and *Transvaal Episode* by Harry Bloom; *Chocolates for my Wife* by Todd Matshikiza; *South Africa: The Struggle for a Birthright* by Mary Benson; *The Ochre People* by Noni Javabu; *Ghana: The Autobiography of Kwame Nkrumah*; *Let my People Go* by Albert Luthuli; *Go Well, Stay Well* by Hannah Stanton, copies of *Africa South* magazine, and other lesser known books that I do not remember now. Banned books!

Matteau Matsha's work makes visible a particular mode of passionate political reading under apartheid – in trade unions, university residences, community groups, debating and discussion groups, people read material deeply, closely and carefully.

In these clandestine settings, books became common property. They resembled the *samizdat* (self-published) literature in the Soviet Union, a widespread system of underground publishing generally produced on typewriters with carbon paper and passed from hand to hand.

In such contexts of oppression, appropriating books for political ends made sense. Indeed, this attitude was widespread in radical circles. The famous American anarchist Abbie Hoffman produced a volume entitled *Steal This Book*.

By analysing the workings of a radical reading culture in South Africa, Matteau Matsha not only opens up a new chapter in southern African literary history, she also offers a case study that invites comparison with other radical reading formations elsewhere in the world.

Isabel Hofmeyr
Department of African Literature, University of the Witwatersrand
Department of English, New York University

Acknowledgements

It takes many readers to create a book and this one is no exception. Various people and institutions have supported me during this journey. While I assume full responsibility for the content and for possible errors, I would like to acknowledge the contribution of those who made this book possible.

First, I would like to express my most profound gratitude to Isabel Hofmeyr, for sharing her vast knowledge of book history while I was her student at the University of the Witwatersrand, and for writing the foreword to this book. She continues to inspire me as I pursue my academic journey. Thank you to Archie Dick for his feedback and support, and to Peter D. McDonald, who first suggested the title *Real and Imagined Readers* and who provided invaluable comments on earlier versions of the manuscript. Thank you to Corinne Sandwith and Christine Stilwell, as well as to the anonymous reviewers and critical readers for their frank and constructive comments. I would also like to acknowledge Lindy Stiebel and Monique Marks, who both encouraged me to take the first steps towards embarking on this project.

I would like to express my gratitude to friends and interviewees for kindly sharing their memories and experiences. Sincere thanks to the late Dennis Brutus and Chris van Wyk, and to Gerhard Maré, Christopher Merrett and Jewel Koopman, who all generously shared their knowledge and experiences, either in person and/or through correspondence, as well as to the other people I interviewed who wished to remain anonymous.

Many thanks to my first readers, Chrystal Rosenberg and Ashley Gresh, for their insightful comments, suggestions and hearty encouragements. Thank you to Deanne Collins for her careful proofreading of the revised manuscript. Some archival documents were originally in Afrikaans and I would like to thank Allison Broster for the translations.

I would also like to thank the team at UKZN Press – Alison Lockhart, Debra Primo, Kholeka Mabeta, Marise Bauer and Sally Hines, among others – who made this process a stressfree and pleasant one. I acknowledge the institutional support offered by the Durban University of Technology towards the completion of this book.

Thank you to Kevin Hendrikse, and to Zola, Dali and Mandla Matsha, who each in their own ways kept me going during the lengthy process of writing and rewriting this book.

Finally, I acknowledge my immense debt to my mother and father, who taught me a love of books and reading. *Merci*!

Abbreviations

ANC	African National Congress
APB	Afrikaanse Pers-Boekhandel
BC	black consciousness
BCM	Black Consciousness Movement
BCP	Black Community Programmes
CNA	Central News Agency
CPSA	Communist Party of South Africa
LIWO	Library and Information Workers' Organisation
NASA	National Archives of South Africa
Naspers	Nasionale Pers
NEUF	Non-European United Front
NEUM	Non-European Unity Movement
NP	National Party
NPU	Newspaper Press Union
NUSAS	National Union of South African Students
OUP	Oxford University Press
PAB	Publications Appeal Board
Perskor	Perskorporasie van Suid-Afrika
SABC	South African Broadcasting Corporation
SACC	South African Council of Churches
SACP	South African Communist Party
SAIRR	South African Institute of Race Relations

SALA	South African Library Association
SASO	South African Students' Organisation
SPRO-CAS	Study Project on Christianity in Apartheid Society

1 | Introduction

> In Africa, when an old person dies, a library burns.
> — Amadou Hampaté Ba

READING IS AN ELUSIVE activity, not easily defined or understood.[1] Book historians have long explored reading through various lenses, as pointed out by book historian Robert Darnton (2002: 20): 'Despite considerable literature on its psychology, phenomenology, textology, and sociology, reading remains mysterious. How do readers make sense of the signs on the printed page? What are the social effects of that experience? And how has it varied?'

This book seeks to interrogate and nuance the widespread assumption that South Africa lacks a reading culture, based on the premise that reading is indeed a complex activity that can take various shapes and forms. While this book does not advocate for an exaggeration and generalisation of reading in South Africa, it focuses on a specific reading culture in South Africa – namely, a modest yet powerful politicised reading culture that

---

1. Several international and South African book historians have studied reading and ordinary readers, pointing to the fact that reading has often been misrepresented and largely remains unknown. See Chartier (1989, 2002a, 2002b); Darnton (1982, 2002); Dick (2004a, 2004b, 2006, 2007a, 2007b, 2013); Hofmeyr (1985, 1993, 1996, 2001, 2004, 2005); Hofmeyr and Kriel (2006); Leach, Verbeek and Stilwell (1994); Lyons and Taksa (1992); Mashishi (2000); Newell (2002a, 2002b); Radway (1984); Rose (2001); and Thale (1995), among others.

evolved in the shadow of apartheid censorship. This particular reading culture did not exist in a vacuum and formed part of a greater reading continuum that spans from the colonial period into post-apartheid South Africa and coexisted with other reading cultures. A probe into reading during the apartheid period reveals the existence of varying definitions of literature, reading and literacy, which foregrounds the need to rethink narrowly defined notions of readers and reading. While relatively few in number, readers of banned books played an important role in cultural, social and political affairs in apartheid South Africa. This critical readership impacted on contemporary reading practices in South Africa, informing a sense of literary, cultural and political activism and it had an influence well beyond the world of books. Indeed, the political struggle and cultural struggle have often intermingled since the early twentieth century (Sandwith 2014).

This book inscribes itself in the book history scholarship, which provides a space and the tools to reaffirm the importance and complexity of ordinary readers in broader literary history, which has long been whitewashed by colonial tenets. Issues relating to the world of books are thus examined, with a strong emphasis on progressive readers, focusing on the social context of reading (Darnton 2002: 21). By socialising texts and embracing literary and political activism, some progressive readers informed the sets of social relations and dynamics developed with regard to banned books. As interconnected activities, literature, books and reading formed part of a broader system of communication that involved writers, publishers, booksellers, librarians and, importantly, readers (Darnton 2002). Censors intruded on the book system and created an exclusive and elitist space, where notions such as literariness and literary merit were debated, effectively construing literary canons and definitions of readers aligned to specific politics and understandings of literature, often underpinned by conservative and purist moral concerns and blatant racism. Through this unusual shared space, readers and censors conversed in an esoteric manner, as censors imagined a series of readers' profiles and speculated on the effects of texts on these readers. This book seeks to uncover the actual effects of these banned books on progressive readers, as far as reading habits can be ascertained, and relying on memory and recollection of the past, with all the epistemological implications this may have.

The world of books is closely connected to freedom of speech, and to the circulation of ideas and knowledge, and therefore it is a politically charged space. As opposed to censored reading, a free and diverse world of books provides a space where contested cultural, political and ideological views are articulated and debated. From the highest levels of governance and bureaucracy to the everyday life of ordinary people, censorship in South Africa sought to curb freedom of speech, circulation, movement and association, and access to information, knowledge and ideas. This book explores how apartheid censorship prejudiced the world of books in South Africa, with a focus on how some progressive readers creatively asserted their political agency in the literary space, using literacy as a political tool for raising consciousness.

By focusing on the readership of banned books during apartheid (1948 to the early 1990s), this book looks at the use of banned literature in alternative book networks, despite the ever-looming censorship apparatus. It focuses on a reader-centric understanding of the impacts of apartheid censorship and legislations on the cultural domain and, more specifically, on the responses they generated in the literary sphere. By focusing on the roles of readers in the alternative book system, the sometimes unusual modalities of sourcing, distributing, reading and sharing performed by committed readers, writers, publishers, librarians and booksellers are highlighted. Beyond focusing on the fact that some readers did read banned books, despite the climate of surveillance and censorship, it shows that these readers were inventive in the ways they accessed and shared books among the largest number of readers possible, using texts in resourceful ways and at times assuming the role of other actors in the book system.

Alternative reading spaces, also considered oppositional and independent, turned reading into an 'activity, the construal of meaning within a system of communication, rather than a canon of texts' (Darnton

2002: 21). In alignment with this definition, reading is understood as an activity embedded in a fluctuating social and political context, in this case in the context of apartheid hegemony. The entity 'readership' is understood as being inclusive, the act of reading extending beyond the primary reader of a text to also include a collective mediation of meaning. Oral networks extended the dissemination of ideas and knowledge contained in books beyond primary readers, opening the space created by books to other readers. In such a context, the precarious line between orality and literacy is blurred and challenged (Ong 1982). Likewise, reading is broadened to include oral discussions of books, which more often than not led to further reading and writing. Through this comprehensive understanding of reading, the nature of 'literature', 'book', 'readership' and 'reading' is redefined. Triangular relations between books, texts and readers are reconfigured and understood in light of their transformative power, emphasising the 'connection between the readable space and the socialisation of the texts' (Chartier 2002a: 51). Books and texts drifted between literary, political and social spaces, informing a culture of committed reading that emerged from these interactions between the literary and the political, and among readers, books and texts.

By rethinking the book system through a reader-centric perspective and in conditions of censorship, some traditional definitions applying to the world of book are probed and subverted. The term 'book' is used in its broad sense to include printed reading material, such as novels, poetry, short stories, newsletters and journals, among others. While defined narrowly by censors as exclusively designating so-called serious literature, in the context of this analysis 'literature' is inclusive and extended to various forms of written texts, including fiction, educational, creative and critical writing. 'Reading' designates reading from a written text, but is also extended to mediated interpretations of texts through oral dissemination by primary readers, where ideas expressed through oral language codes are processed and interpreted by what are termed 'secondary readers'.

The use of 'black', 'white', 'coloured' and 'Indian' to designate South African peoples, writers, readers or readerships is confined to the categories adopted during the apartheid era and used by censors and is employed for purposes of clarity in the context of the historical period on which this book focuses – apartheid South Africa.

Overview

Chapter 2 addresses the development of state censorship in South Africa. Following an overview of censorship from colonial times to publications control and censorship legislation enacted during the apartheid era – more specifically the Suppression of Communism Act No. 44 of 1950, the Publications and Entertainments Act No. 26 of 1963, the Publications Act No. 42 of 1974 and the Publications Amendment Act No. 109 of 1978 – the ideas of readers and literature construed in each Act are discussed. Through an examination of the changing definitions of readers elaborated by successive censorship boards, the workings and ideologies of the censorship bureaucracy are linked to the literary considerations articulated by censors, linking their discourse to that of the various actors in the field of the book. A reader-centric analytical lens to examine the censorship discourse makes explicit the ways in which censors imagined readers and reading, participating in broader and competing definitions of readerships, reading and literature. The ways in which these definitions underpinned efforts to promote specific reading practices and canons of texts, from colonial days to post-apartheid South Africa, thus come to light.

The third chapter explores the alternative literary industry that developed alongside the mainstream one and the effects of censorship on the book trade. Following a succinct overview of mainstream publishers in South Africa, highlighting the ways in which some publishers were in fact extensions of the censorship system, a detailed account of several alternative publishers in relation to the strand of anti-apartheid resistance that emerged sets the broader context in which alternative readers interacted. The links between the various stakeholders in the literary industry are discussed, with specific emphasis on censors and readers, shedding light on the dynamics of competing publishing interests during the apartheid period. The analysis of the strategies adopted by alternative publishers to counter censorship highlights the effects of censorship on progressive booksellers, librarians, publishers and readers. This chapter reveals the cracks that appeared within the mainstream publishing and book industries, leading to an alternative order, where progressive readers interacted with oppositional publishers, booksellers, writers and librarians to create independent creative and socio-political spaces.

Chapter 4 provides a detailed account of the workings of the alternative book industry from the point of view of readers. This chapter focuses on how, when, why and where alternative readers read and exchanged banned books and on alternative literary networks and the formation of reading communities in the shadows of censorship. It discusses the ways in which banned literature was an integral part of the diverse anti-apartheid movements and strands of activism, made possible through the reading strategies adopted by readers. The active role of readers in independent literary networks is discussed in the light of their involvement in the life cycle of books and examines 'the world behind the books' (Darnton 1982: ix). Reading, writing and publishing became an integral part of oppositional and alternative politics. Radical reading practices emerged alongside and informed political resistance and committed readers used committed literature to suit their particular interests. Communities of readers espousing different – though at times similar – ideologies converged in various literary, political and social spaces. In some ways, they provided a sense of continuity in an otherwise fractured South African literary history, in great part as a result of the silencing of writers caused by censorship in the 1950s and 1960s, a period referred to as the 'Great Gap'.

The fifth chapter examines the changing definitions of readers as developed and imagined in selected censors' reports, focusing on sets of reports on Es'kia Mphahlele's *Down Second Avenue*, selected poetry of Dennis Brutus and Ravan Press's *Staffrider* magazine and series. In analysing the censors' close readings of submitted publications, the practical application of censorship and the underlying ideologies and literary notions covered in the previous chapters, this chapter highlights the ways in which socio-political considerations interacted with literary concepts to create a complex and intricate literary discourse, influenced by politics, the socio-political environment and alternative readers. Conversely, it examines how literature and books influenced politics and society and how the world of books extended to the everyday life and activism of ordinary readers. These reports at times read like literary essays and form part of a broader discourse that informed South African literary criticism. The censors' take on the mutual influence between politics and literature at times unexpectedly resonates with similar views within the academic and even oppositional literary spaces, punctuating the debates on the function of literature in society.

Real and imagined readers are thus understood in the light of their actual or assumed roles in the world of books, both alternative and mainstream. This book is based on theories drawn from the history of the book, the sociology of literature, South African literary history and on data from secondary and primary sources, such as archival material and interviews with and testimonies from readers, writers and publishers. It is also influenced by historiographies of reading, which draw from archival material, authentic publications, such as journals and newsletters, semi-structured interviews with some librarians, writers and publishers and ordinary readers (some of whom requested anonymity) and secondary sources such as autobiographies, memoirs and literary studies. This collection of information from official and unofficial, and written and oral sources, speaks to the lack of a definite authority on the history of reading in apartheid South Africa. Writer and literary critic Lewis Nkosi points to the importance of autobiographies to retrieve knowledge on South African social history: 'However stylistically flawed they may seem, collectively these narratives, so incurably inflected with the voice of actual "lived" experience, constitute the most significant source of knowledge we have regarding the feel and texture of black life in South Africa' (2016a: 257).

Using these sources of information – some of which were classified and/or banned during apartheid – to retrieve a period of South African literary history, this book seeks to shed light on a perhaps lesser known aspect of South African book history, where the assumed silence imposed by censorship on the literary industry was in fact challenged and broken by oppositional writers, publishers, booksellers, librarians and readers, who conversed in and out of the literary space in order to make sense of – and change – the course of a much broader social and political order.

2 | Censorship in Apartheid South Africa

> The greater the visible order, the greater the hidden disorder.
> — Ben Okri, *A Way of Being Free*

THIS CHAPTER IS underpinned by the assumption that censors and readers entered some kind of dialogue, articulating ideas of art and literariness in unique ways. Perhaps unexpectedly, readers and censors were closely linked to one another, as noted by J.M. Coetzee (1996). This chapter highlights the implications of censorship legislation in the sociocultural sphere from a reader-centric perspective, providing an overview of the changing legislation, while highlighting how the censorship apparatus produced fluctuating definitions of the reader. South African censorship had profound consequences far beyond the field of literature, impacting on the political, social and cultural fields, and it altered cultural production and readership formations. While operating under moralistic pretences, censorship in apartheid South Africa was used as a political tool to silence opposing voices. The workings of the censorship system were shielded in secrecy, creating a general climate of fear. Writing on censorship was itself a risky endeavour and it comes as no surprise that most works addressing this issue in South Africa were published from the 1980s onwards, when censorship legislation started to undergo reform.

Lifting the secrecy on censorship
The broader conversation on South African censorship includes a publication produced by the Institute for Race Relations entitled

Censorship (Coggin 1983), which contains five critical essays on censorship by André Brink, Allan Boesak, Ian McDonald, André du Toit and Johan van der Vyver. Each focuses on a particular aspect of censorship, such as public morals, politics, literature and law. In 1984, Louise Silver published *A Guide to Political Censorship in South Africa*, focusing on the legislation and legal perspective. This was followed by a detailed account by J.C.W. van Rooyen, himself a censor, in 1987. Van Rooyen's *Censorship in South Africa* focuses on the Publications Act No. 42 of 1974 and subsequent amendments and provides insight into the system's internal procedures and administrative workings. In *A Culture of Censorship*, published in 1994, academic librarian Christopher Merrett highlights the role of censorship in South African intellectual history, arguing that it was intrinsic to colonialism and then apartheid, with far-reaching consequences in the cultural field. Coetzee's *Giving Offense* was published in 1996 and discusses the various forms of censorship across history and geographical space, illustrating the intricate complexities hidden behind political agendas in the application of censorship in South Africa and abroad. In *The Muzzled Muse*, Margreet de Lange (1997) focuses on literary production during apartheid censorship and on the relationship inevitably forged between writers and censors. Other works, in the form of shorter essays, articles or chapters also focused on censorship, including several essays published in *Staffrider* and *Censoring Reality*, which presents in the form of conference papers a brief survey of the biased information disseminated through textbooks and newspapers as a consequence of publication control, propaganda and the manipulation of information.

Several South African anthologies of literature also address the issue of censorship. Michael Chapman's *Southern African Literatures* (2003) provides insight into the history of literature in South Africa and includes a chapter focusing on the apartheid era, inevitably covering censorship and political issues. Chapman gives an overview of 'resistance' literature and of the 'silent decade' of the 1960s, otherwise known as the Great Gap. Chapman's *Soweto Poetry* (2007) also looks back on literary production during apartheid and discusses the surge of black poetry in the 1970s.

An important contribution to understanding the workings of South African censorship under apartheid and its effect on the cultural sphere is Peter D. McDonald's *The Literature Police*.[1] Published in 2009, it focuses on the world of books and literature and offers new insight into the practical functioning of the censorship apparatus. Drawing on recently released archival records, it explores the complexities of the censors' application of the law and the cultural consequences of apartheid on literary production. McDonald discusses the ever-changing censors' ideology, offering new ways of envisaging their relationship with writers, publishers and readers. The complexities of this ideology, caught between literary and political considerations, are highlighted, and the secular and intellectual minds of censors are analysed in the light of their reports and archival evidence.

Censorship and the colonial gaze

Censorship was a pillar of the political economy of colonialism (Merrett 1994: 9). Indeed, official control of cultural production and consumption pre-dates apartheid. European colonialism could itself be read as a form of censorship on a massive scale, repressing the voices, ideas, cultures and identities of the colonised people. While promoting a culture of reading and writing, and indeed playing a major role in the formation of a black intelligentsia in South Africa, colonial missionary education was coercive in its workings, propagating an elitist notion of civilisation, modernity and Christianity.

A string of laws further institutionalised censorship prior to apartheid, including the Obscene Publications Act No. 31 of 1892, which targeted imported pornographic material; the Customs Management Act No. 9 of 1913, which controlled the importation of publications deemed objectionable; and the Entertainments Censorship Act No. 28 of 1931, initially aimed at controlling the circulation of motion pictures and public

---

1. See http://www.theliteraturepolice.com/, which 'is intended for anyone curious to know more about the subject and for those interested in doing further research into the vast topic of apartheid censorship'.

entertainment in general, but eventually extending its power to include control over imported books and periodicals in 1934.

When the National Party (NP) came to power in 1948, substantial components of publications control were already in place that would subsequently be developed into complex and strict censorship machinery. As under colonialism and imperialism, censorship became part of the foundation of grand apartheid. However, the apartheid government added numerous additional layers. One of the pieces of legislation that had a critical impact on the availability and circulation of publications was the Suppression of Communism Act No. 44 of 1950, which was initially promulgated to outlaw the Communist Party of South Africa – the CPSA, later renamed the South African Communist Party (SACP) – and gave the state the power to ban any person or organisation suspected of promoting communism.

The suppression of communist readers
As the building blocks of apartheid were gradually laid under NP Prime Minister Daniel François Malan, silencing any opposition became the only way to subjugate the South African population. With censorship being essential to the apartheid nationalist plan, the Suppression of Communism Act was a defining moment in the consolidation of state censorship. Enacted in 1950, this legislation empowered the minister of justice to ban and list organisations or individuals, detain or deport people without trial, seize documents and prohibit printing, publication and circulation of publications allegedly promoting 'communism' (Merrett 1994: 21). Through this Act, the minister of justice exercised censorship by serving bans on alleged communist persons and publications, in a bid to counter 'communism', 'terrorism' and 'treason'. The Suppression of Communism Act's general objective was 'to declare the Communist Party of South Africa to be an unlawful organization; to make provision for declaring other organizations promoting communistic activities to be unlawful and for prohibiting certain periodical or other publications; to prohibit certain communistic activities; and to make provision for other incidental matters'.

Section 1 of the Act defined the key terms of this broad objective. 'Communism' was relatively loosely defined, as 'the doctrine of Marxian socialism', promoting 'dictatorship of the proletariat', 'aiming at bringing about political, industrial or social or economic change within the Union', either through internal or foreign assistance, and encouraging 'feelings of hostility between the European and non-European races of the Union'. In this light, a 'communist' was, 'a person who professes to be a communist' or more implicitly, 'a person [. . .] advocating, advising, defending or encouraging the achievement of any of the objects of communism'. The definition was eventually extended to anyone opposing the apartheid regime or opposing the NP's political agenda, giving the minister of justice the power to label dissident individuals, groups and institutions as 'communists'. A statutory communist was to be silenced and strategies ranging from house arrest to intimidation, detention without trial, forced exile and in some instances torture, at times fatal, were used.

Section 6 (a), (b) and (c) of the Act also makes provision for prohibiting certain publications promoting 'the spread of communism', 'published or disseminated by or under the direction or guidance of an organisation which has been declared an unlawful organization', serving 'as a means for expressing views propagated by any such organization' or 'calculated to further the achievement of any of the objects of communism'. According to the Act, the governor general was mandated to, 'without notice to any person concerned, by proclamation in the *Gazette*, prohibit the printing, publication or dissemination' of a publication, designated in section 1 (1) of the Act, as any 'book, pamphlet, record, list, placard, poster, drawing, photograph, picture, newspaper, magazine, book or handbill'. The foundations for publication control were consolidated with the Suppression of Communism Act, introducing the notion of 'undesirable' writers and publications and, by extension, undesirable communist readers.

In terms of the Act, a banned person had to report to a police station on a regular basis and could not participate in any organisation's activities or publish documents. It is estimated that by 1956, some 4 000 publications were banned, some under the provisions of the Suppression of Communism Act (Merrett 1994: 34) and from 1950 to 1974, a total of 1 240 banning orders were served on people and organisations (52).

The apartheid system progressively consolidated its bureaucratic structure and hegemony in public and private spaces. In 1950 alone, the Group Areas Act, the Immorality Amendment Act, the Population Registration Act and the Suppression of Communism Act were passed. The years that followed saw the implementation of the Bantu Authorities Act of 1951, the Bantu Education Act of 1953, the Criminal Law Amendment Act of 1953 and the the Public Safety Act of 1953, to name but a few.

The Post Office Act No. 44 of 1958 (an amendment to the 1911 Act) also had implications for literature, through the control of posted parcels and documents. Empowered by the Customs Management Act No. 9 of 1913, customs agents acted as censors although, as Merrett (1994: 34) puts it, they 'would peruse [books] at 6s. per 50 pages'. The minister of the interior published a list of authors – from South Africa and abroad – whose work had to be seized at borders. Imported books and periodicals were inspected and customs agents had discretionary powers over the entry of publications into the country. In fact, they scanned books and publications, rather than read them, and often based their decisions on extra-textual elements, rather than the text itself. The aim was to remove such publications from the public eye and to make them unavailable to readers in South Africa.

Over the years, however, several books published overseas by banned authors clandestinely entered South Africa, such as Bloke Modisane's *Blame Me on History*, Alex La Guma's *A Walk in the Night* and several of Dennis Brutus's poems (Thompson 2000: 206). Loopholes were found in the way publications control operated. Disparities between books covering the same topic but published inside and outside South Africa exposed the arbitrariness of the system. For instance, following the events of Sharpeville in 1960, Ambrose Reeves' imported book *Shooting at Sharpeville* was systematically embargoed at customs and banned under the pretext that it represented a danger to the apartheid regime (Merrett 1994:

46). Meanwhile, a book on Sharpeville written by South African Bernard Sachs and published in South Africa, *The Road to Sharpeville*, was initially proscribed, but the ban was overturned because it was a South African publication and could therefore only be banned if found to be promoting communism (Merrett 1994: 46).

Despite the stringent measures supported by the Suppression of Communism Act, and the ensuing large-scale alienation of writers from their readership, the government sought to further tighten publications control and called for a commission to report on the way apartheid South Africa was portrayed in the media. The Press Commission was set up in 1950, following NP Member of Parliament A.J.R. van Rhyn's suggestion in 1948 to monitor the printed media. He called for a probe into the alleged 'sensationalism', 'misrepresentation' and 'subversive' and 'misleading' nature of mainly English press reports in South Africa and their effect on the country's international reputation and on internal race relations (Hachten and Giffard 1984: 52).

The main objectives of the Commission included an investigation into the possibilities of increased state control over internal and external media reporting, monopolistic propensities and the work of foreign correspondents in South Africa (Merrett 1994: 36; Hachten and Giffard 1984: 54). The Commission was also tasked with an inquiry into the accuracy, responsibility and patriotism of South African journalism as well as incidences of sensationalism and triviality in the press. The minister of external affairs, Eric Louw, voiced the opinion of several parliamentarians when he declared in 1959 that 'a great deal of South Africa's international trouble is due to political articles in the English Press' (in Merrett 1994: 37).

While the Commission did not table a report until the 1960s, the psychological effects of being consistently scrutinised and subjected to intimidation for nearly a decade took its toll on the press (Merrett 1994: 37). Between 1950 and 1955, the Press Commission undertook thorough surveillance and recorded the activities of the written media. Press releases, published reports and clippings were assessed and dossiers were compiled on journalists and editors (36). Journalists subjected to such surveillance often resorted to self-censorship (Hachten and Giffard 1984: 58). Several foreign correspondents were deported from South Africa during this period, notably British correspondents Basil Davidson, John Hacht and Doris Lessing (Merrett 1994: 37).

As Brian Bunting wrote in *New Age* in 1959, *Post* and *Drum* were among the few South African publications at that time to truly challenge the apartheid regime, with highly controversial topics and reports (in Merrett 1994: 38). Segregation of churches, farm labour conditions and jail conditions are some examples of the topics tackled by the *Drum* team of journalists and photographers who exposed the impact of apartheid on the black majority. Unsurprisingly, investigative journalism was a primary concern for the authorities. Newspaper offices were under security police surveillance, attempts were made to recruit staff as informers, newspapers' vendors and employees were intimidated, offices were raided, material was confiscated and journalists assaulted.

The final report of the Press Commission was approved by Parliament in 1964, after a draft report had been tabled in 1962. The recommendations included declaring foreign reporting on South Africa 'extremely undesirable' (Hachten and Giffard 1984: 64) and setting up the Press Council to replace the existing Newspaper Press Union (NPU), which was perceived as lacking disciplinary powers. According to the report, the Press Council would maintain press freedom in South Africa, encourage accurate reporting and informed and responsible comment, encourage and maintain the dignity of the state and its officials, receive complaints, try these matters and pass judgement (Hachten and Giffard 1984: 64). However, the NPU was kept in place and the Commission's recommendations were shelved, only to be implemented through various laws and amendments to existing Acts in the decades that followed, especially after John Vorster was elected as prime minister in 1966 by white minority vote.

Accusing the press of 'stabbing South Africa in the back', Vorster declared in 1971: 'I am looking at a legislation now which will contain a clause providing that if a newspaper continues to be guilty of publishing articles inciting racial hatred it will simply not appear on the streets' (in Hachten and Giffard 1984: 68). This kind of rhetoric provided an impetus for large-scale publication control and the NPU amended its constitution in 1973, giving more power to the Press Council by allowing it to fine those who contravened the newly established code of conduct. Besides promoting the need to 'accurately' report news and inform the South African public, the amended code warned against reports likely to stir up racial, ethnic or religious tension and demanded 'due compliance with agreements entered into between the Newspaper Press Union and any department of the Government of South Africa with a view to public safety or security or the general mood' (69).

An antidote to 'spiritual poison'

With control of the press, general publications control gained momentum. Parallel to the Press Commission, which primarily targeted the media, the Commission of Enquiry in Regard to Undesirable Publications targeted publications in the broadest sense of the word. It was led by Geoffrey Cronjé, a professor of sociology and influential apartheid ideologue, who wrote several books and had a passion for literature. Referred to as the Cronjé Commission, it was launched in 1954. Its aim was to investigate the production, possession and circulation of imported and local publications in South Africa. Its findings were published in September 1957, after being tabled for the first time in October 1956. The Commission's report formulated several recommendations with far-reaching impact on the development of subsequent censorship laws, from the 1960s onwards. In addition, through this Commission, the basis of various definitions of readers emerged, marking the beginning of an esoteric dialogue between censors and imagined readers.

The aim of the Cronjé Commission was to identify so-called 'indecent, offensive or harmful literature' (McDonald 2009: 23). Notions of literature being 'indecent', 'offensive' or 'harmful' laid the foundation for the literary rhetoric typical of apartheid censors' discourse. These notions contributed to the concept of 'undesirability' and informed literary criticism and semantic considerations articulated by censors to justify censorship in subsequent decades. Several notions of 'readers' emerged from these concepts, as the 'evil of indecent offensive or harmful literature' could manifest itself in various ways through its readers. For example, readers needing protection from 'indecent' and 'offensive' material were portrayed as puritans, easily shocked and offended, innocent and naive. In contrast, readers from whom the general public needed protection could include the easily influenced reader, the subversive reader and the communist reader, as defined in the Suppression of Communism Act. These definitions would form the basis of the main understanding of readers that would more or less consistently underpin the censors' arguments with regard to issues of readers and readership throughout apartheid, where the fine line between citizens and readers became invariably blurred.

The Commission advocated the creation of the Publications Control Board, which would compile a database and formally license all book professionals in South Africa, as well as a monitoring system for local and imported literature (Merrett 1994: 35; McDonald 2009: 23). It recommended the adoption of an official definition of literature, an idea that would spark intellectual debate among censors, literary experts and writers in general, for many years. Undesirable literature, or in the Commission's words 'spiritual poison', would include material considered 'indecent, offensive or harmful to the ordinary, civilised, decent, reasonable and responsible inhabitants of South Africa' (Merrett 1994: 35). This citizen would become the benchmark reader against which undesirability would be evaluated. The Commission proposed the suppression of publications found undesirable, with the exception of reading for academic and research purposes, as it was assumed that there would be few erudite readers. It recommended the prohibition of possession and importation of alleged communist literature and the formation of a Publications Appeal Board, linked to the government, which would review appeals.

From the Commission's discourse emerges the concept of an ideal reader, according to its definition, ordinary, civilised, decent, reasonable and responsible. This ideal reader coincided with the ideal citizen, embodying nationalist values and beliefs and participating in a broader nation-building project underpinned by specific ideas of reading, literature and culture as unifying forces, a stance echoing the colonial nation-building mission. As opposed to the easily enticed or reactionary reader, the 'ordinary' reader had strong Christian values and morals. Along these lines, the censors' mission was to prevent any harm or offence caused by undesirable literature to the so-called law-abiding citizen, a euphemism for people who endorsed and were privileged by apartheid laws.

Following the Cronjé Commission's recommendations, the deputy minister of the interior, P.W. Botha, proposed the Undesirable Publications Bill in 1960, which was never enacted, but was seriously considered. This Bill advocated censorship before publication, unprecedented – at least officially – in South Africa. It targeted any form of cultural expression, from the press to films, theatre, literature and printed publications in general. It was denounced for trying to achieve, in the words of the leader of the South African Labour Party and Member of Parliament Alexander Hepple, 'political censorship of the most restrictive kind' (in De Lange 1997: 34).

Cronjé, a strong advocate of separate development and apartheid's racial classifications, wrote several essays in which he discusses the issue of readers and readership. In *'n Tuiste vir die nageslag* (A home for posterity), Cronjé discusses two kinds of readers: the reader who reads with a magnifying glass, 'searching for evidence to present to the natives and Coloureds that the Afrikaner is their greatest enemy', and the *volks* reader, who has the ability to read between the lines and 'put back into the text what has been censored out', forming an 'esoteric reading community' that is assumed to be unaffected by censorship (Coetzee 1996: 169).[2]

---

2. The *volks* reader is the ideal reader imagined by censors. The idea of the *volks* reader is moulded on an ideal citizen, who supports and participates in the National Party's vision for the Afrikaner nation (the *Afrikanervolk* or *volk*). The literary world was one of many spheres of influence that were expected to contribute to this NP-aligned nation-building project.

According to Cronjé's argument, the reader needing control is the one with a magnifying glass, who is the 'liberal reader', and the 'native' and 'Coloured' readers, who are presumed to be easily influenced. The liberal reader was imagined as educated and harmful to the status quo. Because of their education and sophisticated nature, the *volks* reader was believed by censors to be able to 'read between the lines', as common values and vantage points would ensure that voluntarily censored texts would be assumed, understood and implicitly restored. Himself a writer, reader and censor, Cronjé posits this privileged reader as an accomplice in the system, revealing an exclusive relationship between the enlightened censor, the patriotic writer and the *volks* reader.

The censors' tendency to identify with and speak on behalf of readers marks the evolution of the modern censorship apparatus from 1963 until the 1990s. South African readers were divided between broad categories, such as 'good readers', whether naive, easily offended or balanced, and the elusive group of 'other readers', a mixed bag of subversive, reactionary and communist readers, who were, in Cronjé's words, 'dangerous' and of whom 'account must be taken' (in Coetzee 1996: 169). It is in this regard that the Commission's report is of utmost importance for the censorship laws subsequently developed, as such imagined readers eventually occupied a prominent place in the censors' arguments.

Cronjé justified the existence of institutionalised censorship as a measure to nurture and protect 'good' Afrikaans literature, while furthering nationalist interests. In this perspective, the ingredients of 'literariness' that made for good literature included an artistically worthy literary piece; a 'Christian outlook on life'; 'consideration for the racial composition of the Union'; and a particular sensitivity when addressing potentially 'subversive' topics (McDonald 2009: 26). The Afrikaans writer was expected to feel and show responsibility towards their nation and to promote Afrikaner nationalist values. Censorship's goal was to guide and promote, through the dissemination of good literature, good reading for good citizens, or what was later believed to be the average and balanced reader.

The Cronjé Commission and Undesirable Publications Bill generated vigorous opposition from a broad spectrum of intellectuals, from both inside and outside the Afrikaner literary establishment (Merrett 1994: 36). As McDonald (2009: 160) points out, 'opposing censorship was itself a matter of dispute'. However, much of the opposition concerned the details of the Bill per se, rather than the idea of institutionalised censorship itself, hinting that debates of a literary nature still occurred within the confines of censorship. Although the Bill was soon abandoned amid pressure and protests, and reworked into the somewhat watered-down Publications and Entertainments Act in 1963, a conversation on the role of literature and of the writer, and on publication control, emerged from this controversy, involving censors, academics and writers. The exchanges were occasionally published, for instance, in *Standpunte*, *Die Burger* and *Huisgenoot* (30-1). Opposition among the ranks of Afrikaners was of concern to the authorities. For example, intellectuals, such as N.P. van Wyk Louw and D.J. Opperman, as well as international organisations, such as PEN South Africa (PEN SA), openly criticised the Bill. In reaction, Abraham Jonker, one of the ideological drivers of the censorship apparatus, wrote in the newspaper *Die Burger* on 30 January 1963: 'This proposal has nothing to do with serious literature. The Bill is directed against filth, pornography, blasphemy, offensiveness and the distribution of communistic propaganda. Everyone who opposes the regulations is in favour of these wrongs' (in De Lange 1997: 34). The idea of serious literature being an ever-contested notion generated ongoing public debate on the essence of literature and the role of writers in society, leading to multiple reforms and reworking of the censorship system.

Van Wyk Louw, a central literary figure in the Afrikaans avant-garde, played a key role in ongoing debate on the new Bill, which involved notions of literariness and the role of the writer as a critical intellectual (McDonald 2009: 28). For Van Wyk Louw, the Afrikaner nation depended not only on a political philosophy such as apartheid to survive as a minority, but also on the creation of an Afrikaner Republic of Letters (30). He considered literature to be a manifestation of the 'national spirit' that should be under the guardianship of avant-garde writers, not politicians (31). In his view, literature's goal was nation building.

Another key player, which shared a similar ideology, was the Afrikaans Writers' Circle, founded in 1934 under government patronage. It was not opposed to the fundamental principles of censorship, but rather to its intricate technicalities, such as the definition of literature and the essence of literariness. Its aim was to consolidate the *volk*'s literary canons and Afrikaans literary canons, but excluded black Afrikaans-speaking writers, such as Adam Small and S.V. Peterson (McDonald 2009: 164). The organisation upheld the sanctity of the literary above politics and believed literature to be the purest art form. For censors, literature was the highest aesthetic form and was not meant for a popular readership, but for a few privileged literary readers (163). Paradoxically, and despite the rhetoric, the fine line between politics and arts was crossed with the very idea of publications control and explicitly so when writers were eventually appointed to the censorship board. Strikingly, the censors' ideas of the literary, and of an ideal, literary sophisticated reader, were at times not so dissimilar from those of some relatively progressive literary actors.

The South African branch of PEN, the international freedom of expression association, was an anti-censorship group founded in Johannesburg in 1927. PEN SA's first chairperson was Sarah Gertrude Millin and from 1950 onwards it also had an office in Cape Town. Although PEN SA opposed censorship in principle, it was implicitly working within the parameters of the apartheid system. Its members were mainly white liberals and included some Afrikaner avant-garde writers, such as Van Wyk Louw, who was also affiliated to the Afrikaans Writers' Circle. PEN SA upheld the position that literature should be apolitical – a stance not that distant from the censors' belief that arts and politics were incompatible – and promoted the advancement of South African literature in English. Freedom of expression was seemingly not a universal right.

The Sestigers were a group of emerging Afrikaans writers in the 1960s, including Chris Barnard, Breyten Breytenbach, André Brink, Ingrid Jonker,

Etienne Leroux, Jan Rabie and Bartho Smit, to name but a few. Their work was frequently reviewed by censors, as they often broke away from the conservative Afrikaans cultural tradition framed by censors. However, as discussed later in this chapter, they would not be directly affected by banning until the end of the 1960s. Despite the commonality between their definition of literature and that of the censors, these young writers felt a sense of alienation in the face of the paternalistic and patronising censorship structures (Chapman 2003: 250). However, as Brink noted in 1971, they never actively challenged state control: 'No Afrikaans writer as yet tried to offer a serious political challenge to the system. We have no one with enough guts, it seems, to say: No' (in Chapman 2003: 402).

Black South Africans were the most directly affected by censorship laws and measures and as a majority were also the most vocal in their opposition to the idea of institutionalised censorship. Albert Luthuli voiced his concerns and those of many black South Africans in an interview with *New Age* in 1957, when the idea of a consolidated censorship apparatus was gaining momentum. He condemned the Cronjé Commission's recommendations not only in terms of poetic licence, but mainly as another building block of apartheid: 'The recommendations of the Commission of Inquiry in Regard to Undesirable Publications create another grave threat to the liberties of the people and constitute an unwarranted attack on the liberty of expression.' This position differs from the opposition that would subsequently emanate from the Afrikaans avant-garde or white liberals, as Luthuli condemned censorship as a political tool. For him, it was simply another step towards the grip of apartheid on the South African population that should be categorically rejected, a stance also shared by Athol Fugard and Nadine Gordimer, among others. Gordimer explains in an article published in *Staffrider*:

> One or two writers, like myself, had opposed the Act from the beginning three years before; you didn't have to look into a crystal ball to see that once you agree to accept censorship conditionally, you have endorsed it in principle and you will have to accept

whatever means are used to apply it, in the end (Gordimer 1988: 13).

The apartheid regime and its series of laws obviously generated opposition well beyond literary circles and in 1960 a state of emergency was declared, following anti-apartheid protests and resistance on a national scale. The late 1950s to the early 1960s saw unrest in the townships of Cato Manor (Durban), Langa (Cape Town) and Sharpeville (Johannesburg), to name but a few. The events of Sharpeville in 1960, where the police opened fire on a protesting crowd, marked a turning point in South African history and politics, but also in South African literature, provoking a stream of literary answers or 'documentary responses' to the tragedy (Heywood 2004: 194). Increased resistance and opposition were met with escalating repression, as the state tightened its control over the flow of ideas and information.

From literary experts to bureaucrats

It was in this general climate of increased protest and repression that the Publications and Entertainments Act No. 26 was adopted in Parliament in March 1963, under Hendrik Verwoerd's administration. Through this Act, publications control became tighter, although censorship existed in more diffuse forms well before that date – in fact, from the early days of colonisation. It is estimated that by 1963, 12 629 publications had already been taken out of circulation in South Africa, mainly through the Suppression of Communism Act, the General Law Amendment Act No. 76 of 1962 and and the Customs Act (De Lange 1997: 7). Literature by black authors was caught in a web of legislation long before it entered the institutionalised publications control system. The new legislation now also affected white authors, who thus far had few brushes with the system.

The Act was vaguely worded, using a language open to interpretation. The central notion of undesirability was detailed in six points in section 5 (2):

A publication or object shall be deemed undesirable if it or any part of it:
- (a) is indecent or obscene or offensive or harmful to public morals;
- (b) is blasphemous or is offensive to the religious convictions or feelings of any section of the inhabitants of the Republic;
- (c) brings any section of the inhabitants of the Republic into ridicule or contempt;
- (d) is harmful to the relations between any inhabitants of the Republic;
- (e) is prejudicial to the safety of the state, the general welfare or the peace and good order;
- (f) discloses with reference to any judicial proceedings
    - i. any matter which is indecent or obscene or is offensive or harmful to public morals;
    - ii. any indecent or obscene medical, surgical, or physiological details the disclosure of which is likely to be offensive or harmful to public morals.

In addition, section 6 (1) of the Act alludes to the notion of the probable or likely reader:

If in any legal proceedings under this Act the question arises whether any matter is indecent or obscene or is offensive or harmful to public morals, that matter shall be deemed to be:

- (a) indecent or obscene if, in the opinion of the court, it has the tendency to deprave or to corrupt the minds of persons who are likely to be exposed to the effect or influence thereof; or
- (b) offensive to public morals if, in the opinion of the court, it is likely to be outrageous or disgustful to persons who are likely to read or see it; or

(c) harmful to public morals if, in the opinion of the court, it deals in an improper manner with murder, suicide, death, horror, cruelty, fighting, brawling, ill-treatment, lawlessness, gangsterism, robbery, crime, the techniques of crimes and criminals, tippling, drunkenness, trafficking in or addiction to drugs, smuggling, sexual intercourse, prostitution, promiscuity, White-slavery, licentiousness, lust, passionate love scenes, homosexuality, sexual assault, rape, sodomy, sadism, sexual bestiality, abortion, change of sex, night life, physical poses, nudity, scant or inadequate dress, divorce, marital infidelity, adultery, illegitimacy, human or social deviation or degeneracy, or any other similar or related phenomenon; or
(d) indecent or obscene or offensive or harmful to public morals if, in the opinion of the court, it is in any other manner subversive of morality.

A thin line was drawn between morals and politics, creating a general climate of secrecy and opening up a space for interpretation in reading the Act. Conservative moral standards were invariably blurred with conservative politics and religion.

The first Publications Control Board, also called the Board of Censors, was composed of nine full-time and part-time appointed members, for the most part academics in literature departments at leading South African universities. The Board was based in Cape Town and was assisted by a panel of secondary readers and subcommittees. Although an autonomous body, it was part and parcel of the broader apartheid project, translating an Afrikaner nationalist political agenda into moralistic and literary pretences. Gerrit Dekker, who identified as an avant-garde Afrikaans literary expert, was appointed as chairperson of the Board and held office from November 1963 to October 1968. His appointment was influenced by the lobbying efforts of prominent avant-garde intellectual and poet Van Wyk Louw. Dekker's appointment could be read as an olive branch from the Verwoerd administration, to ease emerging tensions within the Afrikaans literary establishment. The appointment of a literary person as chairperson of the Board also contributed, as McDonald (2009: 39) points out, to placing issues with regard to literariness at the core of apartheid censorship. The appointment of Dekker and his team of literary experts and academics as members of the first censorship board indeed appeased the *volks* avant-garde, who believed that literature should be dealt with by literary experts and not lay administrators. McDonald (2009: 161) remarks that the inclusion of Afrikaner literary experts in the censorship board made it 'difficult to construe the writer-censor relationship in the South African case as straightforwardly rivalrous'. The dual identity of the censor as a writer sheltered a political discourse disguised as literary under the pretence of legitimacy, revealing the bias of mainstream South African literary canons' formation from an early period. The insistence of the avant-garde on preserving the purity of literature above the political proved futile and ambiguous.

With its literary experts and readers, the Board mainly targeted potentially undesirable South African publications in English (McDonald 2009: 42) and imports, such as paperbacks and popular mass fiction. A staggering 60 per cent of South African English books submitted to the censors were banned (45). Since the Press Code was implemented parallel to the Publications and Entertainments Act, the Board mainly dealt with novels, essays and literary magazines. Afrikaans literature and writers enjoyed a privileged status in this first decade of censorship, while, as noted above, literature from African authors was often suppressed before it even reached the censorship bureaucracy, through other apartheid legislation. Once a book was declared undesirable, it was banned and could no longer be quoted, reprinted or distributed. In total, 52 per cent of all publications submitted to the Board in the 1960s and 1970s were banned because they were judged 'undesirable literature' (Du Toit 1983: 81).

The conservative Afrikaans Writers' Circle did not formally object to the Act, but an anti-censorship petition led by PEN SA and independent writers was signed in April 1963 by some 200 white writers and a handful of coloured writers. McDonald (2009: 37) observes that half of these signatories ended up having some works banned, while the other half eventually played a role in the censorship bureaucracy. The credibility and impact of this petition could, however, be questioned, as it was submitted a couple of months *after* the Publications and Entertainments Act was passed. More importantly, with the exception of five coloured signatories, it was only signed by white writers and artists (171). Through their rhetoric and biased application of censorship laws, censors aimed to divide South African writers along racial lines. The polarisation of the literary world, mirroring the segregation imposed on the population in general, prevented the creation of an inclusive notion of 'South African literature' or the 'South African writer', leading to parallel, though at times intersecting, ideas of writers, literatures and readers. This inevitably led to multiple definitions of the role of the writer and literature in society, each elaborated from a specific position.

Customs officials and police sent the bulk of potentially undesirable literature to censors for review, although post office personnel, publishers, librarians and booksellers also submitted publications. In a few instances, members of the public collaborated directly in their personal capacity. However, it is estimated that official agencies such as the departments of police and customs submitted 95 per cent of all publications examined by censors (Du Toit 1983: 85). The first book banned under the Act was the explicitly titled *An Act of Immorality*, penned under the not-so-subtle pseudonym Des Troye (Merrett 1994: 62). The police sent it to the censors after an officer's wife bought it in a local bookshop (McDonald 2009: 49). It was thereafter listed in the *Government Gazette*, as were future banned books. However, noting the inefficiency of the system in picking up potentially undesirable publications, Dekker appointed a full-time inspector, J.J. Bloom, who had the task of travelling across the country in search of suspicious literature (41). The nation-wide hunt for undesirable literature could be said to have planted the seed of a shift in the way censorship operated, whereby the literary veil was slowly lifted to reveal a more obvious political face.

Literary censors were a very elitist and privileged group of readers, confident of their self-proclaimed authority over everything literary by virtue of their academic rank, and of the firm belief that they were, in the words of Merrett (1994: 62), 'enlightened censors'. By using their own standards for good reading, they had the power to decide what constituted literature, playing an increasingly significant role in the definition of South African literary canons. The literariness of a publication was a potential mitigating factor against banning, as it was assumed that it would be of interest to a limited literary readership. However, literariness was itself a contested notion, over which censors had the last say.

Censors took on the responsibility of protecting readers from undesirable reading material and promoting what they thought to be good literature. The notions of 'undesirability' and the 'average reader' were central to their thought process, as they developed readers' profiles against which morals and offensiveness were assessed. The imagined average reader was similar to the *volks* reader that Cronjé addressed in *'n Tuiste vir die nageslag* and was sympathetic to nationalist values. What constituted literature was assumed to be universally understood and as McDonald (2009: 36) argues, censors became the embodiment of the reasonable man whose morals and literature they jealously safeguarded. In the course of their duties, censors became at once intrusive readers and censorious bureaucrats and functionaries, but also readers who upheld aesthetic literary values and posited themselves as 'the literature police', to borrow McDonald's phrase (2004: 299, 2009).

In 1965, Ruth First of *New Age*, Margaret Smith of the *Sunday Times*, Paul Trewhela of the *Rand Daily Mail*, Hugh Lewin and Raymond Eisenstein were some of the 1 095 detainees arrested under the 90-day detention provisions (Merrett 1994: 48). On 1 April 1966, some 46 names were added to the list of banned persons in South Africa (53), among them several contributors to *Drum* magazine. Politically motivated trials were the order of the day, with publications being used as evidence of communism or a threat to the state, serving as proof and grounds on which to effectively sentence and ban an individual or organisation. Moreover, under the

1963 Publications and Entertainments Act, bans could be served on entire series and genres. For example, in 1964 Penguin's African Library series was banned, as it included banned authors such as Brian Bunting, Ruth First, Govan Mbeki and Ronald Segal.

Following Verwoerd's assassination in 1966, John Vorster became prime minister in 1967 and Parliament adopted the Terrorism Act No. 83 of 1967, which allowed for indefinite detention for the purposes of interrogation. Two years later, the General Law Amendment Act of 1969 made provision for the suppression of all information or publications that could jeopardise state hegemony, effectively silencing opposition and dissent. Suppression of information worked hand in hand with propaganda, through organs such as the South African Broadcasting Corporation (SABC), the *Government Gazette*, Radio Bantu and several pro-apartheid newspapers, such as *Die Vaderland*.

A climate of fear prevailed, as readers, writers and publishers were under constant scrutiny. The Central News Agency (CNA), a major commercial press outlet in South Africa, was one of many that would not stock so-called leftist publications (Merrett 1994: 65). Fear of communism, a concept yet to be clearly defined, was behind the decision to reject the idea of bringing television to South Africa during a parliamentary session in 1963, for fear it would be used by communists to contaminate a mass viewership. Censorship in South Africa rapidly developed into a complex system designed to silence social and political dissent. By this point, it had a far wider reach than debates on literariness.

In search of literary references: The Great Gap

Through the General Law Amendment Act No. 76 of 1962, a blanket ban silenced 102 anti-apartheid activists, including many black leaders, writers and artists (McDonald 2009: 33). Between 1964 and 1974 more than 10 000 publications were banned under the Publications and Entertainments Act. During the same period, an estimated 1 240 banning orders were served in terms of the Suppression of Communism Act (Merrett 1994: 52). And, as Mbulelo Vizikhungo Mzamane (1991: 180) points out, many left the country: 'The large-scale emigration of actors and musicians paralleled the drainage of intellectuals, writers and politicians.'

The marginalisation and suppression of South African oppositional writing, and of that by black authors in particular, created a situation where many works were only available abroad or not available at all. The 1960s became known as the 'silent decade' (Chapman 2003: 246). In 1966, many South African writers living abroad were listed under the Suppression of Communism Act, such as Mazisi Kunene, Todd Matshikiza, Bloke Modisane, Es'kia Mphahlele, Lewis Nkosi, Cosmo Pieterse and Can Themba, while Dennis Brutus, Alfred Hutchinson and Alex La Guma were among writers already banned prior to that date (Chapman 2007: 5). Gordimer denounced the large-scale suppression of black voices in 1972, saying that 'black writing had been wiped out by censorship, bans and exile, and that black writers had become just names' (Merrett 1994: 63). She spoke of the fear instilled in would-be black fiction writers:

> Aspirant writers are intimidated not only by censorship as such but also by the fear that anything at all controversial, set out by a black in the generally explicit medium of prose, makes the writer suspect, since the correlation of articulacy and political insurrection, so far as blacks are concerned, is firmly lodged in the minds of the Ministers of the Interior, Justice and Police (Gordimer 1973: 51).

The climate of fear and massive banning created an irreversible gap in South African literary continuity, and as independent publisher David Philip (1990: 12) explains: 'It was a period of swinging censorship and became known as the "Unbridgeable Gap" in South African literature because so many classics of South African literature became unavailable to us South Africans.' This interrupted the flow of literature by black writers, wiping out cultural and literary references for future generations. The gap is unbridgeable, as when some titles were unbanned years later, they had lost some of their immediate relevance. These conditions placed

South African readers in a constrained literary landscape, where reading material was limited to so-called good books or else sourced clandestinely, as discussed in the next chapter.

Miriam Tlali describes the inevitable sense of loss experienced among readers and writers alike, in relation to the Great Gap: 'They say writers learn from their predecessors. When I searched frantically for mine, there was nothing but a void. What had happened to all writings my mother had talked about?' (in De Lange 1997: 126). Merrett (1994: 201) echoes this sentiment, noting that 'a generation of readers was deprived of ideas, attitudes, role models and cerebral stimulation'. Lack of access to books became the foremost challenge to reading.

A crack in the Republic of Letters

In 1968, Dekker was replaced by Jannie Kruger as chairperson of the Board of Censors, inaugurating a new era in South African censorship, by then still mostly in the hands of Afrikaans literary experts cum bureaucrats. Kruger was a literary reviewer, former editor of Afrikaans newspaper *Die Transvaler* and a cultural adviser to the SABC. The Board members remained virtually the same, with the exception of the replacement of C.J.D. Harvey with J.M. Leighton in 1969 and the addition of G.S. Nienaber, R.E. Lighton, A.J. van Niekerk and J.P. Jansen in 1971 (McDonald 2009: 53). Under Kruger, the number of banned publications increased sharply; whereas in 1968 the Dekker board banned 53 per cent of publications submitted (426 out of 798), the Kruger board banned 72 per cent of those submitted in 1973 (889 out of 1 230) (52).

Kruger's board continued more or less the same political tone as the previous administration, at least during the first few years. The focus remained on mass-market fiction and political fiction in English, while a new focus on poetry emerged, with the banning of *Cry Rage* in 1972, an anthology edited by James Matthews and Gladys Thomas (McDonald 2009: 53). This coincided with the poetry boom of the 1970s that was mainly rooted in the Black Consciousness Movement (BCM). As Chapman (2007: viii) notes with regard to the so-called 'new black poetry' of the 1970s, 'Soweto poetry tapped the imagination, ideas and issues of a Black Consciousness challenge to the apartheid police state'. This surge of writing was in contrast to the void left by the Great Gap of the 1960s and gave a new direction to writing by black writers that quickly found its readership, as witnessed by Gordimer (1973: 51): 'There are signs that, for the first time, black writers' works are beginning to be bought by ordinary black people in the segregated townships, instead of only by liberal or literary whites and the educated black elite.'

Steve Bantu Biko became the first president of the South African Students' Organisation (SASO) in 1968 and Barney Pityana succeeded him as SASO's second president. SASO was initially a black students' movement, the result of a breakaway from the National Union of South African Students (NUSAS) (Thompson 2000: 206). Soon much more than a student movement, SASO was a platform for the articulation of the black consciousness (BC) philosophy and movement. Biko was editor of SASO's newsletter, which could be considered a militant publication in the vein of *Classic*, *Donga*, *Staffrider* and *Wietie* (Mzamane 1991: 182). Editorials and essays focused on the state of politics and society under apartheid. The newsletter's editorials revealed the essence and core of the BCM and aimed to be simultaneously 'informative' and 'educative' (Biko 1970: 1). The newsletter published poetry, prose, columns and socio-political comment and analysis. Artistic merit blended with politics and student politics was discussed as a serious alternative to mainstream politics, giving literature, reading and writing new definitions.

SASO's newsletter opened up a public space for the convergence of a readership rallied around the BCM. This readership was young, educated, politicised and black, making new voices heard in the mainstream public discourse. In 1973, Biko and several of his colleagues were banned under the provisions of the Suppression of Communism Act, which meant that they could no longer speak in public, write, be published or travel (Stubbs 2004). Biko was listed as a banned person and confined to his hometown of King William's Town, where he pursued his political activism clandestinely despite the banning order served on him (Wilson 1991: 46).

While it began in the academic space and despite its main leaders being banned, BC ideology rapidly grew in popularity, gaining currency in urban and rural areas alike. Beyond the political sphere, BC played a major role in South African popular culture in the 1970s and generated a new wave of resistance to the apartheid regime, including a corpus of committed literature. As Chapman (2007: 11) points out, 'Soweto poetry' or 'black urban poetry' was initially 'directed in protest at a white "liberal" readership'. However, with the shift brought about by BC philosophy, it changed in tone and style and in its approach to politics and society:

> By the mid-seventies, however, the emphasis had shifted with Serote's Black Consciousness voice (predictably less popular with Whites) finding its full power in an uncompromising poetry of resistance. This is a mobilising rhetoric utilising epic forms (in a highly contemporary, almost Brechtian sense) and traditional African oral techniques of repetition, parallelism and ideophones. By these means the poet seeks to impart to a Black communal audience, often in a context of performance, a message of consciousness-raising and race pride (Chapman 2007: 12).

Inevitably, the BCM and literature fell under close scrutiny from the security police, who paid particular attention to its leaders, writers and readers. Merrett (1994: 98) explains: 'The course of the 1975–76 SASO-BPC trial of 13 activists in Pretoria illustrated the fact that Black Consciousness as an ideology, and its documents, speeches and philosophy, rather than individuals, were on trial.'

While black writers made their voices loud and clear, and carved their place in the highly contested public discourse, substantial changes to the censorship system emerged from the Kruger Commission initiated in May 1973, following the crisis regarding the first ban on an Afrikaans novel, which caused a stir in Afrikaans literary circles. Published in 1973, Brink's *Kennis van die aand* is the story of coloured actor Joseph Malan, who awaits execution for the murder of his white lover. According to the back cover of the 1974 English version, titled *Looking on Darkness*, 'André Brink panders to no one's political, ideological or religious beliefs in a controversial novel which has achieved international significance and abundant acclaim'. While acclaimed by critics and reviewers, the book was banned under section 5 (2) (b) of the Publications and Entertainments Act in February 1974 (De Lange 1997: 47). It was found undesirable because it was judged blasphemous or 'offensive to the religious convictions or feelings of any section of the inhabitants of the Republic', as per the Act's wording. Brink and his publisher unsuccessfully appealed the ban. Judge J.T. van Wyk found that the novel in fact contravened all sections of the Publications and Entertainments Act (48) and concluded that it 'was obscene, harmful to public morals, and blasphemous' (McDonald 2009: 57).

However, the ban had a highly political undertone, as Brink had broken all conventions underpinning the aesthetics and definition of the role of literature in the Afrikaans Republic of Letters. Afrikaans poet Breyten Breytenbach commented in *Die Transvaler* of 2 October 1974: 'The book reflects a South African reality, but the Government does not want the people to know about it. The ban indicates absolute panic and clearly shows the climate of fear and repression' (in De Lange 1997: 49). Censors were seemingly concerned for readers who needed to be sheltered from Brink's depiction of South African society. Unsurprisingly, they believed that *Kennis van die aand* presented a false view of the country. Judge Van Wyk stated that 'a large majority of probable readers will get the impression that the author has tried to write a historical novel which pretends to be based on facts' (in De Lange 1997: 49). This alleged bias included white employers abusing black domestic employees, a coloured theatre director running into trouble with censors and security police, interracial relations, forced removals and racism, among other social issues plaguing apartheid South Africa.

By all accounts, *Kennis van die aand* and *Looking on Darkness*, the English translation also banned in 1974, marked a turn in Afrikaans literary aesthetics. By writing protest or committed Afrikaans literature, or by staging a reality other than that of conservative Afrikaners' world view, Brink opened up a crack in the Afrikaans literary establishment. As McDonald (2009: 54) reminds us, strong feelings against protest literature prevailed within the Afrikaner literary elite, which was vehemently against politics in literature. This unprecedented case shattered the definitions of *volks* literature and of the readers imagined by censors and led to debates on the elusive notion of the likely readership, which would have far-reaching consequences for the censorship system.

D.J. Opperman, a prominent Afrikaans avant-garde poet and ally of Brink's, testified during the appeal on the ban in 1974. Touching on the heart of the censors' definition of literature and readers, Opperman argued: 'The function of the art work as a mirror is no longer accepted; your likely reader sees a novel as a soap-bubble which offers a spherical vision, curved reflection of reality' (in McDonald 2009: 56). This position argued against the supremacy of one reader over another and denounced the concept of the likely reader being static and immutable. Opperman's argument did not have much effect on the Appeal Board's decision to uphold the ban on the novel, but it revealed dissension within the Afrikaner intelligentsia, with implications for literary discourse in South Africa. Brink wrote an open letter to Kruger, asking whether 'uncle Merwe, uncle Theuns and uncle Apie – Merwe Scholtz, Cloete, and Grové – were so broad (i.e. wide-girthed and broad-minded) that they could straddle the stools of the literature they promote and the stools of the literature they condemn' (57).

Two Afrikaans groups expressed the opposing views of censorship: the pro-censorship Federasie van Afrikaanse Kultuurvereniginge (Federation of Afrikaans Cultural Associations) and the newly formed anti-censorship Afrikaanse Skrywersgilde (Afrikaans Writers' Guild) (Merrett 1994: 80). In the face of stricter measures against Afrikaans literature, the Guild organised a conference on censorship in 1975. The conference was closed to the press and public, raising suspicions that it was aiming to mobilise progressive Afrikaans authors, who had been relatively unaffected by direct censorship until then (De Lange 1997: 38). The progressive Afrikaans publishing house Taurus was formed in the wake of the conference and would play a critical role in the development of South African literature, as discussed in the next chapter.

In the face of increased opposition and polarisation among Afrikaans writers, and increasingly organised resistance, the apartheid regime tightened its grip on public discourse and, in doing so, looked at ways of strengthening its publications control apparatus, which became more repressive from the mid-1970s onwards.

Launched in May 1973 by deputy minister of the interior, J.T. Kruger, the Kruger Commission advocated a complete reworking of the censorship system, focusing on countering the influence of alleged international communist infiltration of South African morals and using anti-liberal and anti-literary rhetoric (McDonald 2009: 58). By promoting a political approach over a literary approach to publications, the influence and powers of literary expert board members were diminished. Despite opposition from PEN SA and the Afrikaans Writers' Circle, which, among other things, pleaded for a more literary approach to censorship, the recommendations of the Kruger Commission were promulgated into law through the Publications Act No. 42, adopted by Parliament in October 1974.

The Directorate of Publications, based in Cape Town, headed by J.L. Pretorius, replaced the Publications Control Board. The minister of the interior had powers to appoint the members of this Directorate. Other new structures included the countrywide censorship readers' committees that were mainly made up of white readers, but also included a few coloured and Indian ones – but not a single black reader – appointed by the Directorate of Publications (Hachten and Giffard 1984: 162). Despite these changes, censorship was still controlled by white administrators, who represented 95 per cent of all committee members in 1975 (McDonald 2009: 62).

The right to appeal to independent courts was replaced by an internal Appeal Board based in Pretoria, an idea initially proposed by the Cronjé Commission. The Publications Appeal Board (PAB) was composed of fourteen members appointed by the state president. J.H. Snyman was appointed as chairperson. The PAB reviewed decisions for a nominal fee should an application be lodged by the Directorate of Publications, an individual or group with a financial interest in the book (such as the author or publisher), or the minister of the interior. The Directorate required that the list of banned titles and the rationale for these bans be published in the *Government Gazette* (McDonald 2009: 60). A new and important provision of the Act made possession of banned books illegal, as per section 9 (3).

The separation of literariness from politics was embodied in the creation of a literary and security committee. As McDonald (2009: 64–5) observes, work by authors associated with BC entering the censorship system were for the most part submitted by police officers and were read by security censors. In such cases, literariness was overlooked to focus on the political content. However, literary and security experts sometimes worked together, such as in the case of Mafika Gwala's *Jol'iinkomo*. This book was initially submitted to a literary committee and reviewed by Merwe Scholtz, who pondered extensively on the literary qualities and politically seditious nature of the collection of poems, finally referring the publication to the security committee. The final decision was reached by a joint literary and security committee, which found the publication not undesirable (but not desirable either), mainly on literary grounds.

The Publications Act of 1974 stipulated that 'in the application of this Act the constant endeavour of the population of the Republic of South Africa to uphold a Christian value of life shall be recognised'. This section of the Act clearly defines the 'average man' against whom undesirability would now be gauged. Section 47 (2) defines the potential reasons for undesirability and reads the same as section 5 (2) of the previous Publications and Entertainments Act No. 26 of 1963. However, section 6 (1) of the Act of 1963, pertaining to undesirability in relation to the likely reader, does not appear in the Act of 1974.

The average reader principle signified a shift from literary to political concerns. Undesirability was therefore measured against community standards, in all regards a highly suggestive point of reference and even more so in a polarised society such as apartheid South Africa. Interestingly, the PAB was seemingly aware of the vagueness of this premise and took on the role of 'social mediator', to borrow a term coined by Coetzee (1996: 188). The PAB affirmed:

> [We are] aware that in South Africa, and indeed in any country, there is in fact no single communal standard, just as no "reasonable man" in fact exists in the determination of negligence in law. Hence, when assessing the community standards the arbiter must endeavour to find a median among the various viewpoints obtaining within the South African community (in Du Toit 1983: 95–6).

In 1978, the Publications Act was amended with the Publications Amendment Act No. 109, this time following an outcry surrounding the 1976 ban on one of the most prominent Afrikaner authors' work – Etienne Leroux's *Magersfontein, O Magersfontein!* The literary committee initially passed the novel, acknowledging its literary qualities. The PAB subsequently overturned this decision on the grounds of obscenity and blasphemy, following pressure from conservative Afrikaner groups. The fact that Leroux received the Hertzog Prize for the second time in his career as well as the CNA Literary Award for *Magersfontein, O Magersfontein!*, in the midst of this controversy, made it even more difficult for the PAB to defend its decision. Afrikaans writers and media increasingly questioned the censorship system and even conservative Afrikaans newspapers supported the argument in favour of the literariness of the novel. An editorial that appeared in *Die Burger* and *Beeld* on 22 November 1977 denounced the decision: 'When a brilliant novel by what may be our greatest writer – a satire whose literary value is not doubted – is summarily banned, our censorship system has become a monster; a threat to the creative artist, our intellectual life and the Afrikaans press' (in De Lange 1997: 40).

One of the main groups opposing this specific ban was Aksie vir Morele Standaarde (Action for Moral Values) led by Eddie van Zyl, who had on previous occasions successfully lobbied the government against the 'moral pollution of South Africa' and organised burnings of offensive publications (De Lange 1997: 39). The review of the literary committee's decision by the PAB was in line with the censors' accommodating attitude towards church and political leaders, characteristic of the application of censorship under Pretorius and Snyman. This meant that Afrikaans works were no longer sheltered by literary arguments from the possibility of being banned. Between 1975 and 1980 Afrikaans works reviewed by censors were for the most part banned, at the rate of about ten out of fourteen (McDonald 2009: 68).

Following the intense debates on his work, Leroux started to doubt his own writing. He expressed his feelings on censorship after receiving the Hertzog Prize in 1979:

> I have to say that, when the book was banned and I was asked whether I would continue to write, I bragged terribly when I said that I would write as though the law didn't exist. Don't kid yourself. This surely has an effect on a person. One cannot suppress the feeling: maybe these people were right? And then you start to check your style, your way of writing. You are very insecure and I believe all people whose books are banned feel the same (in De Lange 1997: 41).

Responses to the pressure caused by censorship varied and were multiple, but all included consideration of the readership, as the act of reading completes the act of writing.

The case surrounding Leroux prompted yet more changes in the censorship system, putting literary committees to the test. Leroux's publisher, Human & Rousseau, contested the PAB's decision before the Supreme Court in 1978, arguing that the undesirability of the novel on the grounds of obscenity was evaluated relative to the average reader and not the likely reader (McDonald 2009: 72). As Silver (1984: 91) notes:

The Board worked with an absolute concept of undesirability, with no allowance being made for the likely reader of the work. As late as 1978, the Snyman Board found that while the Publications and Entertainments Act 26 of 1963 made allowance for the 'likely reader', the present Publications Act of 1974 did not.

The ban remained enforced on the basis of blasphemy, but this high-profile case highlighted the divisions within literary circles and initiated discussions of the idea of reintroducing the concept of the 'likely reader' into literary and censorship discourse.

In part because of its readership and in part because it was a cornerstone of Afrikaans culture and *volk*, Afrikaans literature enjoyed a privileged status, at least until 1978. As noted above, the events surrounding Leroux's case marked the beginning of the end of Pretorius and Snyman's reign as chief censors, paving the way for the reformist approach typical of the 1980s' censorship bureaucracy (McDonald 2009: 72–3).

The 'repressive tolerance' of the 1980s

Vorster resigned as prime minister in 1978 and was succeeded by P.W. Botha. The end of the 1970s and beginning of the 1980s was a decisive period for the apartheid regime. The intensity of the generalised popular uprising was matched by heightened repression, in a cycle of increased violence.

Following the tensions between the literary establishment and the censorship board caused by Leroux's case, the Publications Act of 1974 was amended by the Publications Amendment Act No. 109 of 1978, implemented in 1980. Two new features were introduced: a committee of experts, which would once again give a voice to the literary elite, and the imposition of conditions such as age and display restrictions, which would defend the interests of the likely reader (Van Rooyen 1987: 9). While this series of amendments contributed to appeasing some literary circles, it was received with scepticism and contempt in others. Gordimer, who was critical of censorship in all shapes and forms from the start, observed that the new provisions were merely the application of 'new gloss on old procedures' (in Merrett 1994: 81). Censorship became even more arbitrary, as mitigating factors such as literariness and likely readership were subjective and acted almost exclusively to the benefit of white writers. As De Lange (1997: 29) points out, 'because the standards, as applied, were so clearly ideologically biased, censorship affected each group of writers differently, depending on its relation with the ruling elite'. Silver (1984: 89) also emphasises the subjective nature of the Act:

> The style of writing is also an important fact in determining the potential effect on the likely readers: if a work is boring, as are many works of propaganda, its likely readers are less likely to be motivated to commit acts of terrorism, subversion or violence than they would be by work written in direct and compelling language.

In 1980 a shift occurred in the censors' approach, with the appointment of J.C.W. van Rooyen as chair of the PAB and Abraham Coetzee as director of publications. Under this administration, the amendments proposed in 1978 were fully implemented, once again shifting concerns towards the literary elite. Literary experts' opinions were taken seriously, in an effort to reinstate good relations with the Afrikaner literary intelligentsia (McDonald 2009: 79). Literary and artistic merit resurfaced as mitigating factors, despite the suggestive and debatable nature of these concepts. Expert committees, appointed after an appellant lodged a request, served as advisers to the PAB (Van Rooyen 1987: 9). In 1983 the Board included black literary experts for the first time, a move typical of Van Rooyen's 'repressive tolerance', an expression coined by Jaki Seroke (McDonald 2009: 77).

The effects of the long-term suppression of so-called undesirable publications were ironically not only felt in the ranks of anti-apartheid resistance, but also by censors themselves. Van Rooyen once wondered 'whether the South African reading public [was] isolated from knowledge about the enemy' (in De Lange 1997: 27). Not only were writers isolated from their readers, but politicians were also out of touch with the general population. It is in this patronising spirit of 'getting to know the enemy' that censorship at the beginning of the 1980s took into consideration the necessity of tolerating committed, or protest literature, as it was called, as a legitimate outlet to express frustration and protest. Official acknowledgement of protest literature led to the unbanning of several publications, such as the Freedom Charter in 1984 and the contested release of John Riley's *Cry Freedom*, even if security police still confiscated copies of the movie based on the novel. A space for moderate political discourse was created in the public sphere and protest was differentiated from sedition, although still under the paternalistic and ever-watchful eye of the censors. However, as McDonald (2009: 78) points out, these seemingly progressive reforms of the publications control apparatus were paralleled by a series of repressive laws that acted as direct forms of censorship, such as the Internal Security Act No. 74 of 1982 and the state of emergency declared in 1985, which empowered the state to ban and detain individuals and organisations. Responses to Van Rooyen's reformist and seemingly conciliatory attitude were far from unanimous. Coetzee saw them as treating Afrikaans writers as 'harmless dabblers' (in Merrett 1994: 81), while Gordimer expressed her contempt for the entire apparatus: 'I really have no concept of an ideal reader. I leave that to the Censorship Board with their "probable reader" and "ordinary, average South African"' (in Gray 2005: 37).

The likely reader test

Given Van Rooyen's desire to recognise the interests of the likely reader, issues of readership took a central role in the censors' preoccupations under his leadership. As Coetzee (1996: 186) observes, censors posed as 'arbiter between contending social forces'. Censors read through the eyes of an imagined reader, or as Coetzee has it, 'via an interposed fictional figure, whether reasonable or likely' (188).

What became known as the likely reader test was applied to assess whether a publication contravened section 47 (2) (d) and (e) of the Act, the articles pertaining to relations between citizens of South Africa and to the safety of the state. The test was carried out to assess the impact of a publication on the likely reader and 'whether a work would have the effect of turning the average, decent-minded man, who embodied the median opinion of law-abiding South Africa citizens, to revolutionary or lawless conduct' (Silver 1984: 63). Therefore, a likely popular readership and mass readership would be an aggravating factor, as opposed to a sophisticated or educated readership, which would be limited in numbers. What reading did to the likely reader was determined on speculation alone.

As Silver (1984: 72) notes, the PAB stated that the effect of a publication on the likely reader should be determined by probabilities and not possibilities. Several categories of readers were developed, such as the pro-revolutionary reader, the communist reader, the academic reader and the literary reader. The case of Mothobi Mutloatse's *Forced Landing* emplifies this idea of imagining the likely reader, as detailed in this archival document:

> The argument, the protestations have the ring of sincerity and, as has been said above, will be regarded by the reader as a matter of opinion. The insight of the South African reader must not be underestimated: he is daily confronted with political news and political comment from the left and the right and is generally not so easily influenced as is sometimes thought. The Act cannot guard against possibilities and the adjudicators must base their decisions on probabilities (in Silver 1984: 73).

Likewise, the case of *A Ride on the Whirlwind*, a novel by Sipho Sepamla, reveals these intricate considerations on the probable reaction of a likely readership:

> Although the readership of this publication cannot be regarded as sophisticated or intellectual, the likely reader would be the more arduous kind who would be prepared to labour through parts of

this book. Parts of it could just as well have been left out. [. . .] The likely readership of the present novel would, as has been pointed out above, come close to a popular readership, but on the other hand, revolutionaries and potential revolutionaries find their inspiration in publications of a more direct and inciting nature (in Silver 1984: 68).

Another example of the censors' operative mind is the case of D.H. Lawrence's *Lady Chatterley's Lover*, which was allowed because of its assumed limited sophisticated readership (Van Rooyen 1987: 10).

These new provisions were intrinsically discriminatory and filled with paternalistic overtones, despite the elaborate literary analysis involved in the process. The censors' bias towards certain genres and authors was the result of the quasi-immunity of literature benefiting from international visibility, a lesson learnt after the uproar caused by the ban on Leroux's *Magersfontein, O Magersfontein!* (De Lange 1997: 139). Merrett (1994: 80) argues that 'Black writers were targeted because they were likely to have a Black readership, especially among the young'. Coetzee (1996: 213) further points out that works with a sophisticated likely readership would be used as 'useful safety-valves for pent-up feelings', in the words of Van Rooyen, where 'disaffected intellectuals could let off steam'. Publications were therefore banned not merely because of their subjects and themes, but because of who was likely to read them and their likely effect on readers. Noting the persisting inequalities in the ways censorship was applied to black and white writers, even within the confines of protest literature, Es'kia Mphahlele denounced the fact that 'the White writer can still get away with a lot in South Africa. A Black man who wrote the same things the liberal-minded among the Whites write, who represented the liberal and egalitarian ideas, would most likely be banned' (in De Lange 1997: 130).

Several examples can be found of publications by white authors being unbanned or passed while publications by black authors treating similar topics were banned. For instance, in 1979 Miriam Tlali's *Muriel at*

Metropolitan was banned at the same time as Gordimer's *Burger's Daughter* was unbanned, although both novels allegedly held Afrikaners in contempt in some passages. Brink's *A Dry White Season* and Wessel Ebersohn's *Store up the Anger* were both not banned, while Mtutuzeli Matshoba's *Call Me Not a Man* was banned, even though all three illustrated some similar aspects of the black experience in South Africa, particularly police brutality, prison conditions and forced labour (Merrett 1994: 80). With respect to this particular example, and given that *A Dry White Season* was considered more radical than *Call Me Not a Man*, Gordimer comments: 'Why may White writers deal with inflammables? It is because the new censorship dispensation has understood something important to censorship as an arm of repression – while White writings are predominant critical and protestant in mood, Black writings are inspirational, and that is why the Government fears them' (in De Lange 1997: 132).

The shift in focus, from the average decent-minded reader to the likely reader, had a great influence on the way the censorship bureaucracy operated. Intrinsically linked, artistic and literary merits were the key factors in defining the likely readership of a given publication. Once identified, the effect of a publication on this readership was assessed and it was determined whether it was undesirable or desirable. This way of imagining the figure of the likely reader prevailed until the 1990s.

Post-1990 developments

The Publications Act No. 42 of 1974, as amended by the Publications Amendment Act No. 109 of 1978, remained in force. Abraham Coetzee was the last chief censor until 1997. In 1990, Van Rooyen was replaced by Louis Pienaar, who was chair of the PAB until 1992. While the end of state censorship was in sight, when Nelson Mandela gave his celebrated speech in Cape Town on 11 February 1990, his writings were still banned for possession (Merrett 1994: 170).

In 1992 the Publications Amendment Act No. 90 came into effect. It provided for speedier appeals, which led to the unbanning of many publications, but books under appeal could not be sold while the process was pending (Merrett 1994: 171). Each banned publication had to be reassessed, as the Directorate of Publications had rejected a blanket unbanning of publications in 1991 (170). Between 1991 and 1992 the PAB reviewed more than 4 000 titles, most of which were unbanned (McDonald 2009: 82), while other publications, such as the journal of the African National Congress, *Sechaba*, were considered dated and were therefore believed to not need unbanning by the Directorate of Publications (Merrett 1994: 171).

Mangosuthu Buthelezi, the minister of home affairs in the government of national unity, commissioned a task team to draft proposals to replace the Publications Act as amended, which aimed at encompassing democratic ideals and the spirit of the new South Africa. However, the new Film and Publications Bill resembled the Publications Act in many respects and some of the twelve members of this working group were high ranking in the previous Publications Board (De Lange 1997: 157). Robert Kirby wrote in the *Sunday Times* at the time:

> This is quite an unseemly loading of the task group with activists of the vintage school of censorship. One wonders what chief Buthelezi hopes to gain by these two inclusions. It certainly can't be credibility, simply because including them looks like a sanction for continuity – you never invite a hangman to the wake. Or is the minister just being fair and giving the pair a chance to fight for their jobs (in De Lange 1997: 157)?

Transformation and change occurred progressively and started with the suppression of some clauses of the infamous section 47 of the Publications Act of 1974, mainly those of a political nature (De Lange 1997: 155). In March 1995, the draft of the Film and Publications Bill was published in the *Government Gazette* and later tabled in Parliament. The Senate approved the Bill with some amendments, turning it into law in 1996. Under the new law, the former Directorate of Publications became the Film and Publications Board and the PAB became the Film and Publications Review Board.

Censors' definitions of the reader

Censorship in South Africa silenced entire generations of writers and artists and isolated writers from their readers. In the early 1970s, Gordimer deplored the climate of isolation created by censorship among writers, pointing out that 'as South Africans we do not know what the rest of Africa is thinking, just as, as Whites, we do not know what the Black and Coloured population is thinking' (in Merrett 1994: 63). However, censorship ultimately failed to entirely alienate writers from one another:

> For a very long time three different streams of literature ran their separate courses: Black, Afrikaans and English. But during the last few years a new awareness of a common identity as writers has arisen, creating a new sense of solidarity in a body of informed and articulate resistance to oppression (Brink 1983: 51).

From 1948 onwards, with the NP in power, a vision for the Afrikaner population, the *volk*, took shape. Particular expectations of the Afrikaans literary and cultural field formed part of this collective project and had a great impact on the evolution of the censorship apparatus. As a historical overview of censorship in South Africa suggests, ideas about readers shifted, with definitions of literature, the 'average man' and the likely reader, and the consolidation of an exclusive and oppressive nation-building project.

The Suppression of Communism Act No. 44 of 1950, which aimed to protect South Africa from so-called communist ideas, implied different ideas of readers. By prohibiting certain publications judged communist, the censors aimed at protecting naive and vulnerable readers from potential contamination and avoiding incitement of alleged easily influenced ones. Subversive or communist readers were thought of as finding ideological affinity in communist publications, which could serve their communist agenda and activities. Moreover, the mere fact of reading or being in possession of an alleged communist publication was enough for an individual to be labelled a communist and banned.

The Publications and Entertainments Act No. 26 of 1963, with its consideration of 'the person likely to be exposed to the effect or influence' of a publication (section 6 (1) (a)), introduced a more nuanced although equally subjective conception of readers. Depending on its degree of literariness and sophistication, among other factors, a publication could attract a sophisticated limited readership or a mass readership. Literary readers were held in high esteem by censors, as they were thought of as grounded, intelligent and enlightened, while a mass readership was in all likelihood easily influenced, reactionary and potentially dangerous. Between these two stood the average reader, who was upholding public morals, religious convictions and the good order of the general public. For censors, the average reader was a reflection of the 'average man' and ideal citizen, whose good Christian morals had to be preserved and who had to be protected from obscene, offensive or harmful ideas and publications.

While censorship pre-dates apartheid through colonial missions and successive censorship laws dating as far back as 1913, censors, who in the early days of institutionalised apartheid censorship were mainly literary academics, experts and intellectuals, had a very elitist notion of what constituted literature (McDonald 2009: 39). They posed as the enlightened and balanced reader (Merrett 1994: 62) and were the self-proclaimed guardians of good Afrikaans literature (McDonald 2009: 26). This notion of serious literature would punctuate the censors' discourse in the 1960s, bringing into play notions of good reading, good book and good reader. The concept of literariness at work was rather vague and it seems easier to grasp what was not considered literature than what was. Literariness translated as artistic, Christian and apolitical. Concerns related to aesthetics, morals, politics, religion, language register, race relations and authorship accommodated a very elitist and exclusive group of readers and writers. While implying an elitist readership, the notion of pure literature was designed to preserve Afrikaans literary standards and to place the literary above the political – a rather paradoxical position since censorship was fundamentally political.

This promotion of good reading coincided with an alleged decline in Afrikaans literary production, occasioned by the advent of imported paperbacks from the West, which were, in the eyes of the censors, mass-market fiction and needed to be curbed (McDonald 2009: 25). Such popular literature was a threat from which readers had to be protected, as it contained potentially dangerous and widely disseminated ideas. Lawyer, judge and academic John Dugard explains the censors' vehement objection to imported popular literature:

> The real objection to the social and cultural freedom of the twentieth century is that, if exported to South Africa, it might release the average Afrikaner from the tenacious grasp of those institutions which at present control both his mind and his voting habits: the Dutch Reformed Church, Afrikaner cultural organizations, the Afrikaans language press and the National Party (in Hachten and Giffard 1984: 158).

In its narrow definition as elitist and serious, literature was used as one of many tools to consolidate the hegemonic position of the NP and to legitimise the censorship system. Debates emerged on the essence of the literary and the role of literature. Reflecting on South African literature, Mphahlele, one of South Africa's leading intellectual figures and literary critics, argued for an anti-prescriptive, anti-elitist, African, humanistic literature that would blend aesthetic and political components into one crafted artistic product (McDonald 2009: 176). This perception was in direct opposition to the censors' official one of literature and offered authors greater freedom of expression and poetic licence.

The fluctuating boundary between the 'literary' and the 'political' in South African literature is a recurrent theme in literary criticism (see Ndebele 1991; Nkosi 1983; Sachs 1990). Some literature was quite explicit in its commitment, while some writers avoided alluding to politics altogether and focused on art for art's sake, which in itself could be perceived as a political act, albeit of a different kind. Njabulo Ndebele (1992: 23) echoes the interconnection between fiction and reality: 'The state of literature in South Africa also mirrors in a very fundamental way the larger historical imbalances in the country and that lasting answers to some of our literary problems are to be found in the manner in which the larger struggle for liberation is finally resolved.' By asserting the inevitable link between politics and literature, Ndebele points to the complexities of a public space where competing cultural, political, social and literary identities coexist and struggle to survive.

A clear sense of otherness prevailed among censors and dislocated the discourses and relations between censors, writers and readers. Gordimer (1988: 16) highlights the relevance writers find in their readers when asserting that 'writers cannot be a cultural force worth censoring until there is a mass population that can, and will have the facilities to, read our books'. The focus on suppressing writers and their publications effectively hindered readerships' growth and prevented reading cultures from flourishing to their full potential. Through the censorship system, most work by black writers was either banned or the writers were in exile. Breytenbach, a strong opponent of censorship, argues that it was not necessary in the mainstream book trade, as the establishment had other more discreet means of dealing with its own dissenters before publication (in McDonald 2009: 99).

Conclusion

From colonial times, censorship was used as a political tool to control and influence public opinion. Numerous publications, both from South Africa and abroad, were banned and removed from circulation; school curricula were heavily controlled and biased; an ambient discourse of positive uplifting was propagated; libraries and bookstores were scrutinised; and the vast majority of writers were directly or indirectly affected by publications control. Propaganda and other coercive tactics were not unheard of and apartheid censorship forms part of a broader continuum of publication control and influence over what readers ought to read, finding its origins in the Cape colony and still rearing its head in contemporary democratic South Africa.

While the censorship apparatus is but one segment of a historical continuity, it created discontinuity and interrupted the flow of cultural production, impacting on literary history, creating particular genres and trends in South African literatures and influencing the formation of readerships, reading cultures and literary canons. Good literature in South Africa formed part of a specific narrative instilled since the beginning of colonialism and contributed to nation building, as it consolidated a propaganda geared towards the idea of an ideal 'average man', that is, embracing a nationalist identity. On the other hand, literature as a social construct and vehicle of culture also contributed to creating a sense of identity among opposing voices. Despite the bans and strict censorship measures, alternative readerships strived to survive. As Brink (1983: 52) observed:

> Censorship in South Africa has created for the reader a new sense of adventure, in literature, a new sense of being 'in touch'. This is illustrated by the increased demand for banned books amongst White readers and in the way in which new publications by Blacks are sold on the streets of Soweto.

The effects of censorship on readers, writers, publishers and booksellers are various and complex and are underpinned by competing interests and positionalities. Censorship in South Africa was a political weapon, integral to the apartheid arsenal. Gordimer summarised the political nature of censorship: 'We shall not be rid of censorship until we are rid of apartheid. Censorship is the arm of mind control and is as necessary to maintain a racist regime as the other arm of internal repression, the secret police' (in Hachten and Giffard 1984: 155).

Successive competing definitions of imagined readers played a role in the censorship discourse. Against these constructs, some actual readers read and sourced books, as discussed in the next chapter.

3 | Censorship versus Publishers, Librarians and Booksellers

> The right to write is a human right.
> — Ngũgĩ wa Thiong'o, *Writers in Politics*

IMAGINING IDEAS OF readers and proposing an elitist notion of literature, apartheid censorship engineered a 'good book' campaign aligned to a much wider repressive political propaganda and cultural programme. Literary responses to censorship were diverse and underpinned by different and, at times, conflicting ideologies, political outlooks and cultural sensitivities, reflecting the various strands of resistance to the apartheid regime. The key actors in the book industry – publishers, academics, librarians, booksellers and actual readers, were caught between censors and imagined reading publics.

One definition of alternative publishers in apartheid South Africa could loosely designate those operating outside the mainstream book trade who took risks in publishing books likely to be banned and at times had to adopt unorthodox means to do so. Despite strict censorship laws, these alternative publishers, who could also be called oppositional or independent publishers, defied the 'good book' campaign engineered by the censorship apparatus and enabled the creation of a progressive and diverse literary space. They developed independent editorial policies without undue interference, were innovative, promoted freedom of speech, took financial risks and were key players in upholding bibliodiversity in a context characterised by hegemony and repression. 'Bibliodiversity', a term coined by a Chilean independent publishers' collective, 'is cultural diversity applied to the world of books', which promotes the circulation of a plurality of voices and is an integral part of democratic ideals.[1] In discussing South African alternative publishers operating under apartheid censorship, this chapter traces strands of anti-censorship resistance that were expressed through the cultural sphere and examines the roles played by booksellers and librarians in disseminating this literature to actual readers, fostering a space for debate and the articulation of alternative voices.

Good books for law-abiding readers: Mainstream publishing in apartheid South Africa

Mainstream publishers generally adopt commercial editorial policies and are market driven. Publications adhere to a predefined editorial policy, are edited to fit within these parameters and are distributed and sold by traditional bookstores and outlets to a general reading public. The aim is to generate sales and profit. In a climate of censorship, this is achieved by conforming to the socio-political factors regulating the public space and the cultural economy. In the case of apartheid South Africa, the dominant public space was controlled by an Afrikaner nationalist nation-building project, where readers were divided into racial categories and channelled towards particular reading materials and patterns. The politicisation of the public space, marked by political, social, economic, cultural and religious interference by the apartheid state, inevitably led to the politicisation of arts and culture, including the book industry. In order to survive as commercial entities, South African mainstream publishers had to conform to the prevailing market diktats, which translated to preserving the status quo. A 'good book' campaign was implemented as an essential tool of apartheid propaganda. The set of relations between the various mainstream publishers and National Party (NP) power circles was complex. Patronage

---

1. International Alliance of Independent Publishers, http://www.alliance-editeurs.org/-presentation-orientation,068-?lang=fr.

and vested interests meant that censors in effect dictated editorial policies and books diverging from their narrow definition of literature ran the risk of being scrutinised and banned. Censors effectively intervened in the formation of literary canons and the establishment of conventions around particular literary genres (McDonald 2009: 84). Major players in the mainstream Afrikaans publishing scene included Nasionale Pers (Naspers), J.L. van Schaik and Perskorporasie van Suid-Afrika (Perskor). As Peter McDonald (2009: 88) notes, these presses 'endeavoured to reshape the market by creating a series of *national* canons of African literature, which reinforced, or at least did not unsettle, apartheid thinking'.

Historically, literature in African languages was mainly published by British missionary presses, established in South Africa during the colonial period. While publishing several novels in African languages, they also published the bulk of textbooks in African languages for their missionary schools, as well as some translations. For instance, Lovedale Press published several novels by African writers, among them Sol T. Plaatje's seminal novel *Mhudi* in 1930. These presses were under white ownership, generally adopted a liberal stance and often employed a black person as editor (McDonald 2009: 87). The transition from the colonial era to apartheid, while marked by continuity in terms of censorship and oppression, was significant for the book market, and more specifically the lucrative textbook market.

Afrikaner nationalism infused the publishing industry from the 1940s onwards, notably through the textbook market, which constituted the bulk of missionary publishing (Mpe and Seeber 2000: 18). The relative independence enjoyed by missionary presses during the colonial period was gradually superseded by the NP government's language boards and the notorious Bantu Education programme, which created a homogenous book market by centrally prescribing textbooks (Davis 2011: 85). Language boards were set up in the 1950s that recommended books to be prescribed by the government's Department of Education, which meant that most books published by missionary presses that were critical of the government's segregationist policies became obsolete (Mpe and Seeber

2000: 18). According to Dumisane Ntshangase (later co-author of the South African Languages Bill), corruption was rife, with members of the board writing the bulk of prescribed (and biased) textbooks (in Mpe and Seeber 2000: 20-1).

Literature in African languages progressively became the terrain of Afrikaner publishers. As McDonald (2009: 89) points out, this partly explains why censorship had little or no direct impact on literature in African languages: by 1973 no books in these languages had been submitted to the censorship board's Bantu language specialist. Mainstream Afrikaans presses' interests in the profitability of the African-language publishing market led to the creation of a canon of African literature revolving around ethnography and oral tradition, praise poetry and animal tales and myths, in alignment with the patronising 'good African' ideal underpinning the newly formed Bantustans (88).

Mainstream publishers' interests were closely tied to mainstream political interests, with some publishing board members also holding public administration positions. A monopoly in the publishing industry rapidly developed, particularly with regard to the textbook market. Perskor and Naspers, two powerful Afrikaner-owned media conglomerates, which enjoyed privileged relationships with the ruling NP, entered and practically took over the lucrative African primary textbook market alongside De Jager-Haum, Oxford University Press (OUP) Southern Africa and Longman Green (Mpe and Seeber 2000: 21-2). Human & Rousseau, Juta & Company and Shuter & Shooter were other mainstream publishers operating in the educational book trade. These publishers pursued profit and focused on market demand, as opposed to alternative and independent publishers who focused on market supply.

In 1935 veteran poet and playwright N.P. van Wyk Louw created the Coalition of the Free Book, a subscription-based publishing initiative offering an alternative to mainstream Afrikaans literary publishers' focus on the textbook market, thus creating a space for the articulation of avant-garde ideals and voices through literature (McDonald 2009: 91). Although short-lived, the Coalition provided a platform for a wider range of Afrikaans literary voices to be heard. In 1945, Van Wyk Louw founded the trilingual literary magazine *Standpunte*, which quickly became a mouthpiece for the Afrikaans literary avant-garde. Contributions were in Dutch, English and Afrikaans, and included writers associated with the Sestigers movement (93). Strikingly, Van Wyk Louw's definition of literature, informed by a very European definition of literary modernity and the creation of a Republic of Letters, was not that dissimilar to the censors' early literary discourse, in its focus on literary aesthetics over politics. Moreover, three censors served on the magazine's editorial board (93), revealing that although it identified as avant-garde, *Standpunte* had a foot firmly anchored in conventional mainstream publishing. Other liberal, left-wing Afrikaans writers of the 1930s in the same circle as Van Wyk Louw included Jacques Malan, Lily Rabkin, Uys Krige and I.D. du Plessis. Malan's Marxist inclinations were well known – he had translated *The Communist Manifesto* into Afrikaans in 1938, with an introduction by Leon Trotsky (Sandwith 2014: 53).

Human & Rousseau and Afrikaanse Pers-Boekhandel (APB) were two mainstream publishing houses that also published works associated with the Afrikaans avant-garde. While their lists of authors were generally relatively similar, including writers such as Chris Barnard, Breyten Breytenbach, André Brink, Ingrid Jonker, Etienne Leroux, Jan Rabie and Bartho Smit, they differed in many other ways. In a nutshell, Transvaal-based Afrikaans fiction publisher APB was closely linked to the elite in power, with Prime Minister H.F. Verwoerd having chaired its board of directors before it merged with Perskor, which was very close to political elite circles (Mpe and Seeber 2000: 20). Although APB counted some Sestiger writers on its list, relations between the publisher and the young writers were tense, revealing an intergenerational clash in terms of literary conventions. Cape-based Human & Rousseau was considered more liberal, before it merged with Nasionale Pers in 1977, a mouthpiece for Afrikaner interests.

Questioning the elitist definitions of literature upheld by censors and at times shared by the most conservative members of the Sestigers, a group of young Sestigers, including Brink, Breytenbach and Adam Small, adopted a sense of political consciousness and inclusiveness. Brink made his position as a writer and co-editor of *Standpunte* clear, in this extract from a piece he wrote in 1968 in the Sestigers' journal *Kol*:

> If I speak of *my* people, then I mean: every person, black, coloured [*bruin* or mixed race] and white, who shares my country and my loyalty towards my country. This is the essence of my argument that our *whole* country must be opened up for writing [*oopgeskryf*, literally 'written open'] and that we writers should start taking account of what 'our whole country' really is (in McDonald 2009: 94).

English mainstream publishers operating in South Africa were, for the most part, subsidiaries of British multinational companies. They included Macmillan, Penguin, Hodder & Stoughton, Heinemann, McGraw-Hill, OUP Southern Africa and Longman Green, to name but a few. While they shared a portion of the textbook market before it was virtually taken over by Afrikaans presses, as mentioned earlier, they mainly focused on importing and distributing books published abroad to a South African readership. In the early 1960s, conditions for the book trade were precarious, not only because of the overarching and repressive apartheid system, but also because of the 1963 censorship legislation, the international cultural boycott against apartheid and a new configuration of the international book trade (McDonald 2009: 105).

British publishers operating in apartheid South Africa were often ambivalent in their editorial policies. Relations between the business and publishing missions were in constant flux, blurring the boundaries between commercial and ideological imperatives (Cloete 2000: 43). The 'dilemmas and contradictions' entailed in the dual policy of juggling both commercial and ideological publishing are illustrated through OUP's operations in South Africa during apartheid (Davis 2011: 79). Supporting her argument with Pierre Bourdieu's model of cultural and economic capital, Caroline Davis (2011: 98) argues that 'cultural capital was accumulated through

OUP's publications for the white academic market and tertiary market, and economic capital through the profitable black educational market'. The publisher balanced this connection between educational and literary publishing through, among other things, Rex Collings's project of creating the Three Crowns series, which would serve 'the importance of embedding "high culture" in the African publishing programme for the purpose of prestige and public relations, [predicting] that Three Crowns might serve an important function in compensating the more commercial activities of the press' (Davis 2005: 227–8). Seemingly, the 'African publishing programme' was regarded as being on the margins of the mainstream publishing programme and was perceived as a 'culture enterprise' (228). The Three Crowns series ended in 1976, but nonetheless served to validate OUP's cultural presence in Africa (227–8). This was the case in South Africa until 1970, when the accumulation of economic capital became OUP's official policy, meaning that concessions were necessary to secure the press's place in the mainstream South African market (Davis 2011: 98). In doing so, OUP eventually compromised its ideological position in favour of profitability, which resulted in it avoiding the publication of oppositional literature and focusing on 'Bantu Education approved texts', such as language textbooks depicting African rural life (79, 86). Seemingly, the line between cultural and commercial publishing had by then been crossed, as OUP's list became increasingly commercial (95).

While OUP remained active in South Africa from the colonial period well into the apartheid era, despite international protest (Davis 2011: 91), some multinational publishing companies closed their South African branches or suspended their activities in the country as a political gesture, refusing to co-operate with the apartheid government. For instance, Heinemann left South Africa in the 1960s, followed by McGraw-Hill in the early 1970s (Mpe and Seeber 2000: 22).

For South African publishers who were not aligned with the NP and found themselves on the outskirts of its close-knit network of influence, publishing almost became a gamble. The space for innovative, creative, independent and thought-provoking publishing aimed at a progressive public was at best curbed and at worst made impossible. Dissent came from within and outside Afrikaans circles and led to the creation of alternative publishing ventures of varying influence and impact, providing alternative books for alternative readers.

Several Afrikaans writers broke away from the mainstream publishing scene and either joined alternative or independent publishers, such as Breytenbach with Buren Publishers, or they founded alternative publishing outlets, such as Taurus; this is discussed in more detail later in this chapter. As McDonald explains, within Afrikaans literary circles the dissent found its roots in a form of resistance to cultural hegemony:

> The cleavage was not so much between the loyal tribal bard and the upstart dissident as between two forms of cultural resistance, one that could be accepted within the terms of the minority *volks avant-garde* and the other that could not. This gives an added significance to the change in the censors' attitudes in the mid-1970s and to the fact that neither of the first Afrikaans titles to be banned was published by a mainstream Afrikaner-owned firm (McDonald 2009: 99).

While the Afrikaans mainstream publishing industry experienced dissension from within and benefited from close relationships with the ruling elite, its English counterpart confronted another set of politics. English-language publishing was – at least until the 1960s – influenced by the British colonial legacy and patronage. As McDonald (2009: 104) reminds us, the Traditional Market Agreement of 1947 divided the international English market between Britain and the United States of America, and Britain gained exclusive selling rights in South Africa, the largest English market in Africa, and other Commonwealth countries until the 1970s. This meant that English-language books were mainly imported and were scrutinised by South African customs. As discussed in the previous chapter, this constituted a precarious and unpredictable form of censorship.

Alternative publishing for alternative readers

The *Merriam-Webster Dictionary* defines the term 'alternative' as 'different from the usual or conventional: such as existing or functioning outside the established cultural, social, or economic system', while 'independent' is defined as 'not dependent: such as not subject to control by others or not affiliated with a larger controlling unit'. In the context of publishing in apartheid South Africa, such alternative or independent publishing ventures could generally be understood as all publishing initiatives situated outside of the mainstream colonial and NP-aligned publishing industry. The reading campaign engineered by censors promoted a Christian view of life that reinforced the powers and legitimacy of the apartheid state and upheld Afrikaner nationalist values in general. Mainstream publishers published books that reinforced or at least did not challenge this view. In contrast, alternative publishing sought to offer a choice to readers, by publishing literature that fell outside of the mainstream body of literature sanctioned by apartheid ideologies, policies and legislation, and a platform for writers who refused to subscribe to the dominant prerogatives dictated by mainstream publishing politics. In all likelihood, these were publishers for whom the 'publishing mission' took precedence over the 'business mission' (Cloete 2000: 43), or in the words of Bourdieu, for whom cultural capital was more important than economic capital (Bourdieu 1994; Davis 2011: 80).

As David Philip points out, the sector of the book trade that was the most affected by censorship was involved in 'academic books and serious trade books for the thinking public' (in McDonald 2009: 84), implying the idea of a thinking readership. Successive censorship boards influenced the scope of academic research through various direct and indirect means, while conservative academics also had an impact on, and at times presided over, government decision-making processes, as was the case with the first censorship board, of which several academics were part. Despite often being seen as progressive, South African university presses were in fact exclusionary and published black authors when their opinion as 'Africans' were sought (Le Roux 2012: 445). University presses active in South Africa during apartheid included the Witwatersrand University Press founded in 1922, the University of Natal Press (1947), the University of South Africa Press (1956), Fort Hare University Press (in existence from the early 1960s to the early 1990s) and the University of Cape Town Press (1993) (439). These presses were modelled on OUP, where the press was a university department run as a non-profit organisation. Eurocentric and conservative in nature, and informed by and informing colonial education, from the 1970s South African university presses adopted the cautious – if not compromised – position of being apolitical (446), which in itself could be read as a political statement in favour of the status quo. While university presses did publish some liberal and oppositional books, they were mainly by white authors, reflecting the limited intellectual diversity and freedom in the academic space. Most oppositional academics found a home in alternative publishers such as Ravan Press, Skotaville or David Philip. Only from the 1980s onwards were black authors published by university presses on a variety of topics (445). This shows the extent of control exercised through censorship by the apartheid government over knowledge and canon formation, a legacy yet to be fully redressed more than twenty years into democracy.

Independent, alternative publishing played a role in building ideological and cultural resistance against apartheid in South Africa. As explained by Dick Cloete (2000: 43), the relationships that developed between the various actors involved in the alternative book world served a set of complementary common interests:

> [These] publications [represented] a community of interest wider than the fortunes of a specific organisation. This community can support publishing activities in a variety of ways ranging from providing a loyal and responsive audience through writing and volunteer support for editing, production, distribution and sales to sponsorships and financial contributions.

The conventions and well-defined roles characterising mainstream publishing were challenged through the creation of this alternative community, underpinned by solidarity around a common cause, a useful notion to understand the readership for these publications.

A community of interest is typically understood as a grouping of individuals united around a shared interest, whose avowed goal is to achieve a mutually beneficial outcome. In the South African context, alternative publishers provided intellectual and literary spaces that were open to various strands of opposition to apartheid, including leftist, liberal, oppositional and radical groupings and individuals, and generally opposed the mainstream publishing industry's discourse. These ventures went beyond the market diktat, promoting innovation and the development of new perspectives (Cloete 2000: 44). Political struggles used artistic and cultural spaces, in order to challenge the commercial book market. Cloete (43) defines alternative publishing as follows: 'Broadly defined, it includes anything outside mainstream commercial publishing, where the market is the final determinant of what is published. In contrast, the publishing mission takes precedence over the business mission in alternative publishing, although there is a point where the line between the two becomes blurred.'

By upholding voices marginalised by mainstream commercial publishers, alternative publishers created a space in the public arena for oppositional discourses to be articulated and perhaps, more importantly, heard (Cloete 2000: 44). In a politicised context such as apartheid South Africa, various strands of political resistance found their niche in the alternative cultural space. It could therefore be proposed that alternative publishers reflected and represented these forms of resistance as they were shunned by, or deliberately distanced themselves from, the mainstream. It is not possible within the limits of this book to include all publishers that could be labelled independent or alternative, as this would require a comprehensive survey of a vast number of anti-apartheid organisations (community-based, faith-based, non-governmental, political, grassroots and so on) as well as numerous oppositional publishing ventures of various scales and scope. Instead, selected alternative publishers of literary books and magazines are discussed.

Before the early 1940s, missionary presses occasionally published an oppositional book, but this was far from common (Philip 1990: 10). In the 1940s, Afrikaans nationalism gained momentum, ultimately leading to the rise of the NP to power and racial segregation. Despite this repressive climate, some alternative publishers worked to make books and ideas accessible through mindful decisions relating to price, language and content. Hailed as the first recognised oppositional publisher in South Africa, the African Bookman was founded in 1943 by Julian Rollnick. Although it closed in 1948, it produced around sixty titles, among which ten were by South African writers, including Govan Mbeki, Es'kia Mphahlele, and Eddie Roux, to name but a few (10).

The South African Institute of Race Relations (SAIRR), founded in 1929, could also be considered a pioneer of alternative publishing in South Africa. While it only started to publish books in the 1960s, it disseminated alternative ideas critical of the successive colonial and nationalist discourses through newsletters and booklets. The annual political review *Survey of Race Relations in South Africa* was one of its key publications. Typically spanning a couple of hundred pages, each edition of the *Survey* discussed the political affairs and developments that occurred in South Africa for a given year, as a kind of socio-political almanac. In its mission to expose facts not made known through the dominant media, the SAIRR inevitably ended up being seen as oppositional (Philip 1990: 17). The 1965 *Survey* contains headings such as 'Political Parties', listing mainstream parties and their respective politics; 'Political Representation of Coloured People'; 'Non-White Political Parties'; 'Secret Organisations', discussing organisations such as the Afrikaner Broederbond, the Sons of England and the Freemasons; 'Security Measures', including an overview of the Suppression of Communism Amendment Act No. 97 of 1965; 'General Protests Against the Suppression of Communism Act and Criminal Procedure Amendment Act', discussing the protest meetings held in Cape Town and Durban; 'Control of Publications'; 'Foreign Affairs', which discusses United Nations proceedings on South Africa and international sanctions against the apartheid regime; 'General Matters

Affecting Africans', which discusses issues such as population control and homelands; and 'Coloured and Asian Affairs', among others (Horrell 1966). The general editorial line aimed to counter propaganda and make facts known. Also published by the SAIRR, the booklet *Action, Reaction and Counteraction: A Companion Booklet to 'Legislation and Race Relations'* is, as explained in the title page, 'a review of non-white opposition to the apartheid policy, counter-measures by the Government, and the eruption of new waves of unrest' (Horrell 1963).

While the SAIRR continued its activities – and is still an active civil society organisation in contemporary South Africa – one of its co-founders, liberal leader Leo Marquard set up the South African branch of OUP in Cape Town. Although OUP could be considered an alternative publisher in its early days of operation, it later became a major player in the commercial book trade (Philip 1990: 13) and in the South African school publishing market (Davis 2011). However, until the early 1970s, OUP published several oppositional books – for instance, Edgar Brookes's *Civil Liberty in South Africa*, David Welsh's *The Roots of Segregation* and Marquard's *People and Policies of South Africa* (Philip 1990: 11).

David Philip, who was Marquard's assistant editor and later editorial manager at OUP, left the company in 1971 to set up David Philip Publishers, with his wife Marie. Also embracing a liberal tradition, David Philip Publishers focused on tertiary education and general publishing 'to provide previously unavailable texts of South African literature for use in universities and in the process going some way towards bridging the "unbridgeable gap" in our literature caused by the banning of the 1960s and 1970s' (Philip 1990: 14). By publishing what they termed 'books that matter for Southern Africa' (Philip 1990: 9), David Philip Publishers contributed to making progressive authors' works available and providing books to readers identifying with anti-apartheid and oppositional politics. The company did not hesitate to take risks or publish books likely to be banned or attract the censors' scrutiny, as was the case with *Student Perspectives on South Africa*. Edited by H.W. van der Merwe and David Welsh, this collection of essays published in 1972 was written by representatives and members of the various students' movements active in the early 1970s, such as the South African Students' Organisation (SASO), the National Union of South African Students (NUSAS) and the Afrikaanse Studentebond. Students' organisations provided sites of alternative reading, writing and publishing, with some producing anti-apartheid newsletters and pamphlets, and playing a central role in South African anti-apartheid and alternative politics – see, for example, Badat (1999).

The first impression of *Student Perspectives on South Africa* rapidly sold out and some of its contributors, among them black consciousness (BC) leaders Steve Biko and Barney Pityana, were declared banned persons, which meant that the book could no longer be distributed in South Africa. Having recently printed a second run, Philip sent it to London for distribution overseas. This example reveals the daring attitude of oppositional publishers such as Philip, who explains:

> If one were actually to read and take seriously the details of their legislation for instance on censorship and banned people, and the penalties for infringements, one would end up publishing nothing. It was therefore necessary for a publisher to develop a blanking of the mind towards this legislation and above all to be careful not actually to be guided by it. This may sound irresponsible but it was better to be irresponsible than scared stiff of publishing anything (Philip 1990: 14).

With its AfricaSouth Paperbacks series launched in 1982, David Philip Publishers sought to keep alternative books in print: 'Many previously banned books were unbanned as the result of our applications to the Publications Committee, and then republished in AfricaSouth Paperbacks' (Philip 1990: 14).

Faith-based resistance and liberal patronage opened the doors to English-language alternative publishers, which would prove to have a significant impact on the South African literary and socio-political scene, such as the Study Project on Christianity in Apartheid Society (SPRO-CAS), funded by the Christian Institute and the South African Council of Churches (SACC). Afrikaner anti-apartheid activist Beyers Naudé founded SPRO-CAS in 1969 'to explore the possibilities and problems of creating a social order in South Africa based on the "integrated thrusts of love and association" as an alternative to the apartheid society' (Stadler 1975: 102). Through its community projects and publications, SPRO-CAS served as an incubator for political debates and analysis. It operated in two phases – SPRO-CAS I and SPRO-CAS II. The former was a study project that focused on an analysis of the situation and enabled the creation of a series of commissions, which resulted in publications such as *Anatomy of Apartheid*, *Towards Social Change* and *South Africa's Political Alternatives*, all edited by Peter Randall in 1970, 1971 and 1973, respectively. The second phase could be labelled as the action project and was aimed at formulating strategies for social, political and economic change. Among other titles, it published Rick Turner's *The Eye of the Needle* and James Matthews and Gladys Thomas's *Cry Rage* in 1972, which were both banned in March 1973 (107). In total, SPRO-CAS I and II produced dozens of reports and some one hundred articles and essays (102), the bulk of which were edited by Randall, who served as SPRO-CAS's director between 1969 and 1972, after having been assistant director at the SAIRR between 1965 and 1969.

The Black Community Programmes (BCP) was established in 1970, under SPRO-CAS II's umbrella. It would serve as an incubator for the emerging Black Consciousness Movement (BCM), with the involvement of anti-apartheid activists such as Biko, Bennie Khoapa, Pityana and Mamphela Ramphele, to name but a few. The BCP also produced several publications through its publishing programme – for example, the periodical collection of essays by black activists titled *Black Viewpoint*; the periodical examination of black political activity, *Black Review*; and the *Handbook of Black Organisations* (Stadler 1975: 108). As Khoapa points out, referring to the body of BCM-inspired literature: 'All these publications are selling much more widely in the black community than any other publications of literary value' (in Cloete 2000: 46). The introduction to the *Black Viewpoint* September 1972 issue, written by Biko, corroborates this view, clearly stating the objectives of the publication and laying down some of the founding principles of the BCM:

> It is significant that in a country peopled to the extent of 75% blacks and whose entire economic structure is supported and maintained, willingly or unwillingly, mainly by blacks, we find very few publications that are directed at, manned by and produced by black people.
>
> *Black Viewpoint* is a happy addition by the Black Community Programmes to all those publications that are of great relevance to the black people. Our relevance is meant to be in the sense that we communicate black things said by blacks in the various situations in which they find themselves in this country of ours. We have felt and observed in the past, the existence of a great vacuum in our literary and newspaper world. So many things are said so often about us and for us but very seldom by us.
>
> [. . .] In terms of thinking, therefore, *Black Viewpoint* is meant to protect and further the interests of black people. We do not intend to venture beyond this. We shall not serve as an exclusive mouthpiece for any particular section of the black community but merely to pick up topics as they come and as they are dealt with by blacks in various situations (Biko 1972: n.p.).

This editorial excerpt raises the question of marginalised yet majority black readerships and the vacuum, as Biko terms it, in the black literature and media spheres. Biko reminds us that relevance and common interests are central to the formation of these readerships, once again highlighting the dichotomy between the mainstream commercial publishing industry and the ideological needs and purpose of the alternative literary space. Biko's editorial also signifies a move away from white liberal resistance to apartheid and oppositional publishing. Despite being banned in 1977, the BCP provided leverage for several black-owned publishing ventures throughout the 1970s and 1980s, with black publishers and editors producing books and publications by black authors for black readers, thus responding to the needs of a reading public that until then had been mostly ignored.

Also an offshoot of SPRO-CAS, Ravan Press was established in 1972 in Johannesburg and played a central role in the alternative publishing scene. Founded by Peter Randall, Danie van Zyl and Beyers Naudé, who were all members of the Christian Institute, Ravan Press was described in the following terms, in line with SPRO-CAS's overall vision and ideology: 'We are part of that section of South African society engaged in changing the present social system . . . we aim to produce books that inform the struggle in the present . . . and that create a climate in which the new society can be discussed' (in Philip 1990: 15).

Ravan Press was a platform for emerging and established oppositional writers, initially focused on BC and liberation theology and eventually including various genres, such as 'class-orientated analysis, trade-union and workerist books, literacy, history and social studies, fiction, and children's books' (Philip 1990: 15). At the core of its mandate was the publication of SPRO-CAS's radical research and the SPRO-CAS commissions' reports (Mpe and Seeber 2000: 5; Cloete 2000: 47). Ravan rapidly positioned itself as a prime publisher of radical creative writing and anti-apartheid social research, inevitably attracting the censors' attention and scrutiny. As Glenn Moss recalls, banning books was not the only way in which the authorities tried to silence Ravan:

> The State and its various organs were predictably antagonistic and this manifested itself in repetitive banning and confiscation of books, general harassment and intimidation, interference in the infrastructure necessary for formal business operations (telephone, postage, relations with printers) and physical attacks on Ravan premises and property. This included the firebombing of Ravan's offices (in Mpe and Seeber 2000: 26–7).

Randall was Ravan's first director, until a banning order was served on him in 1977 and he was replaced by Mike Kirkwood. Kirkwood, who had been editor of *Bolt*, had contacts with writers and artists such as Mothobi Mutloatse and Jaki Seroke, among others (Cloete 2000: 48). Writers and publishers worked in close collaboration and were involved in the different stages of production. The idea of a magazine where artists would also be editors matured, leading to the creation of *Staffrider* in 1979. Around the same time, at the end of the 1970s, Mutloatse became director at Ravan while also working at *The Voice*, a newspaper edited by the SACC. Seroke was also closely involved in the running of *Staffrider*, co-ordinating the relations between the magazine and community-based arts groups and organising workshops with artists, focusing on writing skills and African literature, from which several contributions to *Staffrider* emerged, including Ingoapele Madingoane's *Africa My Beginning* and Mtutuzeli Matshoba's *Call Me Not a Man*. As explained by Seroke, relevance and immediacy took precedence over literary qualities: 'The intention was not to achieve the highest aesthetic standards but to produce a literature of poor communities, a little rough perhaps, but able to express their life' (in Cloete 2000: 48). The *Staffrider* magazine and series aimed at reaching reading communities in black townships (McDonald 2009: 144). Mutloatse further expresses how literary conventions and forms were owned, transformed and subverted and consciously rejected, and how literature was used to assert identities and channel anger in a creative manner:

> We are going to pee, spit and shit on literary convention before we are through; we are going to kick and pull and push and drag literature into the form we prefer. We are going to experiment and probe and not give a damn what the critics have to say. Because we are in search of our true self – undergoing self-discovery as a people (in Mpe and Seeber 2000: 25).

Far from producing solely reactionary and oppositional literature, the BCM instilled self-realisation and empowerment in this literary impulse. Unsurprisingly, *Staffrider* rapidly ran into trouble with censors and the first issue was banned a month after its publication in 1978 on the grounds of obscenity, harm to race relations and sedition, and for portraying the South African police force in an unfavourable and undermining manner (McDonald 2009: 147). Ravan adopted a policy of non-cooperation with censors and refused to appeal the ban through the Appeal Board. However, Kirkwood engaged in meetings with J.C.W. van Rooyen, a reformist who was soon to be chair of the Board, and initiated dialogue with censors through Ravan's lawyers.

The correspondence between Ravan and censors was published in the subsequent issue of *Staffrider* and highlights the discourse relating to the issue of readership at stake in the debate, emphasising the close relationship Ravan had with its contributors and readers. In this extract from a letter from Kirkwood to Van Rooyen, note Ravan's reply to the paternalist rhetoric typical of Van Rooyen's 'new pragmatic language':

> The authority and image of the police are, let's face it, in considerable disrepair as far as blacks are concerned . . . Nevertheless all the black readers we consulted (did you consult any?) thought that the depiction of the police in the magazine was fair. Moreover, they felt that the depiction, openly published, would relieve tension rather than exacerbate it: a 'safety valve', if you like (in McDonald 2009: 147).

Staffrider would often be examined by censors in the following years, provoking debates between the conservative and reformist censor factions. The magazine was somehow tolerated, as the new reformist censorship discourse tolerating protest literature and considering questions of 'likely readership' gained currency (McDonald 2009: 148).

In 1982 Chris van Wyk was appointed editor of *Staffrider*, community groups having edited the magazine before that. In 1987, Kirkwood resigned and was replaced by Moss as managing director and Randall returned after his ban was lifted. This era marked a change in Ravan's publishing programme, with less fiction and poetry published. The change was caused by several factors, including the shrinking market for oppositional and resistance literature, and the withdrawal of international funding for cultural and political activism with the imminent defeat of the apartheid regime (Cloete 2000: 50). In 1990 *Staffrider* fell under the control of the Congress of South African Writers and Andries Oliphant became chief editor. In 1996 Ravan's personnel was retrenched and it was integrated into mainstream publisher Hodder.

A situation involving Kirkwood and Mbulelo Vizikhungo Mzamane sheds light on the debates that occurred in the alternative publishing space and the complex set of relations between white publishers and black writers, which are in turn reflective of the inclusive versus separatist approaches characterising the political resistance movements in South Africa (McDonald 2009: 154). The contentious issue at stake in this case revolves around Matshoba's *Call Me Not a Man*, which was published by Ravan in the Staffrider series in 1980 and banned soon after publication. Mzamane reviewed Matshoba's book and criticised it for having been rushed into production (150). He criticised Ravan's editorial policy or lack thereof, advocating for a more rigorous pre-publication editorial process that would contribute to instilling a greater sense of self-criticism in writers. In doing so, Mzamane directly confronted Kirkwood in his capacity as editor, emphasising the importance of craftsmanship in literature and believing in the idea that the art of writing is rewriting, thus emphasising the important duty of an editor. Kirkwood responded by arguing that as editor of a publishing company promoting black empowerment and supporting BC writers, he did not want to interfere and preferred to act as a 'transitional editor' or 'outsider' (151). *Staffrider*'s editorial non-interference approach sought to provide a free space for emerging black writers, but inevitably impacted on overall quality. This debate led to the pressing issue of black ownership and Mzamane concluded that the problem was directly linked to leadership: 'Ravan is in your hands and not mine or Mothobi's, for that matter' (in McDonald 2009: 151).

Tensions of this nature, on the position of black writers in a white-dominated alternative publishing industry, culminated in the breakaway of several prominent black writers from progressive literary and intellectual spaces such as Ravan and PEN SA. The African Writers' Association was founded in this context, leading to the creation of the independent black publishing house Skotaville Publishers. Skotaville was founded in 1982 in Soweto, Johannesburg, by Seroke, who was later joined by Mutloatse. Besides Seroke and Mutloatse who served as executive directors, the board only comprised black people and included Es'kia Mphahlele, Sipho Sepamla and Miriam Tlali, among others. In the words of Mutloatse, Skotaville aimed at being a 'truly independent black printing and publishing house', providing 'affordable books aimed at a mass market' (in Cloete 2000: 51). It gained publishing rights to some of the International Labour Organization's and World Health Organization's publications. Its list also included some educational and children's books, as well as prominent anti-apartheid activists' works, such as Desmond Tutu's *Hope and Suffering* and Nelson Mandela's biography *Higher than Hope*. It also published the socio-literary magazine *The Classic*. In total, Skotaville published almost one hundred titles in the 1980s, which consisted of mainly political, theological and educational publications, with a fifth of its total output being literary books (McDonald 2009: 151).

Skotaville's objectives were to provide a space owned by and for black writers, free from the white-dominated publishing industry – both mainstream and alternative, providing a platform for black voices and viewpoints, and reclaiming the legitimacy of African literature, breaking away from Bantu Education's textbook reductive view of literature by black South Africans (McDonald 2009: 152). Skotaville's political stance espoused BC, visible in the selection of board members, authors, content and general editorial policies. The idea of providing an alternative to the white-owned commercial publishers positioned Skotaville in direct competition with Ravan and several of Ravan's black writers moved to Skotaville, with a view to providing black literature to black readerships.

In the late 1980s, as the political climate in South Africa grew more tense, Skotaville's contributors and offices were often subjected to harassment from the security police. Seroke was arrested in 1987 for furthering the aims of the Pan Africanist Congress and was only released in 1991 (McDonald 2009: 154). These political factors, combined with a change in the book market, led to a partnership between Macmillan's Nolwazi Publishers and Skotaville. In 1999, however, Skotaville was revived and repositioned 'as an alternative to the predominantly white-owned commercial and media houses', targeting a black readership (Cloete 2000: 52). Nevertheless, the bulk of its publishing output occurred in the 1980s, which made it the last major publishing house founded during apartheid (McDonald 2009: 512) and one of the leading anti-apartheid publishers of struggle literature (Berger 2000: 83).

From Skotaville grew another powerful yet short-lived publishing venture, Seriti sa Sechaba Publishers. Seriti sa Sechaba was founded in 1988 by Dinah Lefakane, who was previously with Skotaville. It was the first publishing house founded, owned and managed by a black South African woman. As Philip (1990: 15) points out, Seriti sa Sechaba's initial intention was to publish feminist literature, but it soon expanded to include children's literature. Its list included Portia Rankoane's *Moment of Truth: A Collection of Poems* and Dinah Lefakane and Seageng Tsikang's *Women in South Africa: From the Heart, an Anthology of Stories*, among others. The aim was to support and empower black South African women writers. Seriti sa Sechaba enabled black South African women to use their voices to portray themselves through literature, making literature accessible to everyone in South Africa, both as readers or writers (Clayton 1993: 30).

While English publishing under liberal patronage arguably produced the bulk of oppositional or anti-apartheid literature and positioned English as the main language of resistance, Afrikaans alternative publishers also provided a platform for alternative voices. Afrikaans literature undeniably enjoyed a privileged status until the mid-1970s, although social pressure and the close-knit relations between censors and publishers resulted in pre-publication censorship. Examples of publishers' interference and pre-publication control include the case of Ingrid Jonker's 'Die kind wat doodgeskiet is deur soldate by Nyanga', a poem condemning the shooting of a child by soldiers in Nyanga township. Jonker's poem was to be included in her poetry collection *Rook en oker* and although the contract between her and the publisher was signed, a member of the publishing house's board opposed the political tone of the poem and requested that it be withdrawn from the collection. Jonker refused, but shortened the title to 'Die kind', only to find that the poem had been relegated to the end of the book in the children's poetry section in the final edition published in 1965 (De Lange 1997: 35).

One of the major players on the Afrikaans alternative literary scene was Taurus, an alternative publishing house founded in 1975 by academics Ampie Coetzee, Ernst Liebenberg and John Miles, who were working in the Afrikaans and Nederlands Department at the University of the Witwatersrand. Taurus's promotional brochure pledged to give 'writers of literature the assurance that it would publish any manuscript of value without any form of pre-censorship being exercised' (in McDonald 2009: 100). As the first major Afrikaans initiative directly confronting the dominant position of established Afrikaans commercial publishers, Taurus exposed the growing internal divisions among the Afrikaans intelligentsia. Its publishing list was definitely engaged in oppositional politics and, to get its books out before censors intervened, the publisher adopted a distribution system reminiscent of Van Wyk Louw's scheme in the 1930s, albeit with a slightly more progressive and inclusive intent. In McDonald's words, Taurus 'was designed to create an opening for more radically interventionist kinds of writing by side-stepping both the censors and over-compromised publishers like H&R [Human & Rousseau]' (2009: 100). Taurus operated in the small space between underground publisher and direct mail orders (101). It maintained a subscription list of readers and distributed its books by direct mail order, thus reducing the financial risks associated with post-publication censorship by ensuring that some copies would be in circulation before attracting the censors' attention. Taurus's first novel was Brink's *Oomblik in die wind* (Moment in the wind), which narrates the story of an interracial love affair in the colonial Cape and it was considered highly likely that it would be banned. To ensure that some copies of the book would be in circulation in the event of a ban,

Taurus sent the novel to its subscribers and also hired the services of an Asian printer who did not read Afrikaans; the first print run of 1 000 copies was sold out within five days (101). In total, Taurus published more than eighty titles, of which several were banned and many more scrutinised by censors.

Other notable South African alternative publishers include Buren Publishers, an interventionist Afrikaans publishing house that released several of Breytenbach's books and some of Brink's; Renoster Books, launched in 1971 by Lionel Abrahams, which published Oswald Mtshali and Mongane Wally Serote's books; BLAC Publishing (Black Literature Arts and Culture), founded by James Matthews in 1974, which focused on radical anti-apartheid publishing by black writers, but closed in 1991 after suffering several bans and constant harassment by the apartheid regime and its censors; Bateleur Press, founded by Lionel Abrahams and Patrick Cullinan in 1974, which focused on poetry; Dutch-born publisher Ad Donker, whose eponymous press initially imported books and eventually opened a South African publishing venture specialising in academic publishing, with anthologies such as *The Companion to South Africa English Literature* destined for a school and university market, and so-called serious literature, including John Conyngham, Athol Fugard, Mafika Pascal Gwala, Bessie Head and Mongane Wally Serote's works; and Prog, a small alternative Afrikaans publisher founded in 1988, which focused on black Afrikaans poetry.

While these alternative presses enabled progressive writers to reach their readers, the majority did not survive more than a few years, for a number of reasons, ranging from censorship constraints to financial issues. They closed down, or were bought by or merged with commercial publishers. Besides David Philip Publishers and Ad Donker, which were not solely dependent on foreign funding for their survival, most alternative presses depended on foreign investment, which partly explains their precarious and sometimes short lifespan, as well as their disappearance with the advent of democracy in South Africa (Oliphant 2000: 19). Moreover, the nature of the reading market for oppositional publishers changed as political alternatives loomed and demand for critical and oppositional political texts diminished (Cloete 2000: 50). Immediate relevance and urgency gradually faded with the changing political landscape, opening a space for new literary developments and alternatives.

Dissemination and distribution of books

As seen in the case of Taurus, alternative or independent publishers often had to adopt unconventional strategies to reach their readers without the interference of censors, even if this meant adopting underground publication and distribution processes. They often used direct distribution, as the idea was to get as many copies as possible in circulation before a publication attracted the censors' attention. This often meant a small-scale operation, in comparison to mainstream publishers, and subtlety was the key to reaching readers. As the case of Brink's *Oomblik in die wind* indicates, marketing and distribution strategies had to be fast and subtle. Nadine Gordimer observes:

> The general idea is that it is better to have the books ship in quietly and sell modestly than to be unable to sell at all. If the book is subsequently banned, the author has the satisfaction of knowing that at least it has some chance to be read, if not widely (in De Lange 1997: 75).

David Philip recalls how in 1987 he published *Detention and Torture in South Africa*, a title at high risk of attracting the attention of censors. Edited by Don Foster and Dennis Davis, it was a strong denunciation of security police practices and was considered a significant contribution to exposing the injustices perpetrated by the apartheid judicial and police systems. Philip recalls how the books were distributed in a swift and secret manner to evade the censors' scrutiny:

> We made a list of 600 sympathetic persons whom we regarded as likely purchasers, before the book appeared in the shops,

> dispatched 600 copies to them, with a letter explaining that we wished to ensure a wide distribution for what we regarded as an important book and that we enclosed our invoice in the hope that they would be prepared to pay for the book, but that if not they could either return it or keep it without obligation (Philip 1990: 14).

This direct contact between publishers, writers and readers reveals a certain degree of proximity, which is often unheard of in conventional mainstream publishing. By adapting the conventions of the book trade to a specific context, relations between its key players were therefore altered and took on the allure of a community of interest. Feedback and outcomes could be received through means other than sales figures. Philip points out that, in the case of *Detention and Torture in South Africa*, they nonetheless failed, as they suffered financial loss and received complaints from some targeted readers, who did not appreciate receiving goods they did not order and being expected to pay for them. Moreover, in an ironic twist of fate, the book was never banned.

Brink (1983: 52) also recalls how his novel *A Dry White Season* was dispatched in this manner, with the collaboration of Taurus:

> A list of subscribers was even established and when, in 1979, it became obvious that my novel *A Dry White Season* was in danger of being banned (in its Afrikaans version), 2,000 copies were quietly printed and dispatched to Taurus subscribers, followed by another edition within a week. By the time the censors pounced [. . .] there were enough copies in circulation to ensure a long clandestine existence.

Brink further speaks of a 'psychological victory' as the novel reached, even if in a limited manner, a substantial reader base that could potentially expand beyond initial expectations through circulation of the available copies.

Transnational distribution also occurred. While imports and exports of books are a common feature of the global book trade, some books were literally smuggled in and out of apartheid South Africa, evading both custom officials and censors, as is the case with *Student Perspectives on South Africa*, published by David Philip. The first impression of this collection of essays from a spectrum of students' movements, ranging from SASO to NUSAS and the Studentebond, sold out. Another print run took place at about the same time that two of its contributors, Biko and Pityana, were banned. This meant that the publication was de facto banned and that the second print run could not be distributed in South Africa. Philip took the decision to quietly ship the books to publisher Rex Collings in London who, as Philip (1990: 13) tells it, said he had been expecting them.

These examples demonstrate how some publishers facilitated contact between progressive writers and their readers despite the climate of fear and reprisal, and also reveal the presence of a progressive readership for alternative or oppositional books existing in the margins of the mainstream book trade. Several continental and international publishing ventures focusing on African literature contributed to the publishing of African and South African writers, in particular. With the advent of independence from colonial rule in many African countries and the Cold War, among other factors, the international book trade reconfigured in the late 1950s and early 1960s. As McDonald (2009: 106) highlights, Seven Seas Books, Heinemann's African Writers Series, Mbari Publications and the East African Literature Bureau proved to be influential players on the African literary scene, attracting several young black South African writers to their ranks:

> Partly because of this, the key group of independent literary publishers in London came to be associated almost exclusively with white writers after 1960. Bessie Head, who was initially published by Gollancz, Peter Abrahams, who remained with Faber, and Lewis Nkosi, who was published by Longman and Oxford University Press, were the main exceptions.

The paperback series Seven Seas (1958-78) was based in East Berlin and promoted 'international socialism', 'anti-colonial resistance', 'the American civil rights movement' and the 'anti-apartheid struggle' (McDonald 2009: 109). Heinemann's African Writers Series (1962-2004) focused on postcolonial African literature and Chinua Achebe was the founding editor. The aim of this paperback series was to develop 'a modern literary canon fashioned by Africans for Africa' and its list of authors included a wider South African representation when James Currey became managing director in 1967 (110). Several South African authors were published abroad and eventually distributed in South Africa. A couple of novels by Alex La Guma were published in Nigeria by Mbari Publications, several of Gordimer's novels were published by Penguin in London, Biko's *I Write What I Like* was published by Heinemann in Oxford, and Mphahlele's *Down Second Avenue* was published by Faber & Faber in London (Mpe and Seeber 2000: 23). As Davis (2005: 232) points out, some African imprints of international publishing companies at times served public relations purposes and publicised 'the press's role in Africa as cultural rather than commercial', but they nonetheless contributed to the development of important lists of African writers and reinforced African literary canons in the postcolonial context.

These international publishers distributed books in South Africa through their South African branches, rendered viable through their commercial publishing portfolios, until some closed their South African operations as a sign of protest against the apartheid regime. For their part, South African alternative publishers operated on the outskirts of the mainstream book trade, at times even going completely underground in order to survive. While some distributed books directly to readers, conventional distribution points, such as formal and informal libraries and bookshops, also disseminated progressive literature.

Libraries as the people's orchard

The struggle for accessible and quality library services for black South Africans dates as far back as the colonial period, when recreation and social welfare provisions – which included libraries – were used as a form of social control of the black South African population (Cobley 1997).[2] In 1818, the first South African Public Library was established in the Cape, funded by a tax on imported wine, and subscriptions were introduced in 1827 (Stillwell 1993: 93). However, such libraries, as well as schemes to expand services and their scope to rural areas, were aimed at the white population (93–7).

A 1911 census reveals that only 6.8 per cent of the African population in South Africa was literate (Cobley 1997: 59). The slow growth of the literacy rate was exacerbated by the lack of public libraries for African readers, which remained mainly unchallenged until the end of the 1930s (60). Prior to 1930, library services were only attached to what were then known as 'native colleges', such as Lovedale and Fort Hare, and the 'native teachers' library' at the Department of Education in Pietermaritzburg, or Inanda Seminary in Natal (now KwaZulu-Natal) (Stillwell 1993: 97). Limited numbers of books were also made accessible through missions and institutions reserved for Africans, such as the Lovedale Institution, Morija Training Institution and Tiger Kloof Native Institution, which allowed their graduates to access their libraries after they had completed their studies (Cobley 1997: 62). Lovedale had a book caravan that travelled to the Ciskei and Transkei (now the Eastern Cape Province) promoting literacy and reading in the area. Having promoted literacy and reading as part of their education and so-called civilisation programme in South Africa, the missionaries eventually realised that the newly educated African elite was politically empowered by these literacy skills (58).

Other initiatives to promote and sustain reading and literacy included reading rooms in townships; the Bantu Men's Social Centre, established in 1924 in Johannesburg, which had a small library; the SAIRR that had a library that was open to 'non-European' members of the institute from 1929; and A.B. Xuma who operated a small 'non-European library'

---

2. The metaphor in the subheading – 'Libraries as the people's orchard' – appeared in an editorial of the *Bantu World* in 1938 (in Dick 2007b: 16).

from his Sophiatown home in the early 1930s (Cobley 1997: 64). Other initiatives providing books to black readers included some self-help organisations, social clubs, discussion groups, Sunday schools ran by political organisations, such as the Lenin Club and Trotskyist groups (Dick 2007b: 17). Although informally segregated well before then, the 1928 South African Library Conference, held in Bloemfontein, sanctioned the official segregation of public library services in South Africa.

A 1929 report on libraries by the Carnegie initiative noted that the geographical area to be serviced by the few libraries was too vast; the infrastructure was inadequate; current librarians were gatekeeping the profession; libraries were not co-operating among themselves; the book stock was inadequate for black readers; and access was limited as a result of the subscription price (Stilwell 1993: 92). An important development in the provision of library services to the black South African population was the Carnegie Non-European Travelling Library, founded in the Transvaal in 1930, followed by the Natal Carnegie Non-European Library Services in 1931 and the Cape Coloured Carnegie Library Services in 1933 (Cobley 1997). The Carnegie initiative demonstrated the need for libraries for black readers. Its collections were based on box library systems that served black readers, through community centres, reading rooms, missions and schools situated in urban, semi-rural and rural areas. For example, the Bantu Men's Social Centre became a depot of the Carnegie initiative in Johannesburg. These initiatives fostered literacy, reading and writing. An editorial in the *Bantu World* newspaper in 1938 noted that this library movement was informing a cultural movement towards the creation of African literature by African authors, for African readers (Dick 2007b: 16). Indeed, the orchard metaphor, attributed to either H.I.E. Dhlomo or the *Bantu World* editor R.V. Selope Thema, in which books are compared to precious fruits needing to be grown and picked, savoured and shared, encouraged readers who did not find relevant reading material on libraries' shelves to write it themselves, to plant their own trees.

Poet and intellectual H.I.E. Dhlomo became Carnegie's first 'non-European' librarian organiser in 1937, tasked with 'organizing reading centres, regulating the supply of books, lecturing and advising on reading matter' (Colbey 1997: 66). However, the availability of books as sources of radical ideas to heighten political and intellectual consciousness among black readers was not welcomed by all, as the government promoted a conservative moralising and civilising mission of libraries and reading (67–8). By the 1930s, the phrase 'undesirable literature' had already entered the national vocabulary, through Ray Phillips, a missionary and member of the Carnegie Non-European Library committee. While it had its flaws, the Carnegie Library initiative countered the argument that there was no demand for books and reading in the black population in South Africa. Despite their general animosity, municipal library services had to cater for an increasing African readership and the first branch of the Non-European Public Library opened in Johannesburg in 1939 when the Johannesburg Public Library took over the library services at the Bantu Men's Social Centre, attracting more than 1 000 readers within its first year of operation (70). Shortly after this, the Winifred Holtby Memorial Library was built in Soweto (71). Under Dhlomo's leadership, reading habits grew substantially (Stilwell 1993: 100) and several cultural and literary events in cities and townships were organised, at times called literary socials. In 1938, Dhlomo wrote in *The Reader's Companion*:

> If you want to become a good reader, and by a good reader I mean a person who can read without difficulty at all, it is necessary for you to read whenever you can. Carry a book around with you, in your pocket or under your arm; and if you have to wait for a friend, or if you have one or two minutes to spare, read a few paragraphs from your book . . . Reading is still the only means by which you can come in touch with the great minds of the world (in Everts 1993: n.p.).

Dhlomo was recalled as librarian organiser in 1941 and joined his brother, R.R.R. Dhlomo, at the newspaper *Ilanga lase Natal* until his death in 1956, in Durban. He played an immense role in fostering a culture of reading, learning and writing. Far from retreating from the creative and intellectual arenas, Dhlomo wrote several plays, poems and essays (Peterson 1991) and in 1944 was a member of the International Club in Durban, which was a multiracial platform for public readings, lectures on yoga philosophy, African poetry and music, theatre and art exhibitions, among other things (Stilwell 1993: 101).

In 1948, the new, white-elected NP government had a severe impact on public services in general, notably education, which was now bundled with the provision of library services (Cobley 1997). The Bantu Education Act No. 47 of 1953 led to the 'purge or closing of many existing black school libraries' (Dick 2007b: 19–20) and many more public libraries or book initiatives. Library services for black South Africans were thereafter managed by the Department of Bantu Education and the system was designed to limit access to books (Stilwell 1993: 104) and promote propaganda in favour of the status quo, creating a scarcity of books that left traces well into democratic South Africa. The report of the 1951 Eiselen Commission on Native Education listed 42 library services in black areas, with a total of 26 944 registered users and a total stock of 130 108 books (Cobley 1997: 76). Under the apartheid government, the authorities closed some of these public libraries. Some survived throughout the apartheid era, often poorly stocked and serviced, while others were literally destroyed or burned down in the wake of political violence and school boycotts, especially in the 1970s and 1980s (Dick 2007b: 20). Popular information networks and resource centres emerged in the 1980s and 1990s to provide alternative library services, filling a gap caused by the biased and inadequate services provided for black people by the state. These resource centres provided alternative reading material inaccessible in public libraries and were established in community centres and on university campuses, among other sites, throughout the country. As with other initiatives, such as the Bantu Men's Social Centre, young African male students were the main users of these resource centres (Stilwell 1994: 304), a gender bias that warrants further research.

The Reservation of Separate Amenities Act No. 49 of 1953, which sanctioned the segregation of public services, was revoked in 1990, technically opening public libraries to all, but insidious means of access control, such as price and the relevance of reading material, still meant limited services for the black majority (Stilwell 1994). In 1990, after more than four decades of apartheid repression, library services in townships were almost non-existent (Stilwell 1993: 104). Despite the strict control of reading exercised by the apartheid government, particularly through Bantu Education and the censorship system, some alternative book distribution schemes and reading communities existed and survived. The informal library and reading initiatives set up in black areas in the 1970s and 1980s were often aligned with anti-apartheid organisations and activism (Dick 2007b: 20) and student political movements (Badat 1999).

Another initiative that contributed substantial anti-apartheid literature and resisted late apartheid hegemony was the Library and Information Workers' Organisation (LIWO), founded in Durban in 1990, with other branches soon following in other provinces (Kagan 2015: 11). The LIWO was launched by a group of anti-apartheid, alternative librarians, who felt that their progressive, non-racial and grassroots values were not represented by existing librarian associations, such as the South African Library Association (SALA) and the African Library Association of South Africa (10). This initiative showed that not all librarians were working for the apartheid system or were apolitical and that some were actively resisting apartheid (13). The LIWO led advocacy and awareness campaigns with a host of cultural and political organisations during the transition to democracy and, among other things, advocated for the public's right to know and for the preservation of archival documents that could be incriminating for the apartheid regime (16). In the mid-1990s, some resource centres merged with the LIWO and some members of the LIWO Natal branch launched the academic journal *Innovation: Journal of Appropriate Librarianship and Information Work in South Africa*, with a sharp focus on progressive librarianship.

As prime sites of intellectual debate, university spaces were full of contradictions, with progressive student bodies operating alongside conservative ones; conformist university presses publishing books alongside progressive academics publishing alternative, anti-apartheid independent literature; and initiatives such as resource centres distributing anti-apartheid readings alongside academic libraries mainly preserving the status quo. While authorised to acquire and stock some banned publications, most academic libraries could not put these into circulation without permission from the censorship board.[3] The South African Library in Cape Town and the State Library in Pretoria enjoyed more latitude, and not only could they acquire banned publications, but they could also make them available for consultation in the library, although strictly for academic purposes.

The limited availability of alternative academic books, and their forbidden status, inevitably had consequences in most fields of research and impacted on the scope and range of research produced at South African universities. This was particularly true in the field of humanities and social sciences, where one out of two political publications submitted to the Publications Committee was banned (Du Toit 1983: 92). André du Toit, from the Department of Political Philosophy at the University of Stellenbosch, was among those who warned that research in political philosophy, among other disciplines, was rendered virtually impossible because of bans on seminal literature in the field (Hatchen and Giffard 1984: 167). Research on South African history, for instance, was often more easily pursued outside South Africa, as the necessary documentation was frequently more readily available overseas (Merrett 1994: 199). The lack of access to documentary sources posed a serious threat to research to the point that, in 1987, the Human Sciences Research Council declared that censorship was a major obstacle to South African academic activities (198).

The official climate of connivance with the censorship bureaucracy in the librarian profession not only limited access to books for potential readers, but also generally limited the production of research and publications. While, as noted above, some legislative provisions made it possible for books banned for possession to be kept in academic libraries,

---

3. http://www.theliteraturepolice.com/.

they were reserved for exclusive usage by researchers who, in the minds of censors, were in all likelihood sophisticated, educated readers, all mitigating factors that were thought to curb the potentially harmful influence of these publications.

However, obtaining special exemptions to consult banned books could be a lengthy administrative procedure and required official authorisation stipulating that the reading of the books was essential to the research. For instance, Dr David Welsh from the University of Cape Town had to provide such a letter to consult five of his own books that had been recently banned:

> When he asked for permission to consult them, he was required to supply a statement from his dean certifying that they were absolutely necessary for his research. The permit was given but the books were kept for personal study only and had to be kept under lock and key, and not loaned to anyone (Hachten and Giffard 1984: 167).

Librarian Christopher Merrett, who, along with other librarians, resisted censorship and denounced the majority of librarians' silence, recalls the forbidden repository at the University of Natal Library: 'At the university library we had a more modest cupboard, it used to stand right in the passage by the head librarian's office, and it was full of banned books.'[4] Banned academic publications were kept in locked rooms and cabinets and accessed on approbation from the Publications Board, which would study the application on a case-by-case basis. However, there was often no response and, as Merrett recalls, the final decision to grant access to banned publications was at times taken by head librarians.

As seen in the above examples, the act of reading more often than not contributed to the writing of more literature. In this light, it could be

---

4. Christopher Merrett, interview, Pietermaritzburg, 23 October 2007.

submitted that academics, as readers, contributed to a certain extent to unlocking – literally and figuratively – the messages and information in banned books. By analysing, discussing, quoting and paraphrasing banned publications, these readers cum writers shared information and ideas in different formats and communicated them through various channels. Ideas contained in these books reached a more popular or mass readership, whether orally or in writing. For example, BC leader Biko read and quoted Aimé Césaire and Frantz Fanon in his speeches and essays, illustrating the dissemination of such complex ideas and writings to a wider, popular audience.

The librarian profession was generally politically aligned to the NP through SALA, a powerful lobby group, against which smaller progressive organisations, such as the Cape Library Assistants Section and the Cape Library Association, would appear as alternatives to the dominant ideology. Even if not all librarians working in formal institutions colluded with the system, the majority supported or tolerated it (Dick 2004a: 35). A climate of self-censorship prevailed among librarians, as they regulated reading by suppressing 'offending books' and promoting 'good books' (36). This attitude was either underpinned by ideological connivance or by a climate of fear. According to Merrett,[5] informers sometimes visited libraries and officials randomly checked libraries in search of prohibited literature, a practice introduced by publications director Gerrit Dekker when he hired the first travelling inspector in the 1960s (McDonald 2009: 41). Librarians held a gatekeeper position, as they had the power to support or hinder access to books, to the extent that they could have – in theory – rendered the Publications Act impracticable (Merrett 1994: 212). Censorship had profound effects on critical points of distribution of information and librarians played a mediating role between books and readers. Furthermore, library directors used their position of authority to have the last word on the availability of and access to books, effectively acting as censors at their own discretion (Dick 2004a: 35).

---

5. Merrett, interview.

Librarianship was a conformist and conservative profession and public libraries played a major role in suppressing so-called undesirable publications. Banned library books had to be removed from shelves and put away and in extreme cases burned, a practice that occurred in several public libraries across South Africa (Dick 2004a: 33). Some undesirable books withdrawn from circulation were sent to central depots or libraries, forming an impressive and probably eclectic collection of literature. Central librarians were responsible for keeping these publications out of circulation and often resorted to destroying them. At times, banned books kept in central libraries were burned, pulped or shredded. In a few instances, they were returned to the supplier (Merrett 1994: 61). Piet Westra remembers one of these book-burning incidents, which ended on an unpredictable note, while he was director at the State Library:

> One good day the Central Police Station in Pretoria wanted to get rid of heaps of items they had assembled and asked us for advice on how to do this. My boss suggested that the material could be burned in one of the enormous ovens that ISCOR [then South Africa's largest steel manufacturer] used for their steel producing process.
> [. . .]
> This oven may have been 20 meters high, spitting flames and smoke from an opening at the top. Hundreds of items were lifted in one scoop by a huge mechanical shovel from the lorry and dumped into the opening at the top of the oven, which resulted in smoke and big flames. But at about the third load that went up something went wrong. Midway between the lorry and the oven the shovel suddenly opened and hundreds of publications, *Playboys*, *Hustlers*, *Men Only* and others, often more explicit, were spilt on the floor.
> What happened next reminded me in a way of a scene out of Dante's *Inferno*. Out of nothing from all dark corners of the hall dozens of helmeted workers in overalls suddenly rushed in,

grabbing as many items as they could carry in their arms and disappeared as quickly into the darkness again as they had come. The news of our operation must have leaked out. But the end result was that we had not only burned publications, but also redistributed quite a few.[6]

The practice of burning books, which is by all accounts contrary to the spirit of librarianship, led to the destruction of thousands of books seized by police or other government agencies between 1955 and 1971, burned in municipal furnaces and incinerators, in what could be termed a 'bibliocide' (Dick 2004a: 31). Book burning was generally perpetrated in a climate of 'unquestioning obedience to authority', 'mindless performance of duties' and an 'uncritical attitude' (35). Initially, only pornography was thrown into furnaces, but when the Publications and Entertainments Act came into effect in 1963, any banned material could be subjected to this treatment. It is reported that in 1964, the Cape Town Library Services burned some 800 books, while in 1968 the number of banned books burned by the Natal Provincial Library amounted to 5 375 (32).

As a professional body, librarians generally did not oppose or denounce this massive destruction of books. Withdrawn or destroyed books were typically replaced with so-called good books, in what would ironically be labelled 'the new library spirit' (Dick 2004a: 35). The fact that librarians performed these destructive acts amid general silence from the profession is hardly justifiable, as the police services announced in 1954 that banned books had to be removed from the shelves and from public circulation, but could be stored in sealed bags in libraries (33).

Distribution and circulation of books in bookshops

Just as librarians were intermediaries between a book and its readers, booksellers played a role in promoting or hindering access to books

---

6. http://www.theliteraturepolice.com/.

for the book-buying public. Engaging in the book trade on commercial terms, booksellers' attitudes were mainly dictated by economic rather than ideological concerns, contrary to the librarians' position in the public system. The financial risk was real for booksellers, as once banned, undesirable books were rendered illegal and could no longer be sold. Besides the financial loss associated with books being removed from shelves, fines or imprisonment were imposed for displaying or selling banned material.

Censorship crept in at various levels of the book trade and impacted on the provision of books as well as the selection of publications made available to readers, creating a situation where booksellers became – at times unintentionally – regulators of reading. The selection of titles and authors that a bookseller would stock was somewhat of a gamble, based on the probabilities of a publication being banned. Although they enjoyed relative independence from government structures, as opposed to public libraries, for instance, they were nonetheless subjected to inspectors and security branch officers' random visits. Chris van Wyk recalls the presence of such undercover officers who scrutinised bookshops' shelves in search of so-called communist and subversive literature.[7] Some zealous customers also informally took upon themselves the role of censors and reading regulators, as this incident recalled by Philip (1990: 17) reveals: 'In the bookshops like CNA, the managers had been reluctant to buy oppositional books because they claimed that their shop assistants' lives were endangered if they stocked such books, and because the books themselves were often mutilated and made unsaleable by ill-disposed customers.' Government officials also harassed individuals selling alternative publications, as illustrated by an incident in the early 1960s, when a seller of the banned liberal publication *Contact* was detained (Merrett 1994: 44).

Precautions were also necessary when ordering imported publications, as customs officials perused incoming publications and redirected them

---

7. Chris van Wyk, interview, Johannesburg, 12 October 2007.

to the Publications Board if necessary. Some wary booksellers would sometimes send a sample to the Publications Board before importing in greater numbers, while local publications were sometimes sent to lawyers for assessment (Hachten and Giffard 1984: 164). Imported written media were also scrutinised and sometimes articles were cut out or blackened before being distributed in South Africa. For example, prominent South African Communist Party (SACP) leader and anti-apartheid activist Bram Fischer's article on South Africa in London's *Observer* was literally cut out of the imported copies, before they were sold through mainstream news outlets (Merrett 1994: 53). Similarly, towards the end of 1963, the last three lines of an article on the Penguin African Library were blackened from the copies of the *Times Literary Supplement* published for a South African reading public, as anti-apartheid activist Ronald Segal was quoted on his anti-apartheid views (51). A portion of an article from a 1965 edition of London's *The Times* was also blackened before it could be distributed in South Africa, as it quoted anti-apartheid activist and banned African National Congress (ANC) leader Nelson Mandela (53). Such measures were sometimes carried out by off-duty officials, or by wary publishers in an act of self-censorship to ensure the commercialisation of a potentially undesirable publication. The South African edition of Monica Wilson and Leonard Thompson's *Oxford History of South Africa* was published in 1969 with 52 blank pages under the heading 'South African Nationalism', a chapter researched and written over a period of two years by Leo Kuper, which inevitably quoted and referred to banned persons and organisations (63). As Davis (2011: 88) observes, the decision was seemingly taken in good faith, although it was heavily criticised:

> [Leo] Marquard, [David] Philip and [Fred] Cannon [managers at OUP] presumed that the volume would be banned on account of this one chapter, and argued that 'the availability of the work should not be jeopardised . . . that the chapter concerned was expendable in the interests of the availability of the rest of the work'. The decision was made to publish the South African edition of the

second volume with 52 blank pages where Kuper's chapter would have appeared, although the international edition was published intact. As a result, the book was not banned, although the censor apparently argued that the missing pages were so annoying that he wished he could ban it. OUP has been criticised for being willingly silenced in this fashion and for not even testing the system.

Through their insistence on protecting so-called good or reasonable citizens from undesirable literature, as a disguise for repressing anti-apartheid and political opposition, censors thwarted the development of a reading culture among the vast majority of South Africans. The climate of fear and repression seemingly infiltrated all levels of the book trade and reinforced conditions of censorship. At times it drove writers and publishers to self-censorship, protecting the status quo through control over the circulation of literature, ideas and information. The gap caused by censorship affected both readers and writers, as booksellers were reluctant to purchase books even once a ban had been lifted. South African author Miriam Tlali, who had several brushes with the censorship system throughout her life, explains how this practice affected literary continuity and exacerbated the gap in South African literature: '*Muriel* [*at Metropolitan*] and *Amandla* [two of Tlali's books] were unbanned since 1985 but they are still unavailable. The booksellers simply do not take the books in their stock. The self-censorship of booksellers presents a significant barrier for the free flow of information' (in De Lange 1997: 144).

Conclusion

The shared spaces between readers and writers, publishers, librarians and booksellers can foster literacy, creativity and a reading culture, or under restrictions can become repressive and sterile spaces. In a context such as apartheid South Africa, censors, through the legislation impacting on thought control, such as the Suppression of Communism Act, the Bantu Education Act, the Publications and Entertainments Act of 1963, the Publications Act of 1974 and subsequent publications control legislation, exercised an influence on the modalities and modus operandi of the book trade.

Some alternative publishers, alternative in that they were set against the mainstream or commercial publishers, adapted conventional modes of book production in order to be able to operate despite prevailing circumstances, at times even going underground in order to produce books for an equally alternative readership, offering a choice in terms of reading material and discourses articulated, even if in a marginal fashion. Alternative publishers were often aligned to – and indeed emanated from – specific strands of anti-apartheid resistance, showing strong yet heavily repressed resistance and opposition to a hegemonic, paternalistic and oppressive system. These oppositional, alternative and independent publishers published books that mainstream publishers would not publish, for ideological or financial reasons.

While the onus of distribution would traditionally fall on libraries and bookshops, in a situation of censorship as in apartheid South Africa, the roles and responsibilities of those involved in the alternative book trade were often multiple and various. Some dispositions contained in the censorship legislation made it possible for some readers to access banned or subversive books in academic libraries, for instance, while post-publication censorship definitely played in favour of readers who knew where to buy potentially subversive books in bookshops, before censors pounced or booksellers became aware of their books' potential undesirability. However, the general climate of self-censorship among librarians and booksellers and the non-viability of the formal book trade led to the creation of an alternative trade, where unconventional and clandestine distribution strategies were adopted and alternative publishers often used creative and unorthodox distribution channels to reach their readers.

Alternative points of distribution existed in the margins of the space occupied by mainstream publishers, libraries and bookshops. Some alternative publishers interacted directly with their readers, as was the case with David Philip, Taurus and Ravan, among others, in order to get some of their titles in the market before attracting the censors' scrutiny. In doing so, they encouraged the formation and development of alternative readerships, involving readers in the communication circuit by encouraging them to perform several functions: readers, writers, publishers and distributors.

The alternative literary space, where writers, readers and publishers interacted on various levels and in different ways, became a space for the incubation of alternative politics. The next chapter discusses how the alternative literary scene and political activism sometimes converged through readers. So-called alternative readers asserted their choice when turning to oppositional publishers to source reading material and by reading alternative publications that were essential to the very existence of the alternative publishing industry as they created a demand and *raison d'être* for these publications. The official climate of concealment surrounding banned books and the alternative book provision initiatives, in response to the lack of alternative reading material, reveal competing views of literacy (Cobley 1997), ranging from civilising to educating, raising awareness and seeking information. While these alternative distribution library services played a significant role in fostering readerships for alternative literature and book production, they could not and probably never pretended to replace comprehensive public library services.

Some challenges remain in contemporary South Africa when it comes to book publishing and distribution, such as the issue of access to libraries in formerly white areas, the lack of services in rural areas and the lack of or inadequacy of libraries in schools (Stilwell 1993: 108). The next chapter discusses how the flow of the traditional book system was disrupted by censorship and how readers stepped in to ensure the sustainability of an alternative book trade.

egramadres
Graphic Address } "INTERIOR."

REPUBLIEK VAN SUID-AFRIKA.
REPUBLIC OF SOUTH AFRICA.

No. 2654/13/32
(Vol. II, nr. 86)

BOARD OF CENSORS
CAPE TOWN
31-7-1963

Navrae }
Enquiries }
Tel. No. ....

AANGETEKEN.

DEPARTEMENT VAN BINNELANDSE SAKE,
DEPARTMENT OF THE INTERIOR,
PRIVAATSAK 114,
PRIVATE BAG 114,
PRETORIA.

Die Voorsitter,
Raad van Sensors,
KAAPSTAD.

RAAD VAN SENSORS
JUL 1963

AANSTOOTLIKE LITERATUUR:

U   29461 - 29470   gedateer   17.7.1963

Die Minister het beslis dat ondergenoemde publikasies aanstootlik is en dat die invoer en verspreiding daarvan verbied moet word:-

✓ BLAME ME ON HISTORY — Bloke Modisane

Die publikasies en lesersverslag is aangeheg.

'n Goewermentskennisgewing sal mettertyd verskyn.

SEKRETARIS VAN BINNELANDSE SAKE.

Figures 1 and 2: Censor's report on Bloke Modisane's *Blame Me on History*

.-61—5,000.   OFFICE OF THE BOARD OF CENSORS,
                                                         ROOM 101, FEDERAL BUILDINGS,
29461.   TULBAGH CENTRE,
                                                         CAPE TOWN.
Mrs. W. A. Joubert.
                                                         5 . 6 . 63

Kindly furnish below your report and views on the undermentioned publication which has been submitted for censorship:—

BLAME ME ON HISTORY —
BLOKE MODISANE.   JAA.
                                                         Secretary.

REPORT OF READER.

(a) Synopsis of publication dealt with:— Bloke Modisane, a Bantu living in Sophiatown, describes how Sophiatown, which the Bantu loved, was razed to the ground. He worked for a Newspaper for the Bantu, but later resigned. He was married & had a daughter. Bloke is embittered by the slum houses of the blacks and the discrimination against them because their skins are black. He joins the A.N.C. whose slogan is: "Drive the whites into the sea", but their strikes & passive resistance have no results. The aim of the whites is to drive the Bantu beyond endurance & then, under the plea of self-defence, to obliterate all blacks. The Bantu are waiting for a Moses to lead them against the whites. Bloke resents his inferiority & the fact that he cannot be admitted to European theatres.
Bloke hates the D.R. Church & their Christianity which says the Angels are white & the Devil is black. He goes to 15 D.R. Churches & is everywhere asked to leave. Laws in South Africa are made to protect only the whites. White domination must be destroyed & S.A. must be ruled by a democratic majority. He urges his people to be daring like the Tsotsis. Bloke fails to get a passport for further study in U.S.A., & after helping to make a film of Native life, he escapes to Rhodesia.

(b) References to pages on which appear passages considered to be indecent, obscene, or objectionable:—

(i) Crime .... Violence 65
    Description of murder .... Sadism
Propaganda against   Ill-treatment of South Africans: 54, 63, 64, 86, 90, 100, 101, 103, 116, 122, 137, 139, 147, 157, 162
(ii) Intimate description of women's bodies 215, 216, 217, 218, 226, 230, 237, 242, 307, 310, 311.
     Passionate love-making ....
     Sexual relations 263, 264.
Anti-white statements: Loose morals: 77, 94, 105, 121, 125, 138, 153, 189, 205, 238, 239, 241, 243, 244,
(iii) Traffic in drugs .... White slave traffic 245, 271.
     The drug habit .... Other vices
(iv) Offensive intermingling between Europeans and Non-Europeans 258, 259, 293.
Statements against Blasphemy: 161, 179, 181, 184, 185, 191. Objectionable language 7, 37.
Rousing natives against the whites: 52, 55, 75, 89, 97, 130, 131, 136, 143, 144, 146,
     Other objectionable features (specify)
(v) Subversive propaganda   224, 225, 227, 231, 232, 233, 246, 247.

(c) Cover Title

(d) General remarks and opinion.
A bitter and biased account of the experiences of a Bantu living in Sophiatown. The writer hates the whites because he is not white. He hates the Government for not legislating in favour of integration & he hates Apartheid because of the stigma on the colour of his skin.
He rouses the Bantu to fight for their rights and to drive the whites into the sea. It is a most dangerous and objectionable publication and will have a very harmful effect on peace-loving Bantu.
I consider it unsuitable for circulation.

Date 11th June, 1963.   W. A. Joubert.
                                                         Signature of Reader.

S.14/1/4 V.13(a)

19.7.1967

Die Voorsitter,
Raad van Beheer oor Publikasies,
Nuwe Arbeidsgebou 541,
Paradestraat,
K A A P S T A D.

KOMMUNISTIESE OF ONDERMYNENDE LEKTUUR
DOWN SECOND AVENUE - DEUR EZEKIEL MPHAHLELE

1. Bogemelde eksemplaar hiermee vir ondersoek ingevolge Artikel 8(1)(a) van Wet 26/1963.

2. Die inhoud van die boek is daarop bereken om 'n gevoel van kwaadgesindheid tussen Blank en Nie-blank aan te wakker. Die hele boek spreek van 'n haat teen die blanke en wys nêrens dat die skrywer sy gevoelens werklik ontbloot om sodoende die haat in hom te ondersoek en sy eie tekortkominge te erken nie. Sy vooroordele is bloot te wyte aan sy eie onkunde en onbeholpenheid maar tog soek hy die rede by die blanke.

3. Volgens beskikbare inligting is dié publikasie nog nie as verbode verklaar nie.

4. Indien u Raad sou beslis dat dit onbetaamlik, onwelvoeglik of aanstootlik is, word dit aanbeveel dat dié asook alle toekomstige uitgawes as verbode verklaar word.

5. Geliewe die bylae mettertyd aan hierdie kantoor terug te stuur.

P. J. D. VAN WYK
n/KOMMISSARIS : SUID-AFRIKAANSE POLISIE

/jcv.

Figure 3: Censor's report on Es'kia Mphahlele's *Down Second Avenue*

19/7/1967

TRANSLATION

S.14/1/4/ V.13 (obscured)

SECRET

19.7.1967

The Chairman,
Publications Control Board,
541 New Labour Building,
Parade Street,
CAPE TOWN

COMMUNIST OR SUBVERSIVE LITERATURE
DOWN SECOND AVENUE – BY EZEKIEL MPHAHLELE

1. The above copy is submitted herewith for investigation in terms of Section 8 (1) (a) of Act 26/1963.
2. The contents of the book are calculated to arouse a sense of ill feeling between White and non-White. The entire book speaks of hate for the whites and nowhere shows that the author is really expressing his feelings so as to study the hate within himself and to acknowledge his own shortcomings. His prejudices are solely due to his own ignorance and ineptitude yet he blames the whites.
3. According to available information, this publication has not yet been declared prohibited.
4. If the Board should rule that it is indecent, obscene or offensive, it is recommended that this as well as all future editions be declared prohibited.
5. Kindly return the annexure to this office in due course.

P.J.B. VAN WYK
pp/COMMISSIONER : SOUTH AFRICAN POLICE

/jcv.

Figure 4: Translation of the censor's report on Es'kia Mphahlele's *Down Second Avenue* (provided by the author)

P78/4/50

1978 -5- 15

Messrs Bowman, Gilfillan & Blacklock
P O Box 1397
JOHANNESBURG
2000

Dear Sirs

PUBLICATIONS ACT, 1974 : PUBLICATION :
STAFFRIDER — Vol 1, No 1, March 1978

In reply to your letter, Ref Mr Jooste/KJ/0.2899 of 25 April 1978, I have to inform you that the Committee's reasons for deciding that the above-mentioned publication is undesirable within the meaning of section 47(2)(a), (d) and (e) of the above-mentioned Act, were as follows:

"1. "Staffrider" is published by Ravan Press as a medium for what the publishers regard as 'new creative writing'. Some of the material is of the same undesirable nature as that published in "Donga", now a prohibited publication. Other material again is not undesirable under the law, and some has decided literary merit. The Committee is not detailing these acceptable parts, as it would amount to pre-censorship. The fact that the publication itself, as a whole, is declared undesirable, does not mean that parts of it, which are not undesirable, may not be published elsewhere.

2. Section 47(2)(e): Amongst the undesirable parts in the publication are those in which the authority and image of the police, as the persons entrusted by the State with maintaining law, internal peace and order, are undermined. These include the articles "Soweto Hijack" (p.12 ff) and "Van" (p.26 ff), and the poems "At The Window" (p.25) and "Stray Bullet" (p.33). Other material prejudicial to the peace and good order include the poem "Nineteen Seventy-Six" on p.21; Keith Gottschalk's poem "Petition to my Interrogators" (p.37); the poem "For Fatima Meer" on p.46; and parts of the article "The Day a Leader Died" on p.57.

3. Section 47(2)(a): Offensive language — such as the use of "fuck" and its derivatives, "poes" and "shitty" — is found in the article "Van" on pp.26 and 27.

4. Section 47(2)(d): Material calculated to harm Black/White relations appears, inter alia, in the poem "Change" on p.11 and the article "Soweto Hijack" on p.12 ff)."

Yours faithfully

R. E. LIGHTON
DIRECTOR OF PUBLICATIONS

BOWMAN, GILFILLAN & BLACKLOCK

Attorneys, Notaries and Conveyancers

A.M. HOFMEYR
C. CILLIERS
H.E. VAN SANTEN
S. DE C. O'GRADY
D.N. WALWYN
B.M. GILFILLAN
A.E.G. TROLLIP
V.H. BACKEBERG
N.B. WEBB
W. NOONAN
D.A. BLAINE
A.P. BOYD
D.R. LAMBSON
L.J. BROEKMAN
C.P. BRIGGS
A.V. PIENAAR
A.P.F. WILLIAMSON
J.K. JASPER
G.A.H. TARRANT
D.E. JOOSTE
M.F. DOHERTY
G.J. LAMPRECHT
H.W. COCHRANE
D.R. SCOTT
L.A. FOSTER
D.G.M. CAMPBELL
J.L. ROBINSON
R.S. HALLATT

CHANGE OF ADDRESS

As from 1/5/78. Communications regarding this matter should be delivered to:
UNITED TOWERS,
160 MAIN STREET,
JOHANNESBURG.

or posted to:
P.O. BOX 1397,
JOHANNESBURG 2000
New Telephone: 28-5120
Telex: 8-0775 SA

UNITED BUILDING,
5th Floor,
Cor. ELOFF & FOX STREETS,
JOHANNESBURG.
2001
SOUTH AFRICA.

TELEPHONE 836-3522
P.O. Box 1397, Johannesburg 2000
Telegraphic Address "JURA"
Telex 8-0775 SA

Please Quote Reference

OUR REF. MR. JOOSTE/KJ/O. 2899
YOUR REF.

25th April 1978

The Director of Publications,
Private Bag X114,
PRETORIA,
0001.

[Stamp: DIREKTORAAT VAN PUBLIKASIES / PRIVAATSAK X9069 / KAAPSTAD / 1978 5 2 / PRIVATE BAG X9069 / CAPE TOWN / DIRECTORATE OF PUBLICATIONS]

Dear Sir,

Re: BANNING OF STAFFRIDER VOL. 1 NO. 1: MARCH 1978

    We have been instructed by the printers and publishers of the above magazine, namely Zenith Printers (Pty) Limited and Ravan Press (Pty) Limited, to enquire from you the reasons for the banning which is referred to in the Government Gazette of the 14th April 1978.

    In your reply would you kindly give some details as to exactly what portions of the magazine were found to be offensive and the reasons for such findings.

Yours faithfully,

BOWMAN, GILFILLAN & BLACKLOCK

Figures 5 and 6: Correspondence between censors and Ravan Press's attorneys regarding the banning of *Staffrider* Vol. 1, No. 1, 1978

G.P.-S.73835—1978-79—2 000   DP 1A

REPUBLIC OF SOUTH AFRICA

Tel. No. 211000 x 22

KONTROLEUR VAN DOEANE EN AKSYNS
PRIVAATSAK 9046
KAAPSTAD
8000

Serial No. P80/1/147
Directorate of Publications
Private Bag 9069
Cape Town
8000

DIREKTORAAT VAN PUBLIKASIES
PRIVAATSAK X9069
KAAPSTAD
1980 -2- 26
PRIVATE BAG X9069
CAPE TOWN
DIRECTORATE OF PUBLICATIONS

Dear..........................

PUBLICATIONS ACT, 1974
PUBLICATION OR OBJECT

APPLICATION FOR A *DECISION/~~REVIEW~~

With reference to your application of........24 January 1980........I have to inform you that the publication or object—

Name and/or description....Stubborn Hope (African Writers Series 208)

Author or producer....Dennis Brutus

Publisher....Heinemann Educational Books Ltd, London

was examined by a committee referred to in section 4 (1) of the Publications Act, 1974, and that the committee decided that the publication or object is—

~~not undesirable~~

*undesirable within the meaning of section 47 (2) (e).................of the said Act.

REMARKS:
The publication is being retained

Yours faithfully

M. J. v.d. WESTHUIZEN
....
Director of Publications

* Delete whichever is not applicable.

Figure 7: Censors' report on Dennis Brutus's *Stubborn Hope*

13 FLINDERS STREET

RIVERLEA

2093

JOHANNESBURG

PHONE: 359349

SABLE BOOKS

REPUBLIEK VAN SUID-AFRIKA
STREEKVERTEENWOORDIGER
DEPT. VAN BINNELANDSE SAKE
1980 -4- 3 1
KAAPSTAD
REGIONAL REPRESENTATIVE
DEPT. OF THE INTERIOR
REPUBLIC OF SOUTH AFRICA

Sirs,

re: Wietie No. 1

P80/3/34

We have learnt, from the 'Rand Daily Mail' published on Tuesday the 25th instant, that the abovementioned publication has been declared undesirable under the Publications Act of 1974.

In the circumstances, we request the following:
  (a) the sections of the publication that were deemed to be undesirable,
  (b) the relevant sections of the 1974 Act pertaining to the undesirable sections of the publication,
  (c) the reasons underlying the undesirability and
  (d) if possible substantiating the nature of the undesirability.

We look forward to your considered and expeditious response in this matter.

Yours faithfully,
for Sable Books

Please reply in English.

EDITORS: FHAZEL JOHENNESSE
CHISTOPHER VAN WYK

Figures 8 and 9: Correspondence between censors and editors of *Wietie*

Republiek van Suid-Afrika  Republic of South Africa

Telegramadres
Telegraphic address FILCEN
Tel No 21-1000

Direktoraat van Publikasies
Directorate of Publications
Privaatsak/Private Bag X9069
KAAPSTAD/CAPE TOWN   8000

Messrs F Johennesse & C van Wyk
Sable Books
13 Flinders Street
RIVERLEA
2093

Verw No
Ref   P 80/3/54

1980 -4- 15

Dear Sirs

PUBLICATIONS ACT, 1974 : PUBLICATION : "WIETIE" - NO 1

With reference to your undated letter, I hereby submit the reasons of the committee for their decision that the above-mentioned publication is undesirable within the meaning of section 47(2)(a) of the Act:

"Although the publication has a lot of merit especially as regards the poetry, it is regretably a fact that some of the obscene words as used are unacceptable. The short story 'Aunty Molly and the Girls' is a case in point. The word 'fuck' is used about six times. See pages 27, 28, 29. Other obscenities appear on the following pages: 3, 5, 26 and 30.

In accordance with section 47(2)(a) of the Publications Act, 1974, the instances referred to are deemed to be undesirable as they are considered to be obscene and offensive."

Yours faithfully

S. F. DU TOIT
DIRECTOR OF PUBLICATIONS

English Academy Conference
4th–6th September 1986

In marking twenty-five years of existence, the English Academy of Southern Africa has called a Conference on English language and literature in South African society, 1961 to 1986.

Given the issues of direct social and political concern at stake in South Africa today, the nature and purpose of this Conference need to be stated clearly.

This Conference is called under the sole aegis of the English Academy. In no way is it associated with the Republican or Johannesburg Festivals this year. The English language is the prerogative of those who use it and it is their concerns which the Conference intends to pay attention to. Furthermore, the focus of the Conference will not be only retrospective — we of the present must consider the future.

It is intended that the nature of the Conference should be shaped by the participants. Cultural, linguistic, educational, political, industrial and social groups, as well as individuals are expected to attend, where *their* concerns, derived from *their* experience can be expressed.

It is for these reasons that the Conference will not consist of a series of formal papers delivered to a largely passive audience. Instead, opportunities for expression and interchange will be the paramount concern of the organizers.

Suggestions for the shape and nature of the Conference are being sought from many quarters. Individuals and organisations are encouraged to make proposals for the Conference programme, a programme which will have sufficient flexibility to meet the needs of all interest groups.

Apart from the many regular conferences on writing, drama, language and publishing which take place in South Africa, two conferences need to be kept in mind. The first is the 1974 conference on 'English-speaking South Africa Today' in Grahamstown. There the concerns of English-speaking middle-class whites received overwhelming attention.

Then there is the 1983 conference on 'Culture and Resistance' in Gaborone. At this conference it was decided that the next such gathering should be inside South Africa. This has not happened as yet.

There is no doubt that to launch a conference on English which will have truly wide representation at this time in our history is an ambitious and risky affair. Any number of circumstances could wreck it. To talk language is to talk politics; to talk about the past twenty-five years of English in South Africa is to talk about the present; and to talk about English in the present is to talk about a future South Africa.

And that is the challenge which this Conference poses. The English Academy's conference is therefore being planned to be representative, flexible and open. What happens will be largely determined by those who are present. This is the spirit in which advice and suggestions are being sought, and those are the terms upon which the Conference is being planned.

Michael Gardiner   Tel: 642-7373 (w)
Conference Organiser   648-0729 (h)
27 St Andrew's Road   Code 011
Parktown
2193

Amandla Ngawethu

Amandla Ngawethu, 'n Afrikaanse debuutbundel van Patrick J. Petersen, het sy verskyning gemaak 11 September 1985 by die Genadendalse Drukkery. 'n Relevante bundel met 'n relevante boodskap. Dertig gedigte wat veral die swartleser sal boei. Dit kan nuttig gebruik word by massavergaderings, skoolboikotte, protesoptogte, begrafnisse, ens.

Prys   R3,92 (AVB ingesluit)
Posgeld R0,19

Rig bestellings aan: Die Morawiese Boekdepot, Posbus 9, Genadendal 7234 en
Die Skrywer, Posbus77, Vredenburg 7380.

Figure 10: Call for contributions from the English Academy Conference published in *Staffrider*, Vol. 6, No. 3, 1986 (inside back cover)

Staffrider

Volume 6. No 3, 1986 R1.50 (excl. GST)

Days with Poona Poon
memories of a poor white childhood

Temba Makunga
remembers Bonnevilles Sof'town and Saville Row suits in

The Masquerade Ball

Language, Literature and the **Struggle** for **Liberation** in South Africa by Daniel Kunene

Exciting new poetry

Figures 11 and 12: Cover pages of *Staffrider* magazines

EDITORIAL

On January 11, South Africa's minister of home affairs and of communications, Stoffel Botha, warned *Work In Progress* that an examination of the publication was underway in terms of state of emergency regulations.

Over a year before, Botha had warned *WIP* that unless it ceased 'systematic publication of subversive propaganda', he would act against it.

The January 11 warning involved possible closure of *WIP* for up to six months, or imposing a pre-publication censor - a state official with powers to censor the contents of the publication.

Over the next weeks, enormous support was expressed for *WIP* and its publishing policy. This came from editors of mainstream newspapers, trade unions, political organisations, religious bodies and a host of other interests and organisations.

The Congress of South African Trade Unions noted that 'censorship of *WIP* is a direct attempt to stifle free and open debate, and to prevent the flow of information so vital to the building of democracy'. The National Union of Mineworkers said that 'every issue of *WIP* that does not come out will be a loss to our members', while the National Council of Trade Unions referred to the publication's 'intelligent and fearless analysis of the political, social and labour trends in our country'.

From within the media world, *Business Day* editor Ken Owen spoke of *WIP* as a 'reliable, intelligent and ethically impeccable publication', while Tertius Myburgh of the *Sunday Times* called *WIP* 'an invaluable source of information which deserves to be heard by all who are interested in serious affairs in South Africa'.

Representatives of foreign governments strongly condemned proposed action against *WIP* and other publications, and a number made direct representations to the South African government.

Two weeks after Botha's warning, *WIP* responded to his threat of closure in a 40-page memorandum dealing with the emergency regulations in general, and the nature of the publication in particular. Botha turned down a suggestion that he meet with a delegation from the publication - and then a blanket of silence descended.

By mid-February, two publications warned at the same time as *WIP* had been suspended for three months, and *WIP* began pushing Botha to respond to the representations made.

Finally, on March 2, Botha's office informed *WIP's* publishers that no action was being contemplated in terms of the media emergency regulations.

It is not for *WIP* to speculate on why the minister has chosen to act against some publications, and not others. The media emergency regulations involve arbitrary decisions and personal opinion. There is little point in seeking logic within arbitrariness.

But it is worthwhile re-stating *WIP's* position on publishing: that not only do all South Africans have the right to be fully and accurately informed by a wide range of opinions, debates and analyses and reporting. In addition, freedom of speech of its nature guarantees the right of publication - and the right of readers to be exposed to diversity and contradiction.

WIP has always been happy to allow readers to make their own choices on the basis of a wide range of information and views. This is the opposite of propaganda, which seeks to impose one view while suppressing others. In this battle for survival with the ministry of home affairs *WIP* has no doubt which side supports the publication of systematic propaganda.

This edition of *WIP* is unavoidably late - held back until the outcome of the threatened closure had been finalised.

No action is currently contemplated against the publication in terms of media emergency regulations at present - although the state still has much in its arsenal.

But *WIP* intends surviving - and sees a long-term future for its publishing programme. One part of this future is financial stability - a crucial component of independent publishing.

Ensuring financial stability, together with ever-increasing costs in paper, printing, reproduction and postage have forced *WIP* to raise its rates. But these increases are modest - way below rates of inflation - and in some cases are the first for over three years.

The editors thank all those who supported *WIP* in its most-recent battle for survival - and look forward to ongoing and increasing support from the most important component of any publication: its readers.

Work In Progress 58 - March/April 1989

Figure 13: Editorial published in *Work in Progress* 58, March/April 1989 (inside cover)

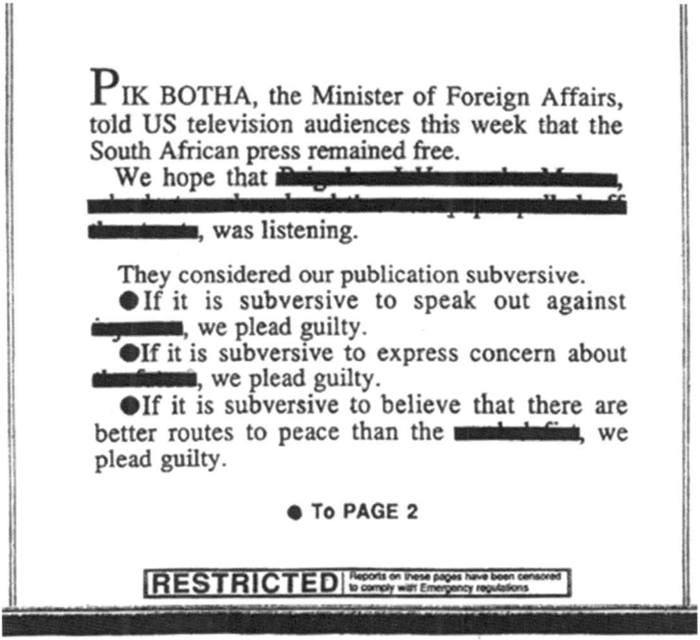

PIK BOTHA, the Minister of Foreign Affairs, told US television audiences this week that the South African press remained free.

We hope that ▇▇, was listening.

They considered our publication subversive.

- If it is subversive to speak out against ▇▇▇▇▇▇, we plead guilty.
- If it is subversive to express concern about ▇▇▇▇▇▇, we plead guilty.
- If it is subversive to believe that there are better routes to peace than the ▇▇▇▇▇▇, we plead guilty.

● To PAGE 2

[RESTRICTED] Reports on these pages have been censored to comply with Emergency regulations

Figure 14: Front page comment of the *Weekly Mail* of 20 June 1986, under the heading 'Our lawyers tell us we can say almost nothing critical about the Emergency but we'll try'

4 | Readers' Roles in the World of Books

> The birth of the reader must be at the cost of the death of the Author.
>
> — Roland Barthes, 'The Death of the Author'

THE LITERARY INDUSTRY in apartheid South Africa was dominated by a mainstream book trade compliant with the dominant conservative ideology, which was closely aligned to the centres of power. Through their zealously crafted censorship apparatus, censors regulated reading and controlled availability and access to books. A 'good book' campaign was engineered and imposed on readers and the various book professionals – publishers, librarians and booksellers. This repressive control was underpinned by the censors' belief that readers' minds had to be protected from undesirable ideas, for fear that readings would translate into political action.

However, despite the censorship climate spanning the colonial era to the apartheid regime (and at times creeping into post-1994 South Africa), a resilient alternative literary industry emerged, upheld by anti-apartheid writers, publishers, librarians and booksellers, and, as argued in this chapter, alternative progressive readers. The alternative book trade influenced oppositional politics and vice versa. This chapter examines the alternative book trade through an analysis of the active roles performed by readers, revealing their agency and creativity. By storing, reading and sharing banned or undesirable publications, readers proved that an alternative space for both oppositional literature and politics was possible, circumventing the censorship-controlled mainstream literary industry and fostering a culture of engaged reading.

Based on semi-structured interviews and several accounts of readers from secondary sources, this chapter examines the social context in which readers performed and activated their reading, and investigates 'the world behind books' (Darnton 1982: ix). Echoing Robert Darnton's call to go beyond the book, Roger Chartier (2002a: 49) emphasises the necessity of treating the history of reading independently from the history of the actual reading material, and Isabel Hofmeyr (1996: 115) argues that 'if we are to address questions of reception properly, then minimally we will have to relativize our understanding of the book and reading rather than exporting this practice out of all other areas of social life'. In this light, the 'social context of reading' (Darnton 2002: 21) implies an understanding of reading in the context in which it occurs and does not focus on a literary analysis of the texts read. In line with this way of reading and thinking, this chapter focuses on how, when, why and where alternative readers read, and discusses the ways in which these readers were not only literary activists through the role they played in the life cycle of books, but also political activists through their use of banned publications in the anti-apartheid movement.

In order to understand the life cycle of books, one must turn to the various elements involved in the book trade and examine how each promotes assorted genres and canons of literature, from production to consumption, including external political, social and economic factors. Darnton (2002: 12) proposes a very useful communication circuit, which involves seven actors: author, publisher, printer, supplier, shipper, bookseller and reader. In this circuit, readers are described as purchasers, borrowers and members of clubs and libraries. They are situated where the process runs full circle because of their influence on authors, both before and after the moment of writing. Within the circle lie 'intellectual influences and publicity', 'economic and social conjuncture' and 'political and legal sanctions' (11). It is in terms of this cycle that the path followed by undesirable and banned books in apartheid South Africa is understood.

In a typical mainstream book economy, publications go through these stages relatively swiftly, as they are published, marketed and distributed for the commercial gain of all involved, thus following market imperatives. Readers are free to choose their reading material, as books are generally available and accessible. However, the cycle exists within a structured society and is not immune to external and internal influences. As Darnton (2002) points out, various intellectual, social, economic, political and legal factors can alter the workings of the system and this was certainly the case with apartheid censorship, drastically altering the application of this model.

The South African censorship apparatus influenced the ways in which books moved from one stage of the cycle to another. Whether books were banned or likely to be banned, the extreme conditions caused by censorship altered the linearity, role and function traditionally attributed to the actors involved in the book trade, prompting the creation of alternative transmission modalities that enabled these publications to reach the end of the cycle despite adverse conditions, but also creating gaps. This chapter explores how some readers assumed the responsibility of filling these gaps, creating and sustaining an alternative life cycle for books in apartheid South Africa.

Readerships of banned books

Based on the data collected for this research from primary (interviews) and secondary (documentary) sources, a portrait of the readership sample emerges. While not claiming to be a comprehensive, definitive survey, it reveals that relations between readers and banned reading material were at times arbitrary and spontaneous. Many readers were often not aware of the banned status of a publication, but were aware that these publications were contributing to a broader conversation that opposed mainstream politics and the book trade. Readers interviewed and cited in the secondary sources include workers, unionists, political activists, students, academics, teachers, writers and publishers, and generally speaking, ordinary readers. Most would not immediately identity as 'readers of banned literature', but rather as political activists or politically conscious individuals. Moreover, depending on the decade and political climate in which reading occurred, the dynamics informing the readership for banned literature would at times operate in a very isolated manner – such as the case of a banned person in the 1950s. A sense of community among readers prevailed in the 1970s – for instance, around *Staffrider* magazine in Johannesburg and other similar alternative literary spaces.

The various readerships of banned political literature included individuals from various social classes and ideologies, although they shared a common interest in anti-apartheid oppositional politics and literature. The readers discussed here are part of a larger and elusive group that could generally be designated as politically conscious individuals espousing various anti-apartheid strands and ideologies, and involved in resistance politics to varying degrees.

Robert Escarpit (1971: 90) defines utilitarian reading as 'the reading of militants or autodidacts. For them the book serves as the instrument of or to combat techniques of social promotion. Thus the book may be read in order to acquire culture, not primarily to enjoy reading.' In light of this definition, readers of banned literature could be identified as utilitarian readers, as reading was integrated in the anti-apartheid discourse, although to varying degrees it also sought to fulfil leisure, educational or entertainment needs.

Black readerships emerged and developed through the activities of religious, voluntary, cultural and political organisations in South Africa (Dick 2007b). Missions, self-help clubs, political organisations and other similar groups contributed to developing literacy and a reading culture among black South Africans from the nineteenth century onwards, parallel to the colonial reading programme aimed at the white population (13) and entertainment literacy to neutralise radicalism (Sandwith 2014). For instance, political organisations active in Cape Town's District Six, such as the Lenin Club and the New Era Fellowship, as well as the Non-European United Front (NEUF), the Non-European Unity Movement (NEUM) and several Trotskyite groups, facilitated intellectual spaces that would lead to cultural and political discussions (Dick 2007b; Sandwith 2014). Readerships were formed parallel to political movements and spaces, and as Archie Dick (2007b: 18) explains, 'the number of libraries and readers grew in this curious mix of cultural and political contexts'. The cultural origins of these politicised readership groupings, which came to play a role in alternative politics, echo Amilcar Cabral's comment that it is 'generally within the culture that we find seeds of opposition, which leads to the structuring and development of the liberation movement' (1994: 56). Cultural debates shaped political activism and while the reverse could also be said to be true, political ideas developed through writing, reading and interpreting literary texts (Sandwith 2014: 130-1). Groupings such as the NEUF, the NEUM and the Communist Party of South Africa became outlets for popular radicalism (138), breaking away from the moderate stance adopted by cultural initiatives operating under the umbrella of colonial missionary interests, for example.

The idea of readership, readers' groups or communities of readers can be understood in different ways. Drawing on Chartier, this book understands these to comprise readers who share common practices, usages and understanding of texts. Communities of readers are individuals who share 'the same reading styles and the same strategies of interpretation' (Chartier 1989: 158). One could complement this definition of readers by studying them in their social context, as readers are 'complex actors shaped by a complex set of institutions and social relations' (Newell et al. 2000: 9) and do not exist in a vacuum.

Readerships can be understood as publics or audiences, as they receive and process messages in the public domain. Michael Warner (2002b: 50) differentiates between various kinds of publics: 'a public', 'the public' and 'the public that comes into being only in relation to texts and their circulation'. He emphasises the importance of noting the multiplicity of publics and the necessity of approaching them historically (2002a: 9). Warner's idea of a public created in relation to texts and their circulation underpins the examination of the South African reading public associated with alternative and banned publications. However, in this particular context, a clandestine or secret public poses an apparent contradiction in terms. Warner (2002b: 50) defines a public as showing 'common visibility and common action'. The concept of a 'counterpublic' (2002a) is useful here to understand alternative readers as forming a dissident public within a broader context, creating a public sphere located in a marginal and alternative social space centred around books and oppositional politics. The readership of banned literature could be understood as being created through the clandestine circulation of illegal texts and ideas. In Warner's words, they become, 'by virtue of their reflexively circulating discourse, a social entity' (2002a: 11-12). In apartheid South Africa, several reading communities coexisted, including the one that rallied behind censors. It is in this context that qualitatives such as alternative, oppositional or progressive are understood in this book.

These considerations regarding the formation of readerships are reminiscent of Brian Street's assertion that literacy is not strictly understood as 'a set of technical skills learnt in formal education, but as social practices embedded in specific contexts, discourses and positions' (1996: 1). Literacy and reading are used in specific contexts and situations and the dominant groups construe the uses of literacy (4-5). These can range from a functional literacy strictly designed to fulfil minimal everyday requirements to higher levels that enable a reader to use highly intellectual and complex texts on ideological and theoretical levels. Street (5) reminds us that literacy practices are embedded in power relations: 'An ideological model of literacy begins from the premise that variable literacy practices are always rooted in power relations and that the apparent innocence and neutrality of the "rules" serve to disguise the ways in which such power is maintained through literacy.' Such power relations were at play in, for example, the entertainment value conferred on literacy and books to moderate emerging radicalism in urban centres, as with the Carnegie initiative and the early years of the Bantu Men's Social Centre, established in 1924 and led by H.I.E. Dhlomo (Sandwith 2014).

By adopting an ideological approach to literacy, one can better understand the nuances and levels of literacy at play in various contexts and, in this case, promote understanding of the practices of reading among politically aware readers such as those discussed in this book. In this light, reading habits, cultures and practices must be understood in relation to the context in which they occur, which is conditioned by several factors, such as gender, religion, geographical location, class and political affiliations (Lyons and Taksa 1992: 8). Oppositional, progressive readers included individuals from various backgrounds, although they all had in common their involvement – to various degrees – in anti-apartheid politics. They also developed various forms of literacy, as the readers' sample ranges from writers to trade unionists and students, and intellectuals to farmworkers. The fact that they read the same books and shared some common reading practices despite these differences shows how a broader community of interest, united around a common oppositional stance, took precedence over class and other affiliations.

Progressive writers discussed in this book, in their capacity as readers, were involved in cultural resistance to apartheid and censorship, at grassroots and leadership levels and in between. The act of reading is often embedded in the act of writing and authors involved with alternative publishers were in most cases avid readers. Several autobiographies, memoirs and literary and socio-political studies reveal how anti-apartheid writers read and used banned and alternative books to inspire their own writings. While these writers' stances on the relationship between arts, literature and politics varied, as debated in *Spring is Rebellious* (De Kok and Press 1990), the politicisation of reading was often echoed in a politicised writing style. Mandla Langa, for instance, remembers how he, Steve Biko and Barney Pityana read Jean-Paul Sartre, Lewis Nkosi and Alex La Guma and found inspiration for their own writings (Wilson 1991: 28-9). Black consciousness philosopher Noel Chabani Manganyi recalls how reading W.E.B. Du Bois, Joel Rogers and Frantz Fanon had an impact on his 1977 work *Alienation and the Body in Racist Society* (Heywood 2004: 210). Censors also performed politicised readings and some were also authors and avid readers. As exemplified in H.I.E. Dhlomo's appeal to readers to write books to fill the gaps in black South African literature, reading led to writing. Dick (2007b: 16) notes that this is what happened 'when Peter Abrahams, who worked at the library in 1937, was motivated as a writer upon reading Du Bois's *The Soul of Black Folks*', an example that draws attention to the transoceanic influences between African-American and South African literature.

South African educationist, poet and political activist Dennis Brutus remembers being an avid reader. He would read an eclectic selection of books, some of them banned, although he would not necessarily be aware of their illegal status at the time of reading.[1] He points out that some members of the Port Elizabeth branch of the Teachers' League of South Africa used to meet to discuss various genres of literature, which inevitably included undesirable or banned books. As Brutus recalls, these meetings often led to broader political debates: 'From these book circles I recall discussions on *On Liberty* by John Locke, *Darkness at Noon* by Arthur Koestler, *Jazz* by Rex Harris'.[2] Among these teachers were opinion-makers and individuals who would disseminate books outside their immediate circles and share them with other teachers and students. Although at a different time and place, writer Chris van Wyk recalls reading Es'kia Mphahlele's *Down Second Avenue* after one of his teachers, who took note of his love of reading, lent him a copy.[3]

Some progressive academics formed part of the readership of banned or alternative literature, accessing, reading, writing and sometimes publishing such books in and outside the university space. In academia, politically active students also represented a portion of the readership of banned political publications. Associations such as the South African Students' Organisation (SASO), among others, provided a space where political activism could develop, often based on ideas and debates sparked by banned and oppositional literature. As Lindy Wilson (1991: 28) stresses: 'Everybody read books outside their university subjects. These provided

---

1. Dennis Brutus, interview, Durban, 25 May 2007.
2. Email from Dennis Brutus, 10 November 2007.
3. Chris van Wyk, interview, Johannesburg, 12 October 2007.

the essence of the debates and the discussion that made the future have some kind of possibility.' Student activists, such as those involved in SASO, borrowed extensively from literary sources and newspapers, inserting elements of political philosophy such as the African-American civil rights movement and quotations from Aimé Césaire, Frantz Fanon, James Cone and Malcom X, for example, into their own speeches and essays (29).

Biko often quoted Césaire and Fanon in his speeches and writing, as did other black consciousness leaders (Ramphele 1995: 55). Biko published a column in the SASO newsletter titled 'I Write What I Like' under the pseudonym 'Frank Talk' to defy the ban served on him in 1973 (Stubbs 2004: 2). SASO became a subculture of the university (Wilson 1991: 28) and political debates and literary criticism were entangled in a space where the issues and identities went well beyond academic concerns. Publications like the SASO newsletter played an important role in South African politics and literature, and, as Christopher Merrett (1994: 83) emphasises: 'Student publications, in some senses the precursors of the alternative press which flourished from the 1980s, were an important target [of censors].'

The example of Biko's writing practices introduces the issue of the use of pseudonyms, whereby an alter ego would allow writers to express themselves in the public domain and also enable readers to access otherwise 'undesirable' ideas and texts. By changing their names, these writers could enter and exist in the public domain and find their way to the mainstream culture, even if precariously, with pseudonyms becoming a means of combating censorship. While Brutus was an alleged communist and terrorist, his poems, written under the pseudonym of John Bruin, were prescribed in the school curriculum, which was directly linked to the censorship and thought-control apparatus. Brutus recalls being surprised, if not amused, when learning of this turn of events.[4] Moreover, the use of pseudonyms to bypass censorship reveals the censors' focus on extra-textual

---

4. Dennis Brutus, interview, Durban, 16 May 2007.

elements as a reading protocol. Biko's 'Frank Talk' is an example of defying censorship by challenging the reading performed by censors, through the alteration of extra-textual elements that could influence the reception of texts. It furthermore provides an alternative to self-censorship. Although of a completely different nature, the choice of provocative pseudonym 'Des Troye' by the author of *An Act of Immorality* – the first novel banned under the Publications and Entertainments Act No. 26 of 1963 – also carried a political statement.[5]

The first issue of *Work in Progress* was published in September 1977. Founded by some postgraduate students at the University of the Witwatersrand, it rallied a community of readers around oppositional politics. The objective of *Work in Progress* was to disseminate ideas repressed by the censorship system beyond the university community and to 'stimulate debate and present views on a wide range of issues', as described on the back cover of all issues. The result was an independent socio-political publication driven by freedom of speech and circulation of ideas repressed by apartheid censorship and propaganda. This was a small-scale production venture and founding editors Glenn Moss, Gerhard Maré and Susan Brown managed all aspects of the publication process, from the selection of content to distribution.[6] It published articles on political and social current affairs, political court cases, strikes and disputes, exposing a reality that censors and, more generally, the apartheid regime, tried to conceal. The publication was often scrutinised by censors and some of the correspondence between the editors and the censorship board was published or discussed in its editorials. Publications such as *Work in Progress* contributed to the circulation of ideas and information in the public domain, stimulating debate and forging a network of writers and readers.

---

5. For more about this novel, see http://bookslive.co.za/blog/2016/07/25/why-the-first-south-african-novel-to-be-banned-under-apartheid-law-is-also-one-of-the-worst-ever-written/.
6. Gerhard Maré, interview, Durban, 24 May 2007.

Some networks were developed among students and lecturers in the academic space. One anonymous interviewee recalls that while studying at a technikon in what was then the Transvaal, 'senior students would come to us first-years [students] to ask us about our political orientation and from there informed us and provided us with banned literature such as W.E.B Du Bois, Mao Tse-tung and Kwame Nkrumah'.[7] Such trust among readers with similar ideologies suggests a relatively close-knit and engaged readership. This tendency is also revealed in Dick's account of a similar practice identified in one of the evening school schemes, primarily aimed at developing reading and literacy:

> Teachers also encouraged learners to use other libraries. Mxolisi Mgxashe, for example, a member of the Kensington night school and a Pan-African Congress activist, regularly used the reference section of the South African Library in Cape Town to read and photocopy passages from books on communism, Garveyism (after Marcus Garvey) and Pan-Africanism (Dick 2007b: 19).

Besides readers that could identify as academics, students or writers, some politically conscious ordinary readers also accessed banned books. Merrett (1994: 96) cites farmworkers circulating banned publications and an incident where a coal delivery man in Heilbron read and passed a copy of Nelson Mandela's *The Struggle is My Life* to another reader, at a time where Mandela and therefore all his writings were banned. Some like-minded family members and friends of professionals involved in the alternative literary industry were connected to alternative literary networks because of their personal relationships and were thus exposed to oppositional ideas and banned literature.[8]

Readers from various backgrounds, with different levels of literacy, from urban and rural areas, and different socio-economic contexts, formed an

---

7. Interviewee 1, Durban, 10 November 2004.
8. Van Wyk, interview.

inclusive readership for banned political publications. This heterogeneous readership rallied around anti-apartheid ideologies and resistance, with 'resistance' being understood as 'a complex, multivalent and mobile set of processes, registering various shades of ambivalence, entanglement and complicity' (Sandwith 2014: 13). Readers were dispersed over time and geographical spaces, although urban areas were more favourable for alternative readerships, in part because of the increased accessibility and availability of books in these settings. The readership for banned literature developed alongside forms, usages and practices of literacy, geared towards political gains rather than 'formal schooled literacy practices' (Street 1996: 6).

Genres of books

The publications that are the focus of this chapter could be labelled as political, oppositional, alternative, progressive and anti-apartheid literature. To censors, they were undesirable, communist, seditious, subversive and dangerous. To ordinary readers, they were important and relevant books. The books read by alternative readers form an eclectic mix of genres including autobiographies, novels, short stories, poetry, socio-historical studies, political theory, philosophy, newsletters, journals and media articles, to name but a few. Censors scrutinised books and publications suspected of being undesirable, as per section 5 (2) of the Publications and Entertainments Act No. 26 of 1963, section 47 (2) of the Publications Act No. 42 of 1974 and later amendments, which pertained to the political nature of publications, as well as those banned indirectly in terms of the Suppression of Communism Act No. 44 of 1950 and later amendments. Readers, publishers and authors of such books were further assumed by censors to support and propagate communist views and the state actively used all means possible to suppress these individuals' freedom of speech and right to information, and to remove banned publications from circulation.

According to *Jacobsen's Index of Objectionable Literature* (1974), the number of items banned over time totalled 14 499 publications. Beside books and publications in the strict sense of the term, bans could be extended to any form of text (including visual material) printed on pens, posters, puzzles, greeting cards, stamps or in the form of lyrics in music, and objects such as novelties, T-shirts, calendars, etc. Section 1 (iv) (xi) and (xii) of the Suppression of Communism Act defines the terms 'publications and documents' to include books, pamphlets, records, lists, placards, posters, drawings, photographs, pictures, periodical publications, magazines and handbills. The Publications and Entertainments Act defined 'publications or objects' along similar lines in section (1) (viii), with the addition of newspapers, printed material, typescripts, illustrations, paintings and lithographs, among other things. This range of material speaks to the varied levels and usages of literacy and the versatility of the printed word as a carrier of meanings and ideas, as well as the censors' determination to cover as wide a range of material as possible.

The eclectic list of banned material is striking in its diversity. Interestingly, this was sometimes created by readers themselves. South African writer and intellectual Njabulo Ndebele's first encounter with banned books testifies to a feeling of amazement and puzzlement at being in possession of such a variety of literature with the common denominator of being banned:

> One day, alone at home and bored during school holidays in the mid-1960s, I began to explore my home. There was that wooden crate at the front right corner of the garage against which the silver bumper of my father's Ford Zephyr 6 sometimes rested. The crate had been there for many years [. . .] On top of it was a heavy layer of unused floor tiles; old copies of *Huisgenoot*, *Zonk*, and *Drum* magazines [. . .] Once I had removed everything from the top of the box, I opened it. Inside, were many books on music, art, and poetry, and others that I thought my father must have used for his degree studies at the University of the Witwatersrand. But as I got closer to the bottom of the box, my heart leaped with disbelief! Here was *Down Second Avenue* by Ezekiel Mphahlele; and *Road to Ghana* by Alfred Hutchinson; and *Blame me on History* by Bloke

Modisane; and *Naught for your Comfort* by Trevor Huddleston; and *Tell Freedom* by Peter Abrahams; and *Splendid Sunday* by James Ambrose Brown; and *Transvaal Episode* by Harry Bloom; *Chocolates for my Wife* by Todd Matshikiza; *South Africa: The Struggle for a Birthright* by Mary Benson; *The Ochre People* by Noni Jabavu of Ghana; *The Autobiography of Kwame Nkrumah*; *Let my People Go* by Albert Luthuli; *Go Well, Stay Well* by Hannah Stanton, copies of *Africa South* magazine, and other lesser known books that I do not remember now. Banned books (Ndebele 2007: 9).

The titles in Ndebele's box are an unexpected mix of popular literature, such as *Drum* magazine, side by side with African literary classics, autobiographies and political philosophy by prominent African intellectuals and public figures such as Kwame Nkrumah, Albert Luthuli and Es'kia Mphahlele. In all likelihood, a reader like Ndebele's father did not fall within the censors' either/or imagined categories. The heterogeneous configuration of books such as the one observed in Ndebele's box transcends the popular versus serious literature debate and challenges the belief that educated readers only read so-called serious literature. The choice of reading material went beyond class affiliations and was unpredictable, in part as a result of circumstances where books were not easily accessible and were randomly circulated. As Ndebele's discovery of a full box of banned books reveals, some readers literally stumbled upon banned books.

Books addressing issues of social resistance and socialism and advocating emancipation were inevitably likely to be banned, especially if written by a black author or imported from a communist country. Some readers were seemingly in search of such books. Often, these titles happened to be the ones relevant to progressive readers in South Africa.[9] An anonymous interviewee listed among the banned books read Biko's *I Write What I Like*, *Sowing the Seeds of Revolution* by Samora Machel and books

---

9. Brutus, interview, 25 May 2007; Interviewee 1; Interviewee 9, Johannesburg, 5 September 2004.

by Mao Tse-tung, Du Bois and Nkrumah.[10] Brutus also remembers reading Du Bois, Malcom X, Marcus Garvey, Fidel Castro and Antonio Gramsci, as well as several titles from Heinemann's African Writers Series.[11] He also cites Govan Mbeki's *South Africa: The Peasants' Revolt*, which was sent to him by a friend abroad.[12] Another anonymous interviewee reveals that this kind of political literature was very popular in the Eastern Cape, where it facilitated political discussions.[13] Librarian Christopher Merrett reiterates this when speaking of library books regularly sought after by progressive readers: 'Some banned titles that were regularly asked for by readers include Govan Mbeki's *Peasant's Revolt* [. . .] Books about South African history, about political history that were written by obvious ANC and PAC writers were much in demand. And some South African novelists like Alex La Guma.'[14]

Although many autobiographies by anti-apartheid leaders were subjected to censorship and other legislation such as the Suppression of Communism Act, South African readers nonetheless managed to find and read some of them. Van Wyk recalls Mphahlele's *Down Second Avenue*, banned in its comic version, as one of the first books to inspire him literarily and Mtutuzeli Matshoba's *Call Me Not a Man* as one of the banned books that were widely circulated among readers.[15]

As books in general and banned books in particular were not readily available in many areas during the censorship years, eager readers often had to be creative and open to the unexpected. Van Wyk remembers that avid readers would sometimes read everything they could lay their hands on, which also explains the interesting combination of books of various genres. Imported popular fiction was sometimes read alongside political publications, even by readers who could be thought of as being

---

10. Interviewee 1.
11. Brutus, interview, 25 May 2007.
12. Dennis Brutus, interview, Durban, 10 October 2007.
13. Interviewee 4, Johannesburg, 22 August 2004.
14. Christopher Merrett, interview, Pietermaritzburg, 23 October 2007.
15. Van Wyk, interview.

highly literate intellectuals, falling into the censors' sophisticated reader category. For instance, Brutus recalls reading popular literature, such as Mario Puzzo's *The Godfather* series and Margaret Mitchell's *Gone with the Wind*. Popular literature – banned and not banned – could create a space for discussion and reflection, as was the case with *Gone with the Wind*, which led to discussions on slavery and oppression.[16]

Seemingly trivial items were also banned sometimes. A Diwali, Eid al-Adha and Christmas greeting card sent by Yusuf Dadoo in 1979 was banned after a police lieutenant submitted it to the censorship board. According to the censors' report, it was 'compiled by a communist in exile', contained 'inflammatory remarks calculated to promote a sense of grievance and action' and 'advocates ANC [African National Congress] leadership'.[17] Some of the printed evidence used during the Treason Trial of 1963–4 is also telling of how an unusual configuration of publications was at times interpreted to suit the expectations of the authorities, in this case labelling the owners of such material as 'communists' and 'dangerous individuals'. Referring to the range of printed material found during the raid of the Rivonia farm and used as examples in the trial, ANC leader Nelson Mandela (1995: 244) recalls: 'One by one, every paper, pamphlet, document, book, notebook, letter, magazine and clipping that the police accumulated in the last three years of searches was produced and numbered: 12,000 in all. The submissions ranged from the United Nations Declaration of Human Rights to a Russian cookery book.'

According to the authorities, documents such as those produced during the Treason Trial were undesirable, as per the Suppression of Communism Act they suggested an affiliation to communism. It was assumed that *what* one read was an absolute indicator of *who* one was. The readers of these documents were alleged communists and these documents served as 'irrefutable' proof.

---

16. Brutus, interview, 25 May 2007.
17. National Archives of South Africa (NASA), Cape Town, IDP 3/62, Ref: P78/12/8. Prohibition of possession. Yusuf Dadoo. 1979.

By 1984, the *Government Gazette* listed some 20 000 items of various types and genres as banned (Hachten and Giffard 1984: 165). The Publications Act of 1974 recommended the creation of a security committee, to work alongside the censors' literary committee. A great number of books were thereafter scrutinised by security readers who determined whether the submitted items represented a security threat. In 1975, 25.1 per cent of publications submitted to the censorship board fell in the 'state security' and 'communist' categories, a figure that reached 53.5 per cent in 1978 (Du Toit 1983: 88). Of these, 24.5 per cent were found undesirable in 1975, against 44 per cent in 1979. André du Toit explains this increase in the number of political publications that were found 'undesirable' by pointing out that 'it corresponds with the increasing role played by the police and security police in submitting material to publications committees, now amounting to almost half of the total' (92). These figures do not include books by writers who were banned in terms of the provisions of the Suppression of Communism Act.

In short, all banned books were not necessarily read in the alternative circuit and conversely not all books read in the alternative circuit were banned. Those that were read – whether banned or not – often led to discussion and debate that would transcend the immediate activity of reading to enter a broader socio-political sphere of action within the alternative space. Challenging the expectations and assumptions of censors, educated readers read popular literature, while semi-literate readers grasped the ideas promoted in so-called serious literature.

Sourcing undesirable publications

Official post-publication censorship ensured that books published in South Africa were most likely distributed before censors reacted. A book could remain on someone's bookshelf for some time before it was declared illegal. Some imported books were seized at customs, while others found their way into South Africa before the authorities identified them. In the case of bans on individuals, in terms of the provisions of the Suppression of Communism Act, all literature, essays, speeches and other communications produced were declared illegal and automatically banned. Books could either be banned for distribution or for possession at any given time after publication. It was illegal to distribute undesirable publications, while radically or extremely undesirable publications were illegal even for possession. The Kafkaesque nature of the censorship bureaucracy made it difficult for readers to be up to date in terms of the status of books on their private shelves.

The *Government Gazette* was – and still is – the official government newsletter and was published in Cape Town. It listed recently banned items on a weekly basis and included both imported and local publications. Librarians generally consulted these gazettes to remove banned books and store them in the banned book sections of the library.[18] *Jacobsen's Index of Objectionable Literature* (1974) was in some ways a non-official version of the *Government Gazette*'s listings. The *Jacobsen Index* was an updated directory of publications prohibited for importation and was available from bookstores and libraries across South Africa (Hachten and Giffard 1984: 165). The list was updated weekly, with loose pages added to the ever-growing list. It mainly concentrated on written texts, although it also listed objects ranging from novelties and calendars to political tracts. Perhaps unsurprisingly, some progressive readers performed a subversive reading of these listings and used them as sources of publicity for significant progressive reading material. For instance, Wilson (1991: 29) notes that the *Gazette* became a marketing tool and was one of 'the main sources of information about relevant books [. . .] that became required reading'.

Some bookshops were known in the alternative circuit for clandestinely selling illegal publications to a limited trusted pool of readers. At least two were identified in Johannesburg by interviewees surveyed for this book – Van Schaik and De Jong.[19] Brutus also recalls such bookshops in Port Elizabeth and Cape Town.[20] Cape Town's Open Books is also

---

18. Email from Jewel Koopman, 22 May 2007.
19. Van Wyk, interview; Maré, interview.
20. Brutus, interview, 25 May 2007.

noted as an independent bookseller that kept some banned titles (Cloete 2000: 50). Some Lutheran bookshops are also remembered as a source of banned books, as well as the United States Consulate (Wilson 1991: 29). However, given the ruthlessness of the system and risks associated with distributing banned books, these outlets gave this privileged access only to trusted customers. Van Wyk reveals his experience of such bookshops:

> Fhazel [Johennesse] and I used to go in there [Van Schaik bookshop in Johannesburg] and browse around, and sometimes we'd ask him if he had banned books. Now obviously he would not tell anybody, 'Yes I've got banned books' – I could have been a policeman. But as soon as he started to trust us, he'd say, 'I've got something; it's under the counter or in the other room, come and look.' And we'd go and he'd give us what we wanted.[21]

In this context of concealment and secrecy, alternative marketing strategies were adopted to make banned or potentially undesirable material known and read more widely. As noted in the previous chapter, publishers sometimes used underground mailing distribution schemes to get books to readers directly. Some mainstream commercial bookshops also had banned books on their shelves at times. It is possible that these booksellers were simply caught unawares or considered mainstream bookshops to be safe places to have banned books. They might also have relied on the assumption that higher prices implied a middle-class, conservative readership and that such books were out of reach to a more popular, mass readership. Mandla Langa recalls rewarding trips in search of progressive literature:

> We started sharing libraries, sharing books and also going to all these bookshops which had all these expensive books which we

---

21. Van Wyk, interview.

needed and, you know, finding a way to appropriate them. We started really widening our vistas and our minds by reading books which the regime never possibly thought we'd lay our hands on, anything from the African Writers Series to, well, we read Marcuse, we read the existential philosophers such as Jean-Paul Sartre. There was Mphahlele and maybe some hidden copies by Alex La Guma, Lewis Nkosi, Can Themba, Nat Nakasa, Bloke Modisane. We read all that (in Wilson 1991: 29).

This passage highlights the resourcefulness of readers in 'appropriating' a wide range of reading material, building their personal libraries from multiple sources.

Some informal book traders operated in black townships in Johannesburg, providing services to readers where formal bookshops were not established,[22] in a similar fashion to the mobile libraries discussed in the previous chapter. Van Wyk recalls street vendors who would stock pamphlets, literary magazines and books from Ravan Press's offices. Because these publications were sourced directly from the publisher, the stock was not necessarily banned, as censorship operated post-publication; however, some of these titles were at high risk of being banned if they attracted the censors' scrutiny, as were a number of books published by oppositional publishers. Van Wyk remembers how writers worked closely with Ravan, as they contributed to *Staffrider* and Ravan's list not only by writing, but also by distributing books in Soweto, for example, where books were not readily available:

So these writers' groups would come and submit their poems and short stories and then we'd phone them when *Staffrider* came from the printers. And they'd take copies – 100 copies here, 20 copies there, 60 copies there – and take them to their various writers'

---

22. Van Wyk, interview.

groups and that's how it got disseminated around the country. I remember when I was working at *Staffrider*, there were vendors – they were actually like hawkers who came to buy books and *Staffrider* magazines in our office – and they went and stood on the pavement, put them on a blanket on the pavement or in cardboard boxes on the pavement and sold these books from there. Some would sell them in the train, walking up and down in the train selling them.[23]

As Van Wyk notes, these informal book dealers eagerly took part in this literary subculture, sometimes at risk of being raided and arrested by the security police and running at a financial loss if they were not able to pay Ravan for the stock.

As is evident from these examples, some readers were actively in search of books and it comes as no surprise that some found ways of obtaining banned books in libraries. Although relatively controlled through registers and other administrative procedures, library books kept in restricted areas sometimes disappeared.[24] Some of these banned books sometimes reappeared in the library, anonymously left on a table.[25]

In a few instances, some librarians knowingly distributed banned books. Commenting during a discussion at the Cape Town Book Fair in June 2006, erstwhile Cape Town librarian Vincent Kolbe described how he would casually leave books in a kit bag and those in the know would equally casually pick them up. These few examples prove that not all librarians and booksellers worked with the system; some made oppositional literature available to readers and ran the risks at both professional and personal levels of falling foul of the apartheid state.

Relations of trust and connivance grew between the various spheres of the alternative literary circuit, as oppositional writers, readers, publishers,

---

23. Van Wyk, interview.
24. Merrett, interview; Interviewee 1; Interviewee 15, Durban, 10 May 2007.
25. Merrett, interview.

booksellers and librarians worked in close collaboration to get books read and shared by the largest possible number of readers. However, they did not always meet in person. As editor at Ravan, Van Wyk had privileged access to some oppositional books that were later shared:

> I also happened to work at a publishing house at that time and some literature was banned from time to time and I'd bring these books home and keep them for myself. You also borrowed books from someone – somebody would give you a book, saying, 'This is banned – read it and bring it back or pass it on.'[26]

The mail services inadvertently became a conduit for banned books. If not intercepted by customs, exiled activists would send literature by mail to friends and relatives in South Africa.[27] Other books were sent by European and American anti-apartheid movements (Bozzoli 2004: 330).

As the court case against political activist Ahmed Essop Timol illustrates, some travellers also carried literature in their luggage. He was arrested for having brought an ANC pamphlet and a draft copy of *Inkululeko* – the South African Communist Party's newsletter – into South Africa (Merrett 1994: 49). Trips to and from Swaziland are also recalled as facilitating the importation – or more accurately, smuggling – of banned books sourced in Swazi bookshops.[28] However, bringing banned books across the borders could be perilous, as the case of Tsoeu Mokhele, who received a five-year sentence in 1981 for having brought literature into South Africa through the Lesotho border, demonstrates (Merrett 1994: 96).

The authorities were on the lookout and one of the standard questions asked by South African customs officials at entry points was if one was

---

26. Van Wyk, interview.
27. Interviewee 8, Durban, 10 January 2005; Interviewee 5, Johannesburg, 8 September 2004; Van Wyk, interview. See also Bozzoli (2004: 330).
28. Koopman, email.

in possession of banned literature.[29] They were aware of the illegal entry of banned publications to the country and apart from questioning and searching air and road travellers, spot checks were eventually ordered on imported cargo in a bid to uncover banned literature (Merrett 1994: 81). Customs officials had played an important role in seizing undesirable publications, even before censorship was officially institutionalised. By 1963, the year the first official censorship legislation was enacted, some 9 000 publications had been prohibited (Hachten and Giffard 1984: 159). In 1979, of the 2 138 publications submitted for scrutiny to the Publications Directorate, 822 – or just below 40 per cent – were submitted by customs officials (164).

After becoming available and circulated through alternative channels, these banned books were exchanged among readers and stored in various, and at times unconventional, ways. In a context of censorship and publication control, prohibited books were cautiously dealt with. In private households, banned books were not always stored in a typical fashion, for fear of attracting undue attention from visitors. Van Wyk says, '[We] never used to store [banned] books, but hide them away.'[30] Another reader reveals how banned books were mixed with church books and other good books, reducing the chances of them being singled out.[31] Banned books could also be hidden in yards and ceilings or even burned once read, as Hilda Bernstein recalls (Merrett 1994: 75). Another hiding place cited was a box hidden in a dog's kennel.[32]

Van Wyk recounts how he managed his personal collection of banned books: 'When I started to buy banned literature myself, I kept it in secret places away from other books, so that people could not see – because you never knew who would come to your house.' During the apartheid era, police raids on private households were likely, especially in the case of

---

29. Merrett, interview.
30. Van Wyk, interview.
31. Interviewee 1.
32. Interviewee 1.

known activists. At times, when such a raid was anticipated, books were temporarily stored at the home of a trusted neighbour who was willing to take the risk out of solidarity.[33]

Entire collections of books were sometimes hidden in order to preserve archival material. Jewel Koopman, librarian and archivist at the Alan Paton Centre in Pietermaritzburg, points out that the bulk of the South African Liberal Party's written documentation had to be hidden when the organisation's existence was threatened by the apartheid government because of its multiracial membership, for allegedly furthering the aims of communism, and because several members were banned:

> When the Liberal Party was forced to disband in 1968, the Liberal Party archives were hidden away by the members, as otherwise they would have been confiscated by the Security Branch, who wanted information, especially the membership list. The archives were hidden away in suitcases, boxes, trunks in people's attics, basements and garages until 1989, when the Alan Paton Centre opened. It was then thought to be safe to remove them from their hiding places and bring them to the Alan Paton Centre, where they were re-assembled as an archival collection. Some of the papers were stored here on the campus of the then University of Natal, in trunks, in the basement of the Old Main Building. Only a few people knew they were there.[34]

The climate of secrecy and the high risk involved in safeguarding banned books, archives, artefacts and ideas, speak to the importance of preserving cultural and institutional memory, at a time when mainstream book professionals curbed freedom of speech, of information and publishing, disrupting the literary industry and reading culture. Alternative initiatives, organisations and ordinary readers sourced and stored banned

---

33. Van Wyk, interview.
34. Koopman, email.

publications in ways that evaded the authorities' undesirable publications campaign. However, as is revealed in several accounts, these books were not only stored and kept idle in the hope of being read once censorship was abolished, but were actively exchanged and passed from one reader to another.

The hand-to-hand network of distribution of undesirable and banned publications was in itself a mode of sourcing banned texts for ordinary readers who had no direct contact with alternative publishers, or access to independent bookshops and banned sections of libraries. Banned publications were regularly shared among readers, both in order to be read by the greatest number of readers possible to spread an idea and a message and to keep the books moving, decreasing the chance of readers being found in possession of banned books. The frequent, hand-to-hand exchange of books implies a fragmented mode of reading, where a book could be passed on to the next reader regardless of whether it was entirely read, only to be encountered again when a copy happened to come to a reader again.[35] Van Wyk recalls how readers casually swapped books, considerably widening and diversifying the readership:

> We always passed books on to each other [. . .] Often people gave me books, sometimes banned books, and [they would] say, 'Read it and pass it on.' [. . .] So it was happening. I remember some friends of mine from Soweto passed books to me and took things off my shelves.[36]

This kind of circulation reveals a situation where ownership of a book was sometimes lost along the way. One copy of a book was read by many successive readers through exchange, lending, and borrowing – effectively creating an informal distribution network, a kind of informal library – and creating a group of readers holding similar values and reading strategies

---

35. Interviewee 2, Johannesburg, 20 October 2004.
36. Van Wyk, interview.

who cyclically took ownership of the book. The expected readership of a particular book might be restricted as a result of factors such as cost and availability, and in this case censorship, but the wider distribution of the few copies in circulation extended the readership beyond expectations (Johns 2002: 59).

A copy of a book could also be shared among several readers simultaneously, through the practice of photocopying. Photocopying excerpts or entire texts from a banned publication was common practice and did not hold moral judgement. Brutus recalls that it sometimes happened for very practical reasons, such as monetary constraints, and was also dictated by the repressive intellectual climate inflicted by censorship: 'Because we did not have [. . .] the money to buy books, or even physical access to books. So we had to source clandestinely. We copied in bulk, for an organisation's discussion or an activity, a teachers' organisation for instance [. . .] and we would then distribute.'[37]

For readers and professionals operating in the alternative space, the materiality of books as a commercial commodity was not nearly as important as getting texts read and spreading ideas and messages. For instance, Interviewee 2 recalls having seen the actual book of Biko's *I Write What I Like* only in the 1990s, even though he/she had read a copy in the 1980s, at the height of political censorship and repression. Books were often acquired and read in photocopied bits and pieces.

Photocopying not only changed the physical aspect of texts, but also initiated a different set of relations between readers and texts. Readers took ownership of the text through this unauthorised duplication, creating their own personal version. These photocopies were also distributed among other readers and photocopied further. Through photocopies, more copies of a book, otherwise considered scarce, widened its distribution. Book piracy can be and often is considered as a means of survival in a political environment prone to banning, as a way to circumvent censors (Johns

---

37. Brutus, interview, 25 May 2007.

2002: 61). This was the case in the context of South African censorship, as banned books and texts were photocopied as a way to bypass censorship and to compensate for the unavailability and inaccessibility of books under the strict publication control measures.

SASO activist Papi Mokoena recalls how books were thus disseminated, even in the most unexpected places, through a series of everyday exchanges in the informal literary space. Mokoena speaks of a 'mobile library' in the Orange Free State (now Free State) through which books would constantly circulate through a network of readers: 'We even had a mobile library – books which moved from hand to hand amongst selected people' (in Merrett 1994: 96). The concept of mobility implies an elusive circle of readers connected through ideology and interests, rather than physical space. Readers had the power to choose the next reader, creating a readership where grassroots readers, for example, read similar texts to academic readers. Brutus points out that sometimes books were shared randomly: 'There could be a single copy brought into the country by someone and then circulated by hand, but even then you were not targeting who you are going to circulate to – you would circulate it to whoever was nearby, your friends or colleagues.'[38] Van Wyk similarly speaks of how books would be distributed from house to house in Riverlea, a township in Johannesburg, in a climate of complicity, camaraderie and trust.[39]

While some readers were actively on the lookout for banned books or exchanged copies of banned literature by fellow readers, others came across banned literature through mere chance. Brutus comments on how he first got hold of La Guma's novels in the early days of the apartheid regime through word of mouth:

> So here I am in a law class at Wits, someone passes the book to me, and I'm quite surprised, at that time I don't know the existence of Alex La Guma and of Mbari Press. There was really a climate

---

38. Brutus, interview, 25 May 2007.
39. Van Wyk, interview.

of isolation and ignorance, of course deliberately created by the government to control importation of books. They were not on display anywhere [. . .] It was by accident, or opportunity, that I got the La Guma books, discovering there is an author called Alex La Guma and that he's published outside of the country.[40]

As discussed previously, Ndebele also coincidentally came across banned books hidden in boxes in his father's garage. As with Ndebele and Brutus, a fair number of readers came across banned books unexpectedly. The status of a book as banned often created a sense of urgency that influenced the reading process, whether the book was procured accidentally or on purpose. Ndebele (2007: 9-10) recalls the thrill and feeling of privilege he felt when reading banned books from his newly found box:

> [I] began to read *Down Second Avenue*. Two days later, I read *Blame Me on History*. I still remember clearly the thrill of reading these two books and beginning to discuss them with myself. How different they were from each other, conveying different aspects of the same overriding political and social reality! [. . .] I had heard about these books and knew it was dangerous to possess them, but despite that I felt privileged that they were right there in my home and that I was going to read them in secret.

Book historian Roger Chartier (1989: 167) emphasises that the classification and designation bestowed on texts often creates expectations and anticipations of meaning in readers. South African writer Christopher Hope notes that a sense of expectation influenced both censors and ordinary readers: 'We knew that anything that looked even remotely interesting, or lively, or original was likely to be either unobtainable, illegal, or would shortly be banned' (in Merrett 1994: 64). An unintended

---

40. Brutus, interview, 25 May 2007.

consequence of banning was that it marketed those banned books: 'There were books for which there were expectations; people often said that if the government had not banned some books, we would have never read them. It would never have sold a hundred thousand copies.'[41] This is summed up by J.M. Coetzee (1996: 43), who notes that 'the book that is suppressed gets more attention as a ghost than it would have had alive; the writer who is gagged today is famous tomorrow for having been gagged'.

Leaders or opinion-makers also informally publicised books by recommending or praising a book, encouraging other readers to read it. The implicit authority of an opinion-maker played a major role in making the reputation of a book. Interviewee 1 recalls how reading choices were often influenced by other readers, as banned books were discussed, praised, recommended and shared. Interviewee 2 recalls that 'the most informed amongst us would suggest some books raising issues related to the struggle, so if one of us happened to come across the book we would get it and pass it on'. Biko, for instance, played an opinion-maker's role to a wider audience by virtue of his compelling leadership, through his public speeches and essays. Biko's charisma was renowned beyond academic circles and university precincts and some black consciousness (BC) literature rapidly reached a wider and more popular audience, either in written or oral form. The potential gap between intellectual, academic and ordinary reader could thus somehow be bridged.

Belinda Bozzoli (2004: 335) observes that readers with direct access to banned reading material could make it accessible to a wider readership, thus playing an active role in the dissemination of banned books: 'While the grassroots comrades straddled the legal and illegal worlds and had some access to ideas from outside generated by their own resourcefulness, they largely depended for access to illegitimate ideas upon a stratum of more highly educated readers formed during the 1980s, who had better access to resources.' Readers in positions of power played an important

---

41. Van Wyk, interview.

role in deciding which so-called illegal ideas and books would be accessible to ordinary readers and thus performed functions not dissimilar to the censors, albeit informed by a different ideology.

While word of mouth played a major role in the distribution of books, oral dissemination also played a central role in the propagation of messages and ideas carried by books and the printed word. Some publications were spread orally, as once read they were discussed and debated, entering oral networks and being given a new form that would reach a new readership/audience. Ideas extrapolated from books entered the oral circuit to join a greater and more inclusive pool of readers at various literacy levels. Those readers in positions of authority, because of their use of literacy, created audiences that would coexist with readers who read the book, once again blurring the traditional dichotomies of oral versus written, elite versus ordinary readers, literate versus semi-literate, and creating new spaces where these seemingly opposed poles would converge and create new forms of reading and literacy. The combination of oral and written cultures constituted an alternative way of reading: 'oral reading' (Lyons and Taksa 1992: 35). These social networks further expanded the readership. As Martyn Lyons and Lucy Taksa point out: 'Book historians should not [. . .] measure a book's popularity solely by its circulation figures. Oral testimony may suggest the true extent of distribution and open a way into the "unknown public" ' (190).

The example of *Work in Progress* also illustrates this aspect of the circulation of banned texts in South Africa. Some essays and articles discussing the latest global and local theories and intellectual trends were made available in South Africa through the journal. As recalled by co-founder and editor Glenn Moss in a special edition marking the tenth anniversary of the magazine, *Work in Progress* often ran into trouble with the censorship board:

> It did not take long to come to the attention of the state's censorship machinery. When issue number 5 was banned under the Publications Act, this began a series of bannings that continued

almost unabated for the next 20 editions and four years. This culminated in 1982, when a censorship committee prohibited all future editions of *Work in Progress* (Moss 1987: 45).

Work in Progress was initially distributed to a limited list of trusted readers in what was then the Transvaal in an artisan-like fashion, although as Maré explains, the readership soon expanded nationally via an informal and sometimes underground network of distributors.[42] Readers at all literacy levels directly contributed to circulation, ensuring that the publication reached other readers.

Reading as translating

Readers of banned books were directly or indirectly, and intentionally or not, involved in an alternative literary scene, where they engaged with oppositional literature production and consumption. Through the peculiar ways in which books were recommended and passed on from one reader to another in the alternative circuit, these readers formed networks. The texts were either read individually or collectively. However, as discussed in this section, individual silent reading often led to collective reading and vice versa, as one reading modality does not necessarily exclude the other and can be simultaneously or consecutively performed by readers.

Individual reading creates the space for an intimate relation between readers and texts and can occur in various places at different times, as reading is incorporated into everyday life activities. For Escarpit (1971: 91), silent reading is both social and asocial: 'It temporarily suppresses the individual's relations with his universe to construct new ones with the universe of the work. Consequently, the motivation to read is almost always dissatisfaction, a lack of harmony between the reader and his milieu.' In apartheid South Africa, the ambient socio-political milieu motivated readers' participation in the alternative political or literary

---

42. Maré, interview.

scenes. The act of reading banned or oppositional literature served to create a new space, or milieu, where readers could interact. Through their individual choices of reading material, social usages and interpretations of what they read, readers collectively affirmed their political opposition to the dominant order, although admittedly this opposition was plural and took on different shapes.

When reading a text, the reader enters into a direct and intimate relation with the discourse it articulates and in this light 'reading is felt to be directly connected to the sovereign power of public opinion' (Warner 2002b: 83). In the case of the banned material read under censorship, the ideological aspect of reading could be understood in relation to mainstream public opinion, which is challenged by the alternative discourse. Interviewee 1 recalls reading *I Write What I Like* after a friend returned from overseas with a copy, photocopying each chapter and reflecting and connecting this particular reading to other readings and to the current situation in South Africa. Readings seemingly consolidated political ideology, while providing a framework against which everyday events could be understood and analysed.

Reading can also be seen as an act of consumption, in alignment with Michel de Certeau's statement: 'Reading is only one aspect of consumption, but a fundamental one' (1984: 168). However, in the context of banned reading material circulating in South Africa, this cannot be conceptualised as commercial consumption, as books were exchanged in a way that circumvented the actual commerciality of books, as pirated photocopies or in oral forms, for instance. Reading banned literature could be perceived as having political and social significance and in this sense literary consumption can be, in the words of Hugh Mackay (1997: 4), 'the articulation of a sense of identity', devoid of commercial objectives.

Silent reading occurred in private households, libraries and other public spaces. In the case of libraries, subversive books could be read concealed in study materials, going unnoticed. Interviewee 1 recounts how he/she would go to the library and choose a seat not too close to the librarian's counter, where he/she would 'pretend to study textbooks, but in fact I was reading banned books', a memory also shared by Interviewee 13.[43] In private households, reading a banned book was sometimes a discreet activity. Banned books could, for instance, be read when everybody in the household was asleep, then hidden away and picked up again when an opportune moment presented itself. Van Wyk recalls the sense of adventure and mischief he felt when reading a book by a banned author: 'I used to read it [*Down Second Avenue*] in my room and hide it under the mattress or in a cupboard somewhere away from other books, even though I was not somebody that police would focus their energies on then.'[44] Individual reading could also occur in public settings, such as buses, train stations or parks. When reading a banned book in public, readers would sometimes deliberately alter the book's physical appearance to render it unidentifiable to passers-by, covering the book in an attempt to dissimulate it, or reading from photocopies.[45]

Readers active in the alternative circuit would often meet to discuss their readings and in the process learn new ideas and recommended reading material, activating meanings and processing subversive ideas, theories and ideologies against their reality. These groups were called different things – 'study groups',[46] 'discussion groups' (Dick 2007b),[47] 'working groups' (Wilson 1991) and 'debating societies' (Newell 2002b). Regardless of the chosen appellation, these groups used culture and literature as a starting point for political discussion and played a role in both alternative politics and alternative literature.

Through these groups, readers created spaces where opinions could be articulated and contested, engaging with texts on various levels. As Bozzoli (2004: 329) points out, such spaces were created as a result of the isolation imposed by apartheid and on black urban township residents

---

43. Interviewee 13, Johannesburg, 10 September 2004.
44. Van Wyk, interview.
45. Maré, interview.
46. Interviewee 2; Interviewee 14, Durban, 27 May 2007; Brutus, interview, 25 May 2007.
47. Interviewee 1; Brutus, interview, 25 May 2007.

in particular. She notes that the climate of isolation characteristic of the apartheid era and censorship allowed these secretive subcultural spaces to protect and nurture the inflow of illegal ideas, contributing to the development of a locally brewed consciousness, political culture and spirit of protest. Alluding to the township of Alexandra in Johannesburg, and probably many other townships, Bozzoli further proposes:

> The illicit ideas flowing into the country and the township were able to take hold on the society within mainly through the actions, ideological creativity, legitimacy and particular characteristics of the internal radical intelligentsia. Radical thinkers of varying degrees of sophistication existed within a variety of strata of township society – ranging from the semi-literate leaders of the comrades, through much more educated adult thinkers, to the key nationalist intellectuals of the time (2004: 332).

Bozzoli's observations offer a glimpse into the range of individuals involved in resistance politics, some of whom were alternative, oppositional readers. Furthermore, she discusses how readers engaged with illegal texts and ideas, and how these in turn served as catalysts for local activism. Through her concept of 'translation' of the illicit into the legal performed by thinkers and intellectuals – in other words, by the more literate readers – banned literature was processed and adapted to suit the general context of the readers' immediate environment and their own individual circumstances:

> The key function performed by these intellectuals was that of 'translation' – between the proscribed and the legal, the ANC ideology and the consciousness of the ordinary people, and the radicalism of the grassroots and the relative conservatism of the adults. It is this process of translation that allows forbidden ideas to become attached to local consciousness (Bozzoli 2004: 332).

This analysis suggests ways in which a heterogeneous group of readers, albeit rallied around a single community of interest, interacted with texts to various degrees and adapted their readings to suit their levels of literacy, their immediate needs and their specific circumstances. Bozzoli, however, warns against an overgeneralisation of the extent and scope of these ideas, as censorship prevented large-scale dissemination: 'A myriad of "dangerous" ideas flowed into South Africa during this period. This gave them an air of romance and a certain power among black township dwellers. But their very illicitness also weakened the capacity of such ideas to operate as mobilising devices on a broad scale' (2004: 349).

Bozzoli further explains the translation concept by alluding to the ways in which African-American literature influenced BC intellectuals in developing a uniquely South African ideology, propagated through literature and speeches. While inspired by highly intellectual concepts, the Black Consciousness Movement (BCM) strived to reach a grassroots audience, to inspire the 'reawakening of black people in South Africa' (Motlhabi 1984: 111). In its mission to integrate the voices of those marginalised and silenced by the apartheid system, from intellectuals to grassroots readers, the literary trend inspired by BC challenged perceptions of poetry and literature as elitist and exclusively for highly literate readers, while recognising the evocative power and reach of oral literature (Mzamane 1991: 189). Jeremy Cronin points out that poetry and mass struggle were thus closely linked, with oral poetry being included in students and workers' demonstrations (in Mzamane 1991: 189).

By reaching the margins of literary and cultural spheres, the gaps between literate and semi-literate readers, and written and oral literature, were somehow bridged. As Mbulelo Mzamane (1991: 191) points out, from the mid-1970s onwards it became common to witness poetry being recited or chanted at funerals, trade union rallies and political meetings: 'Black Consciousness saw the folly of ignoring the resources of orature in raising consciousness, transmitting values and reintegrating the African majority with their culture and history.' Bozzoli (2004: 334) remembers how an Africanist poem was read at a meeting of 300 youth activists in St Michael's church hall in Alexandra in March 1986.

The links between BC and literature were strong (Chapman 2007). Foreign literature and political philosophy not only inspired BC ideology, but BC ideology also served as a driving force for the development of new poetry in urban South Africa in the 1970s. Michael Chapman (2007: 11), among others, considers this new poetry a leading socio-literary phenomenon of the 1970s in South Africa. According to Chapman, this poetry, which came to embody the literary translation of a new form of political resistance, over time, became known as 'post-Sharpeville poetry', 'township poetry', 'New Black Poetry of the 1970s', 'participatory poetry', 'people's poetry' or 'Soweto poetry'. It embraced new literary and aesthetic conventions, adopted 'a stark English idiom' and 'ghetto-derived imagery' and embodied a 'communal ethic' and a 'black nationalist ideal' (11–16). Chapman further explains this poetry's stylistic characteristics and its impact on readers as a mobilising factor with regard to BC philosophy: 'This is a mobilising rhetoric utilizing epic forms [. . .] and traditional African oral techniques of repetition, parallelism and ideophones. By these means the poet seeks to impart to a black communal audience, often in a context of performance, a message of consciousness-raising and race pride' (12). Nadine Gordimer (1973: 52) discusses how this 'New Black Poetry' came into being as a shift from prose, which had been vulnerable to censorship: 'Out of this paralytic silence, suspended between fear of expression and the need to give expression to an ever greater pressure of grim experience, has come the black writer's subconscious search for a form less vulnerable than those that led a previous generation into bannings and exile.' For Gordimer, the new generation of writers' choice of poetry as the privileged mode of expression in the 1970s was instinctive and showed a need to express 'feelings in a way that may hope to get a hearing' (53). These poets wrote to be read and readers could identify with and link their reading with 'the individual struggle for physical and spiritual survival under oppression' (54).

The constant shift between a literary and a socio-political focus was common to most readers' groups and was often unplanned and spontaneous. Readers – and in some cases audiences – used literature as a channel for political activism and vice versa, and literature was discussed and dissected through socio-politicised lenses. Not all books discussed in reading groups were banned, but the ideas they conveyed and the discussions they elicited were judged as subversive by the authorities.

Dick (2007b: 17) notes this interaction between politics and literature, citing among others, the radical group called the Fifteen Group, which convened in libraries for political debates and discussions. He also refers to resource centres that provided black townships with library services, complementing poorly stocked public libraries or replacing destroyed ones, as incubators of political resistance through the use of illegal ideas and banned material. While these resource centres served as documentary centres that contributed to the development of the political consciousness of activists, 'some activist groups also used municipal libraries in townships to plan protests, debate political strategy and exchange banned material' (20).

Imported books and ideas were localised, as readers used local reading aesthetics to adapt foreign texts to their reality. Practices of reading that developed with regard to banned literature were characterised by transnationalism and hybridity in terms of interpretive strategies and uses of texts. This is reminiscent of Bozzoli's concept of translation referred to above, which emphasises the activeness of readers in creating meanings from texts and using them to consolidate a form of political resistance. As Bozzoli (2004: 349) notes:

> The rebellion could only work because of a developing alliance between these ideas and the local cultural and ideological networks of rebelliousness within the country and the township and because radical ideas did not 'flow' in a disembodied form – they were carried, sent, received, or blocked in ways that varied across time and place. Many of them underwent a process of conversion from being totally proscribed to possessing some legal currency.

Subversive literature and banned ideas often led to larger debates focusing on the South African situation. For instance, Brutus recalled a community hall, which also served as a cultural centre in Port Elizabeth, where he would co-ordinate cultural evenings showcasing various events that invariably integrated literary and political discussions:

> [The owner] wanted me to organise a cultural club to make use of the hall. So I accepted the idea and talked to the others to discuss the opportunity and how we'd do it. I was able to bring someone from the ANC as a resident talker, and then I'd bring someone to give a talk on jazz, someone on political consciousness, etc. In one of these jazz talks we talked about New Orleans, where they were not allowed to play drums, except once a week because the drum was banned [. . .] My audience was white and black – anybody interested in cultural events.[48]

Brutus also remembers 'discussion groups' in the Eastern Cape in the 1950s, around Port Elizabeth and East London, where activist writers and teachers would meet and discuss foreign texts in relation to South African politics. He adds:

> We had a regular study group, which met maybe once a month and consisted mainly of activists and possibly their wives [. . .] The stuff we read was not so much standard classical political texts – I think one of the books we discussed the most during our surveillance, and we were very careful, very tense and had a lot of debates about it, was a contemporary novel, whether it was William Green or even something very light like Margaret Mitchell's *Gone with the Wind*, which discussed the South in the United States, and slavery and so on.[49]

---

48. Brutus, interview, 25 May 2007.
49. Brutus, interview, 25 May 2007.

Brutus was banned in the 1960s because of his political activism under the Suppression of Communism Act and was therefore unable to participate in some of these gatherings. He explains: 'Unable to attend these meetings I enquired what they had discussed: a paper circulating discussed the topic of Négritude and the ideas of Césaire, Senghor and others. I realised they were using the covert discussion of literary theory as a way to discuss political ideas and actions.'[50]

Van Wyk also recalls public reading events in the 1970s, against the backdrop of independent publisher Ravan Press's activities:

> We never launched books in a formal way, like a cheese and wine affair. There was that, of course, but there were also readings [. . .] I remember when Jeremy Cronin came out of prison he wrote a collection of poems called *Inside*, which was about his life in prison. We launched his book at Wits University [. . .] There were lots of poets in the audience and just people who liked literature. Jeremy spoke about the prison's conditions, about the ANC and read his poetry. Later, Njabulo Ndebele released *Fools and Other Stories*. We organised a gathering in Soweto and we launched the book there. So there were these kinds of launches.[51]

The cultural, social and political background of readers influenced the ways in which they perceived, read, understood and interpreted books and texts. Interviewee 1 recalled how students would gather in college residences where alternative literature would be discussed, linking messages to the South African political situation. Interviewee 2 remembered: 'We used to organise political meetings, not literary clubs, but banned books were almost always discussed there.' Maré also recollected such reading groups at the University of the Witwatersrand, where political issues were invariably raised and linked to the books under discussion.[52]

---

50. Brutus, email.
51. Van Wyk, interview.
52. Maré, interview.

Mamphela Ramphele (1995: 61) remembers similar discussion groups, where readings were directly linked to BC activism on campus: 'We organised many discussion sessions on campus, canvassed for active membership, and got involved in work camps as part of our commitment to active engagement in the problems which plagued oppressed communities.' She also recalls that discussion groups often gathered informally in university residences and other venues on campus, highlighting the fusion of everyday concerns with literary and political preoccupations:

> We used to have parties on weekends at which we drank beer and sat around in the smoke-filled room of one of the members of the group, talking politics, listening to Malcom X's speeches on tape, as well as those of Martin Luther King, discussing banned books which were secretly circulated amongst friends, sharing jokes, and also singing and dancing (Ramphele 1995: 58).

The manipulation of ideas and selective reading were also observable reading strategies and useful tools for opinion-makers, as pointed out by Daniel R. Magaziner (2010: 49):

> Readers manipulated ideas to their own ends – not the other way around. 'I always go to find something from a book,' Biko said. Another activist confirmed this, noting that students 'read selectively, looking for particular quotes, ideas rather than entire philosophies'. Ideas were inanimate until an agent with a particular experience and perspective sought them out and deployed them.

In the late 1970s and 1980s, Braamfontein, in downtown Johannesburg, was considered as one of the hubs of poetry and cultural life, where literature and politics intermingled on a daily basis.[53] These gatherings

---

53. Van Wyk, interview.

were usually openly called 'poetry readings' and the poetry generally had political and social overtones. As Van Wyk recalls, police informants randomly attended these literary events, under cover in the audience:

> Sometimes we did [hide the nature of these gatherings], but mostly we'd say it's a poetry reading. There is nothing wrong with having poetry readings. But the cops knew. In fact, sometimes there were so many of these events that happened all over the place that cops did not bother to attend all of them.[54]

Public readings blending literature with everyday concerns and politics took place in private homes and in public spaces, such as community halls, social clubs, churches, libraries and on university campuses. Writers, poets and readers attended and banned authors were sometimes quietly sitting in the audience, clandestinely defying their bans. Van Wyk speaks of such a literary event at the United States Consulate, where Don Mattera, despite his banning order, sat in the audience.[55]

Quotations from and references to readings occurred at these literary meetings. Quoted passages provided legitimacy and authority to discussions and debates, adding weight to a speaker's arguments and often extending the scope of debate beyond the actual text, allowing the literary to enter the cultural and political area. For instance, while a political prisoner on Robben Island, Ahmed Kathrada was made librarian in the 'Segregation Section', where senior political prisoners were detained. Dick (2007a: 31-2) notes that Kathrada used his position 'to communicate information and have discussions with General Section political prisoners when he delivered, collected and took stock of library books'. Dick adds that reading aloud and quoting from the Bible, for instance, was not uncommon during arrest and detention of political prisoners (29). Biko, who worked at university and community levels, borrowed extensively

---

54. Van Wyk, interview.
55. Van Wyk, interview.

from Césaire and Fanon and used quotations in his speeches and public addresses (Ramphele 1995: 55). Through oral translation or written literature, books transcended their immediate literary imperatives as physical, material commodities. Messages and ideas were extracted, quoted, paraphrased, actualised, translated, shared, discussed and syncretised to suit readers' everyday lives. Reading went beyond mere entertainment and education values were conferred on literature, resulting in a utilitarian and practical dimension to literacy.

Readers creating an alternative social order

The relations between readers and texts are complex and mutual. Darnton (2002: 21) frames the parameters informing the history of reading as follows: '[They] will have to take account of the ways in which texts constrain readers as well as the ways that readers take liberties with texts.' In the South African context, readers were constrained not only by texts, through issues related to relevance, immediacy and language, but also by extra-textual constraints, such as literacy levels, access and availability of texts. Nonetheless, they 'took liberties with texts' and linked the issues they raised with the South African reality, popularising and translating them into an oral form and making them more accessible. In this context, reading could be described as a holistic experience, 'an experience which involves the entire human being, both his individual and collective aspects' (Escarpit 1971: 87). Stephanie Newell (2002a: 6) echoes this when observing:

> The sense of public and private amongst African readers was not caught in the net of an 'either-or' dichotomy. Rather the public and private were combined in a 'both-and' situation, where readers interpreted texts and generated meanings which related both to their own personal lives and also to society at large.

Escarpit's holistic view suggests that public readings could be considered a means of publication and distribution, promoting a text's ideas and discourse to a new pool of readers (1971: 48). Public readings reached new readerships that could be understood as an alternative 'counterpublic', to borrow Warner's terminology (2002a, 2002b). In such sessions, whether or not they were initially intended to be political meetings or literary events, banned books were discussed and oral culture played a major role in the dissemination of these books' messages. Ideas contained in the texts were popularised by some readers and rendered accessible to others at various literacy levels through orality. This weaving between oral and written cultures underlies the variety and particularities of observable reading strategies and the multiplicity of practices adopted by readers' groups. Books informed arguments, debates and discussions, actualising the meanings created out of these texts and generating more literature to be read and discussed in this manner, widening the conversation. Readings were unpacked to resonate with everyday life and this public literary platform allowed readers to interact and discuss books in an otherwise repressive society, where oppositional anti-apartheid views had no space in the official public domain. As Dick Cloete (2000: 47) points out, expressing political positions through poetry was also a way to circumvent censorship: 'Oral poetry was an ideal medium as it could not be banned and required minimum resources.' Peter McDonald (2009: 133) echoes this when noting that unpublished revolutionary poetry, disseminated in manuscript form, from hand to hand and through public performances, was a way of bypassing censorship and the white paternalism prevailing in the literary world.

Politically engaged readers used banned publications – novels, fiction, non-fiction, poetry and newsletters – as an expression of a shared and complex identity, asserting a pleasure of recognition (Fiske 1987). This transferred books from their literary quality and physicality to enter the domain of ideology and practicality, creating a platform for alternative and critical thinking. The ideological and symbolic value of books supplanted their economic value and characteristics as manufactured goods and commodities. The ways in which books were used as focal points in poetry readings and political meetings, among other things, speaks of a translation of culture and ideas into political activism. Banned books were not merely entering the literary circuit as commodities in the traditional sense, but rather existed in a parallel and customised network of production, distribution and consumption. Books were not used as commodities to be displayed; they were used as tools and instruments to convey a message. The physical and material aspect of books in this context was not essential, as the concealment and physical alteration of books by readers reveal. Readers assumed an important role in the life cycle of banned books. Readers 'socialise the work' (Escarpit 1971: 19) and it is through readers that texts have meaning (Chartier 2002b: 134). South African readers of political publications socialised these works by integrating and discussing them in everyday socio-political life.

Alternative literary platforms became spaces for the articulation of personal experiences, relating these to alternative ideas and discourses. In this sense, in response to, or in spite of, the censors' discourse, a 'counter discourse' emerged (Warner 2002b). The relationship between the alternative reading public and the discourses they participated in was reciprocal. In rejecting the ambient and dominant discourse, they also made their own voices heard explicitly and implicitly. This readership was an audience ready to adapt and engage with alternative discourses, producing and participating in an alternative culture. Such internal organisation, characteristic of any kind of public, is described by Warner (2002b: 59) as 'the self-organisation of the public as a body of strangers united through the circulation of their discourse'. However, the unity felt among members of a public is ideological (84).

By socialising literary works, readers enabled books to transcend the theoretical and ideological and to enter the realm of reality. Censorship, as a political tool, aimed to prevent social change by curbing critical thinking and reading. Many banned books circulated in the alternative networks promoted new ideologies and an alternative social order. By slipping in between the cracks in the everyday lives of their readers, banned books, as carriers of ideas and ideologies, became drivers of political and social change. Alternative reading publics could be perceived as social entities, as 'they acquire[d] agency in relation to the state' (Warner 2002a: 89). Through their interpretation and readings of books, alternative readers claimed a space in the public sphere, introducing discourses and ideas that challenged the status quo.

Books had a socio-political purpose, in addition to their literary character. This relates to Interviewee 1's experience – informed senior students would discuss banned texts with first-year students, using books for political activism and mobilisation. Reading banned texts was an integral cultural and political experience, linking readers to their environment and the broader socio-political context. This is the process of 'actualization' referred to by Chartier (2002b), where the meaning is performed by readers to suit their reality. Even if South African readers read foreign literature, like Fanon and Césaire, their comprehension was developed from a South African vantage point and ensuing discussions integrated theories and ideas from abroad into local realities.

Through their use of books, readers became social agents and books conversely became agents of change through the uses readers made of them, creating subcultural spaces. Utilitarian readers, to borrow Escarpit's expression, extract from texts what fits their reality. This practice is reminiscent of De Certeau's notion of 'poaching' (1984). Reading as poaching, underpinned by concepts of readers' agency and resistance, implies that reading is the moment where, as Chartier (2002a) describes it, the world of the reader meets that of the text. In other words, reading happens at the point where the socialised individual meets the socially constructed text, in a particular social context. However, texts are assigned connotations and values. In the case of South Africa, censors were often the 'supreme' readers of texts, or De Certeau's 'manipulative elite reader' (Chartier 2002a) – as, at times, were some alternative readers in positions of leadership as opinion-makers – since they had the final word over the official status of books and further distribution, and thus channelled readers towards a set of predetermined and authorised meanings (Warner 2002b). The 'authorised meaning' was the one against which others would be judged. Readers differing from this authorised reading could be regarded as a 'counterpublic' (Warner 2002a, 2002b). Margreet de Lange (1997: 1) sheds some light on the censors' reading protocols:

> One of the first readers of a literary text produced under censorship restrictions is the censor. The censor is in several respects a special kind of reader. He is a reader with the power to suppress a text and make it unavailable for other readers. He is also a reader who often does not honour the aesthetic conventions for the interpretation of literature. He reads a literary text as a statement about the world, as a message with only referential function, ignoring its poetic function. There is, therefore, a discrepancy between the censorious reader and the literary reader.

Readers are positioned at the centre stage of literary consumption and production, as they constantly negotiate overlaps or interstices between their personal understandings and perceptions of texts, the dominant values bestowed on them and the limitations contained in the texts and those imposed by their milieu. For instance, while deemed undesirable by the authorities, political literature deriving from the BCM articulated the aspirations of many South Africans, such that through its propagation 'cultural liberation [became] inseparable from political liberation' (Chapman 2003: 328).

Through 'oppositional reading' and 'inflected reading' (Fiske 1987: 64), readers challenged and questioned preferred or authorised meanings. In this context, various strands of resistance could manifest through the act of reading, expressed through the choice of reading material and the meanings construed from texts. This constitutes the counterpublic Warner (2002b: 87) describes as one that 'incorporate[s] the personal/impersonal address and expansive estrangement of public speech as the condition of their own common world'.

The act of reading in this context was closely linked to socio-political issues. De Certeau (1984: 172) emphasises this relationship, explaining that 'the creativity of the reader grows as the institution that controlled it declines'. The plurality of possibilities contained in texts opened a space for a plurality of interpretations and uses, reminiscent of De Certeau's definition of reading as poaching: 'By its very nature available to a plural reading, the text becomes a cultural weapon, a private hunting reserve, the pretext for a law that legitimises as "literal" the interpretation given by socially authorised professionals and intellectuals' (157).

Gradually, the exchange of ideas occurring in the literary space links to the broader socio-political space. As Dick (2006: 4) has it: 'The history of reading can tell us about the history of ideas that shaped historical events in South Africa.' The ways in which readers use books speak of the social environment in which both exist. As Ndebele (1991) emphasises, the struggle involved people, not abstraction. By internalising and socialising meanings from texts, readers positioned books as factors for social and political change in South Africa.

Literacy, of which literature and reading are one of many expressions, could be said to have empowered communities, prompting readers to use banned books for political gain. James Paul Gee (1996: 37) suggests that 'literacy only empowers people when it renders them active questioners of the social reality around them'. By debating and actualising texts, readers did precisely that, as texts encouraged critical reflection, creating alternative ideologies and modes of reading. This interaction between texts and readers could be seen as highlighting readers' agency, inventiveness and activeness. Dick (2004b: 43) echoes this value conferred on literacy when stating that 'what people do *with* reading is even more surprising and imaginative than what reading does *to* people'. Reading underpins nation building (Dick 2004b), a fact that both censors and alternative readers were aware of. Alternative reading publics, such as the one for banned literature in apartheid South Africa, 'enter the temporality of politics and adapt themselves to the performatives of rational-critical discourse. For many counterpublics, to do so is to cede the original hope of transforming, not just policy but the space of public life itself' (Warner 2002b: 89).

By simultaneously being at the receiving end and being a driving force behind alternative literature, the counterpublic that was shaped through banned literature participated in creating an alternative canon of 'national literature', understood by Fanon (1994: 47) as literature that does not merely react, criticise or denounce the oppressors, but rather one in which the 'writer progressively takes on the habit of addressing his own people'. Although much has been said about the protest and reactionary character of fiction by black South Africans (see, for example, Nkosi 1983, 2016a, 2016b, 2016c, 2016d; Ndebele 1991; Sachs 1990), some authors, through novels, plays, poetry, essays and other writing, did not give censorious readers precedence over alternative readers and in this sense subverted and defied the power relations existing between readers, authors and censors.

Conclusion

Readers of banned material were involved in socio-political affairs through different spaces and at various levels. This was a relatively small readership that was limited because of censorship, accessibility and literacy rates, among other factors. However, despite their relatively small numbers, these readers were influential. Acquiring and distributing banned material was a political gesture and statement, so far as politically motivated bans are concerned. Some readers actively read banned texts and distributed them and disseminated their ideas to the largest number of readers possible. They used books to raise consciousness and facilitated debate on South African culture and politics.

Following the blanket ban imposed on writers in the 1960s, a resurgence of writing found a home in, and was inspired by, literary magazines and alternative publishers. Van Wyk remembered the 1970s as 'a kind of burgeoning, an avalanche of art'.[56] Literary gatherings often became socio-political events. The 1970s saw a renewal of anti-apartheid strategies, mainly through the activism of students' organisations espousing BC in urban communities (Chapman 2003: 328).

Participating in this effort, trade unionists mobilised resistance at grassroots level (Johns and Davis 1991: 190) and the Congress of South

---

56. Van Wyk, interview.

African Trade Unions and Council of Unions of South Africa were formed in the early to mid-1980s. Through the work of the unions and BC, demonstrations, boycotts, community-based activities and self-help projects were organised for and by the youth, workers and cultural groups, which contributed to the escalation of the crisis faced by the apartheid state (Thompson 2000: 215). These combined efforts culminated in the fall of grand apartheid in the 1990s. This political climate fostered activism on various fronts, with cultural entities and individuals playing a role in the production, elaboration, importation, dissemination and translation of illegal ideas and messages in book and oral forms, and vice versa. Readers were themselves active distributors as they exchanged magazines, papers, books and other publications. They also took on the printing role in photocopying banned books, bridging the gap in accessibility and availability.

Some progressive publishers and booksellers agreed to deal in banned books or those subject to banning, dissociating themselves from the popular adage that the best books are those that sell (Darnton 2002: 13). Through these oppositional publishers and booksellers, some banned books entered and formed readers' networks, facilitating the exchange of these books among readers who asserted their agency in the peculiar life cycle of banned books in apartheid South Africa.

Many activities occurred at the readers' stage, as readers had to be creative and polyvalent in their approach in order to obtain prohibited reading material. Traditional roles were blurred and altered due to external systems impacting on the literary industry. Some readers took on an active role in the communication model followed by banned books and reading material in general, as they contributed to their existence at every stage of Darnton's circuit, and facilitated their passage between the various phases through their assertive strategies. Readers of banned texts appropriated these texts into their daily lives, creating literary platforms where they shared interpretive strategies. Most importantly, books had an ideological rather than economic value, as they were used to further political and social gains. Consumption was conferred with political significance, and through the various uses readers made of their proscribed readings, they posited themselves as active agents in society.

Readers and censors mutually influenced one another and in this way readers played a role in the censorship apparatus itself. The readership for a given publication was a determining factor in censors' decisions, given the correlation between the size of a readership and a publication's chances of being banned. Conversely, censors impacted on readers' choices of reading material and their reading strategies.

Returning to the reading strategies performed by censors and how they connected literature with culture and politics, the next chapter discusses censors' reports and archival documents to examine the reading strategies and interpretive protocols at play, shedding light on the literary discourses and debates that occurred behind closed doors during apartheid censorship.

5 | Imagined Readers in the Censors' Reports

> There can be no true culture when there is no freedom.
> — Dennis Brutus, *Poetry and Protest*

THE NUMEROUS CHANGES to the censorship apparatus were informed by the prevailing socio-political events in South Africa. Readers and censors established a clear link between literature and politics through their readings. Censorship was implemented during the colonial period and gradually incorporated literary considerations in the 1960s, shifting towards a more politicised reading of submitted publications in the 1970s, before adopting what Jaki Seroke called a 'repressive tolerance' in the 1980s (in McDonald 2009: 76). Chief censors personified these changes, including the literary-inclined Gerrit Dekker, politically inclined J.J. Kruger, and Abraham Coetzee and reformist J.C.W. van Rooyen, for example. Through these fluctuations, various notions of literature and readers emerged, notably through the imagined figure of the 'likely reader'. This notion was first introduced in the Publications and Entertainments Act No. 26 of 1963, discarded and replaced with the figure of the 'average man' in the Publications Act No. 42 of 1974 and later reintroduced and refined with the Publications Amendment Act No. 109 of 1978. Various ideas of readers corresponded to this 'likely reader' or 'average man', as is observable in the reports discussed in this chapter.

This chapter examines, from a reader-centric point of view, the application of and connections between the concepts of readers, literature and politics developed by censors through a close reading of selected censors' reports. Three sets of reports focusing on Es'kia Mphahlele's *Down Second Avenue*, Dennis Brutus's poetry and *Staffrider* provide examples and insights into the workings of the censorship system, shedding light on the censors' aesthetics and interpretive protocols, and on their definitions of literariness and literary value. An overview is presented of the various definitions of readers discussed in previous chapters, foregrounding the analysis of the reports in their historical context. The censorship discourse and administration is thus positioned as an unlikely site of literary discourse, where the relationship between arts and politics, and the idea of the book as a weapon of struggle, at times unexpectedly overlap with similar debates in writers', activists' and academic circles. Selected censors' reports are analysed in terms of the ideas of literariness, readership and the role of literature.

The reader in the pre-1963 legislation

During the colonial period and in the context of the Union of South Africa, a host of legislation directly or indirectly affected publications control, including the Obscene Publications Act No. 31 of 1892, the Customs Management Act No. 9 of 1913, the Entertainments Censorship Act No. 28 of 1931 and the Suppression of Communism Act No. 44 of 1950. However, these laws did not propose a reader figure as explicitly as the Publications and Entertainments Act No. 26 of 1963 and subsequent amendments to censorship laws. The Publications and Entertainments Act of 1963 was administered by the Ministry of the Interior and initially targeted imported films and all forms of pictures and graphics, eventually including imported books and periodicals from 1934 onwards (McDonald 2009: 21).

The Customs Management Act of 1913 made provision for undesirable imported publications to be seized, with a particular focus on publications aimed at a general reading public. Over and above their discretionary powers, customs agents had a list of undesirable authors and titles drafted by the Ministry of the Interior. By blocking imported undesirable publications, customs agents, on authority from the Ministry of the Interior, seemingly ensured that the South African public would be sheltered from 'undesirable' ideas.

The Entertainments Censorship Act of 1931 mainly targeted films and pictures. It covered the general public who had access to 'public exhibition and advertisement of cinematographic films and of pictures and of the performance of public entertainments'. A selection of prohibited topics was listed in the Act, based on a list developed in 1916 by T.P. O'Connor for the British Board of Film Censors (McDonald 2009: 21). While the public was alluded to as a general entity, the text also provided for a 'class or classes of persons specified by the board' (Act No. 28 of 1931), who could have conditional access to a given film, picture or other form of public entertainment. The 1931 text specifies in section 5 (1): 'The board shall not approve any film which, in its opinion, depicts any matter that prejudicially affects the safety of the State, or is calculated to disturb peace or good order, or prejudice the general welfare or be offensive to decency.'

The Suppression of Communism Act of 1950 mainly targeted the Communist Party of South Africa and the authorities had the power to ban any person or organisation allegedly promoting the ideology of communism, which was loosely defined and directly linked to the 'safety' of the state, which generally protected white privilege and interests aligned to the National Party (NP). Publications allegedly supporting communism were declared illegal and banned, as were all publications and utterances produced by an alleged communist. The censors' report dated 1970 on Alex La Guma's *The Stone Country* evokes La Guma's status as a listed communist as a factor to justify the ban, as the 'About the Author' text at the back of the book contravened the Suppression of Communism Act:

> The book is about prison life in RSA [Republic of South Africa]. While it presents a brutal picture of prison life, it is not sufficient for banning. However, (i) the author is on the banned list, I think, and (ii) 'About the author' (back inner dust jacket) and the text on

the back cover condemn the book. In addition, the story gives an exaggerated picture of what is going on in the country's prisons. Ban.[1]

A book written by an alleged communist was considered a 'communist publication'. Readers of such publications were seemingly considered potentially dangerous revolutionaries whose readings could trigger more subversion. According to the Act, the doctrine of communism, as propagated by communist publications and individuals,

> aims at bringing about any political, industrial, social or economic changes within the Union by the promotion of disturbance or disorder, by unlawful acts or omissions or by the threat of such acts or omissions or by means which include the promotion of disturbance or disorder, or such acts or omissions or threat (section 1 (1) (ii) (b) of Act No. 44 of 1950).

While the earlier legislation operated on the basis of a generic and sometimes vague idea of a vulnerable South African public, the figure of the reader became more precise with legislation focusing on publications control. From the 1960s onwards, with the consolidation of a formal censorship apparatus, a series of concepts such as 'community standards', 'public morals', 'likely readers' and 'probable readership' emerged, although no official studies surveyed readers until Charles Malan and Martjie Bosman's commissioned *Sensuur, literatuur en die leser*, in 1983. However, the connections between literature and politics, and between reading and political activism, were already foregrounding debates from the 1960s onwards.

---

1. National Archives of South Africa (NASA), Cape Town, IDP, Ref: 210/70. Objectionable literature. *The Stone Country*. Alex La Guma. 1970.

The reader in the Publications and Entertainments Act No. 26 of 1963
The involvement of Afrikaner literary intellectuals and more precisely of the *volks* avant-garde in debates on censorship in South Africa ensured that questions of literary judgement featured in the legislation (McDonald 2009). While prominent intellectuals such as N.P. van Wyk Louw, often considered the 'unofficial conscience of Afrikaner nationalism' (27), opposed the idea of censorship, when it became clear that the system would go ahead, he sought to populate its structures with Afrikaner literary intellectuals from his circles.

Van Wyk Louw was an influential political and cultural nationalist who believed that culture was intrinsically apolitical (McDonald 2009: 29). For Van Wyk Louw, literature constituted the essence of a nation's identity and a manifestation of the national spirit, which belonged to avant-garde writers, not politicians (30). As seen in early debates regarding the idea of a systemised form of publications control in 1947, he opposed censorship, writing in the *volks* avant-garde's mouthpiece *Standpunte*: 'We must learn from history that it is almost always new mass-revolutionary or antiquated and insecure cultures that trust the power of censorship; that stable and powerful cultures do not need it' (in McDonald 2009: 30). Van Wyk Louw was advocating for the development of a strong cultural Afrikaner identity through literature, which would evolve independently from a nationalist political culture, of which politicians would be guardians. He conceptualised his cultural vision in the form of an Afrikaner Republic of Letters, which, as Peter McDonald points out, 'he construed as an autonomous and contrary cultural space in which a new, modern Afrikaans literature and, indeed, Afrikaner identity could flourish' (30). Corinne Sandwith (2014) also discusses the genesis of these public debates occurring in the shadows of literary magazines and oppositional newspapers, among other spaces, and the ways these discourses informed early apartheid cultural and literary debates.

Prior to the enactment of the Publications and Entertainments Act of 1963, the NP government, then led by H.F. Verwoerd, responded to the commissioned Cronjé Report by drafting repressive legislation advocating a centralised pre-publication censorship system that also applied to the press, which was widely opposed. Essentially, the Cronjé Report advocated for 'nationalistic cultural idealism', showed 'hostility to the mass' and promoted the 'idea of literature as the "mirror" of the "community"' (McDonald 2009: 31). It assigned social responsibility to the Afrikaner writer and advocated for 'stricter censorship measures' and 'a positive programme of uplift' (26). Anti-censorship sentiments from within and outside the Afrikaans community were ignored and some procedures were revised into a new Bill and passed in 1963. The Act of 1963 was not as repressive as the draft Bill or even the Cronjé Report, as it favoured post-publication over pre-publication censorship and referred appeals to an independent judiciary not appointed by the censorship board (33). The severe attack by prominent members of the Afrikaner establishment had little impact on the enactment of the Bill, with politicians upholding the view that the censorship legislation would not have an impact on 'serious literature', as this message from Abraham Jonker, published in *Die Burger*, reveals: 'This proposal has nothing to do with serious literature. The Bill is directed against filth, pornography, blasphemy, offensiveness and the distribution of communistic propaganda. Everyone who opposes the regulations is in favour of these wrongs' (in De Lange 1997: 34).

The idea of serious literature punctuated public debate on South African literature until the end of apartheid censorship, being articulated differently – but at times surprisingly similarly – in circles of various political and ideological persuasions. In the early 1960s some Afrikaans writers and PEN SA members had signed a petition against censorship, prompting the inclusion of section 2 (2) in the Act of 1963, pertaining to the appointment of the Publications Control Board, comprising nine members in total and including at least six 'persons having special knowledge of the art, language, literature or the administration of justice' (Act No. 26 of 1963). It is clear that censors were assigned a literary task, or rather that through Van Wyk Louw's persuasion and influence, literary experts were given a censorship task (McDonald 2009: 38). Louw campaigned for Gerrit Dekker, a prominent Afrikaans literary critic, to chair the first Board of Censors, ensuring that neither NP politicians nor Writers' Circle members controlled the censorship apparatus. By having an avant-garde writer at the helm of the censorship board, the question of literature took a central role in the application of censorship, with issues of intentionality, literariness and readership being at the forefront of the censors' discourse (40). Together, Van Wyk Louw and Dekker selected literary experts and academics, adopting a conciliatory approach towards nationalism and the avant-garde as members of the board, rallying three Afrikaans literary professors (T.T. Cloete, A.P. Grové and H. van der Merwe Scholtz), a professor of English (C.J.D. Harvey), a professor of political philosophy and expert on communism (A.H. Murray) and a professor of African languages (T.M.H. Endemann) as members of the board (39).

Censors performed a selective reading of publications submitted and their functions were defined in section 7 (3) of the Act of 1963. These included the examination of all publications submitted, further examining all forms of public entertainment if there were reasons to believe that it may be offensive on religious or moralistic grounds, advising the minister and, quite loosely, 'perform[ing] any other function assigned to it by this Act of any other law'. The readers' report template provides a glimpse of the workings of the system and the reading performed by censors. After 'examining' a publication, censors cited the pages where undesirable passages were identified, after having provided a synopsis of the publication. The list of topics required to be identified in the report included 'passages considered being indecent, obscene, or objectionable' in terms of crime and violence, sexual intercourse and loose morals, blasphemous language, offensive intermingling, subversive propaganda and any 'other objectionable feature' (Act No. 26 of 1963). These templates were available in English and Afrikaans.

Under Dekker's leadership, censors applied their literary expertise, with some reports at times reading more like literary essays than bureaucratic documents. Censors were performing a form of interpretation that could be labelled 'displaced reading' (McDonald 2009: 191). Their goal was to read a publication through the eyes of the readers they imagined for reviewed publications and therefore they could be considered 'intrusive readers' (286), imposing their interpretive protocols between actual readers and the texts. Moreover, as pointed out by McDonald, the concept of the 'likely reader', as introduced in section 6 (a) of the Act of 1963, led to inconsistencies: 'In particular, the references to the "likely reader", which contradicted the absolute criteria of Section 5 (2), introduced a complication in the legislation's construction of the reading public that would be directly addressed only in the early 1980s' (36).

Section 5 (2) of the 1963 Act refers to 'public morals' and 'any sections of the inhabitants of the Republic' as the benchmarks against which undesirability is measured. These references are vague and inclusive, superseding the application of the concept of the 'likely reader', which was left to the discretion of censors. The role of the censor could from then on be described as the 'general arbiter of printed public discourse, responsible for deciding what was or was not "undesirable", and the most powerful if least likely guardian of the literary' (McDonald 2009: 39). Section 6 (2) specifies that these criteria are totally independent from the intention or purpose of 'the person by whom that matter was printed, published, manufactured, made, produced, distributed, displayed, exhibited, sold or offered or kept for sale'. Besides moral subversion, the Act also alludes to political subversion in section 5 (2) (e): 'A publication or object shall be deemed to be undesirable if it or any part of it is prejudicial to the safety of the State, the general welfare or the peace and good order.'

The criterion of undesirability was defined in relation to the so-called average law-abiding resident of the Republic and also sometimes in relation to the reader likely to be exposed to a publication. Section 6 (1) of the 1963 Act, particularly articles (a) and (b), complements section 5 (2) and refines the various factors of undesirability relative to the probable readership and public morals, and emphasises definitions of indecency, obscenity and offensiveness against which the likely reader must be assessed:

> 6 (1) If in any legal proceedings under this Act the question arises whether any matter is indecent or obscene or is offensive or

harmful to public morals, that matter shall be deemed to be –
(a) indecent or obscene if, in the opinion of the court, it has a tendency to *deprave or to corrupt the minds of persons who are likely to be exposed to the effect or influence* thereof; or
(b) offensive to public morals if, in the opinion of the court, it is likely to be *outrageous or disgustful to persons who are likely to read or see it* (emphasis added).

The ideas formulated with regard to readers were highly politicised and tended to typecast them in relation to their reading material and their position in a highly hierarchical and segregated society. For instance, a 'sophisticated' readership, while considered a minority, was imagined to enjoy literature purely for its aesthetic qualities and not likely to perform a politicised reading. Censors cast imagined readers in predetermined reading protocols, including the intellectual reader appreciating literature on an apolitical aesthetic level (the *volks* enlightened reader), the reactionary reader in search of inspiration and motivation to challenge the status quo (the subversive reader) and the easily influenced reader who was part of a mass or popular readership (the vulnerable reader). These and other readers imagined by censors can be further understood through a close reading of selected censors' reports.

Imagined readers in selected censors' reports

A July 1963 report signed by W.A. Joubert strongly recommends the banning of Bloke Modisane's *Blame Me on History*. As noted by Lewis Nkosi (2016b: 52), *Drum* staff member Modisane's seminal autobiography, published in 1963, paints a profile of Sophiatown and 'shows a dedication to a superior form of realism which succeeds partly because the author is alive to the fact that reality itself is elusive to the process of Time as an orderly sequence of events'. The synopsis of the fairly short censors' report highlights some of Modisane's critiques of injustices inherent to the apartheid state. As a reader, Joubert performs a biased reading whereby the meanings attached to the texts are read from the censors' viewpoint and read as a list of undesirable topics for censors:

> Bloke is embittered by the slum houses of the blacks and the discrimination against them because their skins are black. He joins the A.N.C. [African National Congress] whose slogan is: 'Drive the whites into the sea', but strikes & passive resistance have no results [. . .] The Bantu are waiting for a Moses to lead them against the whites. Bloke resents his inferiority & the fact that he cannot be admitted to European theatres. Bloke hates the D.R. Church and their Christianity which says the Angels are white and the Devil is black [. . .] White domination must be destroyed and S.A. must be ruled by a democratic majority. He urges his people to be daring like the Tsotsis.[2]

Advocating a ban, Joubert concludes that Modisane 'rouses the Bantu to fight for their rights and to drive the whites into the sea. It is a most dangerous and objectionable publication and will have a very harmful effect on peace-loving Bantu. I consider it *unsuitable* for circulation.' This conclusion clearly evokes the nature of Modisane's autobiography, establishing a clear link between literature and politics. In light of section 5 (2) (e) of the Act of 1963, which mainly deals with political subversion, this publication would represent, in the eyes of the censors, a threat to the safety of the state, welfare, peace and order or the potentially harmful character of the publication to sections of the inhabitants of the Republic. Seemingly, Joubert conceives the probable readership of Modisane's autobiography as moderate 'peace-loving' black readers, among whom the book's alleged 'propaganda against the government', 'anti-white statements', 'statements against the church', 'violence' and 'rousing native against the whites' passages could spark unrest and revolt.

---

2. NASA, IDP, Ref: 2654/13/32. Objectionable literature. *Blame Me on History*. Bloke Modisane. 1963.

Joubert's report on Modisane's autobiography portrays a black readership that would read it as a call to action, if not one to take up arms. The report further assumes that the 'peace-loving Bantu' does not share the feelings expressed by Modisane. It denies the notion of reading as offering a 'pleasure of recognition' (Darnton 2002) with one's personal circumstances, whereby readers identify with and relate to what they read, finding gratification in seeing their experiences articulated and shared in the public domain through literature. The censor as a reader fails to recognise that the environment in which Modisane lives is well known to the majority of South Africans, who as readers could find relevance and identify with the experiences he relates. He disdainfully dismisses Modisane's account of daily life in a South African township as perhaps not sufficiently literary, but rather bordering on a journalistic style, a sentiment strangely and possibly controversially echoing the debates with regard to arts and politics in various intellectual and literary circles. An example is Nkosi's denunciation of South African literature as

> the journalistic fact parading outrageously as imaginative literature. We find here a type of fiction which exploits the ready-made plots of racial violence, social apartheid, interracial love affairs which are doomed from the beginning, without any attempt to transcend or transmute these given 'social facts' into artistically persuasive works of fiction (Nkosi 2016b: 50–1).

While Nkosi is of course by no means advocating censorship, he pleads for 'greater subtlety, technical originality and sustained vigour' in literature by black South Africans (Nkosi 2016b: 49–50), denouncing what he calls 'naïve realism' (2016c: 233).

Literariness could save a book from banning, in part because of a projected limited readership. C.J.D. Harvey's 1964 report on Breyten Breytenbach's *Die ysterkoei moet sweet* argues in favour of letting the book pass, as Breytenbach was considered a serious author and his poetry collection serious literature. Harvey's main argument is that 'serious poetry in Afrikaans is read by a very small group of highly intelligent and educated people. I do not think that any of these poems have "a tendency to corrupt or deprave the minds" of such people'.[3] The allusion to this assumed small readership denotes an elitist view of literature, where a highly educated and literate readership performs a literary reading on a higher level of understanding. Opposed to this reader is the 'very young or uneducated person into whose hands the book might fall', who 'would understand so little of it that he could not be affected by it'. This implies an uneducated reader, who cannot grasp higher intellectual and literary works such as Breytenbach's and who forms part of the dismissive and vague category of the 'mass readership'. These readers seemingly pose no threat to the censor as far as 'serious Afrikaans poetry' is concerned, as they are believed to be unable to understand poetic language, reading superficially and at face value. However, the Afrikaans section of the report denounces the poem '*Breyten bid vir homself*', which literally translates as 'Breyten prays for himself'. The poem supposedly evokes an undesirable religious connotation, which will most likely offend '*die naïewe leser*', or the naive reader. Public morals and religious convictions are brought into play and assessed via the three types of readers mentioned in the report, namely the 'intelligent educated reader', the 'very young or uneducated reader' and the 'naïve reader'. Highlighting by the same token the desire to protect 'serious' Afrikaans literature, Harvey's report concludes:

> To ban this collection on the grounds of its irreligious or irreverent attitudes would be to make an exception of it (because it is in Afrikaans?), for irreligious and irreverent poems in English and other languages by Blake, A.G. Swinburne, D.H. Lawrence and many other poets, both major and minor, are freely in circulation amongst the very small group who read poetry.[4]

---

3. NASA, IDP, Ref: 841/64. Objectionable literature. *Die ysterkoei moet sweet.* Breyten Breytenbach. 1964.
4. NASA, IDP, Ref: 841/64, Breytenbach, 1964.

The reader of popular literature is also alluded to in some censors' reports, including, among others, in the report on Wilbur Smith's *When the Lion Feeds*. Seemingly, readers' morals had to be preserved and saved from potential contamination by popular fiction, which was believed to promote low morals and values, as the book was unanimously banned, 'although with some hesitation' by the Board of Censors in 1964.[5] The idea of serious literature is observable in this passage of the 1964 report, written by Harvey: 'Though not strictly a work of literature, it is a purely episodic "thriller", it is well enough written to be highly entertaining and would undoubtedly have a big sale amongst the general public. It is a very easy read.' 'Easy reading' and potentially high sales figures suggest the possibility of a wide and popular readership and these factors combined with the book's alleged lack of literary merit played a role in the decision to ban it in terms of section 5 (2) (a) of the Act pertaining to public morals and section 5 (2) (c) relating to blasphemy and offensiveness to religious convictions. According to censors, *When the Lion Feeds*, which turned out to be the first major case of court appeal against a ban under the 1963 Act, contained sufficient scenes of sex and violence to justify a ban, prompting censors to ignore issues of aesthetic unity (McDonald 2009: 51). While the report recognises that this is a difficult case, as Smith's book appeals to a large South African readership, censors are seemingly worried that some passages might deprave the morals of a naive, prudish and conservative readership, as noted in Harvey's report:

> It has no real literary merit but in a clever way supplies popular reading with an open eye to the taste of a wide public and will undoubtedly succeed in appealing to the type of reader it caters for. Unfortunately the author indulges in offensive sex episodes and references to sex which in their drastic description do not convince as functional but in their would-be daringness belong to

---

5. NASA, IDP, Ref: 649/64. Objectionable literature. *When the Lion Feeds*. Wilbur A Smith. 1964.

his apparatus for giving this novel the popular appeal of a 'tough book'.[6]

H. van der Merwe Scholtz's section of the report also focuses on the alleged negligible literary merit of the novel, which would in his opinion attract a specific readership, alluding to literacy levels and age: 'The style in so far as one can use this term is flashy and shallow. All these features ensure that the book will appeal to a broad and differentiated reading public. Also, young people will eagerly consume the book.' Furthermore, he argues that the book has the potential to be a best-seller in South Africa, as the simplistic and popular language and style do not call for a profound reading, in other words for high reading skills. With reference to all these considerations, revolving around literariness, offensiveness, morality and readership, the book was unanimously banned with five votes, as 'several passages considered to be indecent, obscene or objectionable appear in terms of the Act', pertaining to, among other things: 'white slavery and prostitution'; 'passionate love scenes'; 'sexual intercourse'; 'loose morals'; 'description of women's bodies'; 'blasphemous and objectionable language' and 'violence and bloodshed'.[7]

The case of the first publication to be banned under the Act of 1963, Des Troye's *An Act of Immorality*, also illustrates how mass fiction was held in contempt. A policeman submitted *An Act of Immorality* after his wife bought it in a bookstore and the novel was banned on the grounds of offensiveness to public morals (McDonald 2009: 49).[8] Censors sometimes discussed issues of morals in the same breath as the popular genre of a novel and its potential political impact, as illustrated through the censors' argument with regard to the novel's interracial 'promiscuous relations':

---

6. NASA, IDP, Ref: 649/64, Smith, 1964.
7. NASA, IDP, Ref: 649/64, Smith, 1964.
8. Chris van Wyk, interview, Johannesburg, 12 October 2007.

It belonged, as Dekker commented, to the genre of the 'topical novel' (*aktualiteitsroman*) (BCS 1084/64). Though Murray, the primary reader, thought it gave 'an exaggerated view of the "unrest", he felt it satisfied the humanistic criteria because it did not 'go to extremes' or 'propagandize a doctrine'. Despite this, it had to be banned, he argued, because it portrayed 'promiscuous relations between the Coloured man [the central figure, Andrew Dreyer] and the white student [Ruth Talbot]'. Dekker agreed with Murray's literary judgment, but anxious about a possible appeal – he noted that the novel was dedicated to the leading Sestiger Jan Rabie and his wife, Marjorie Wallace – he questioned ('rhetorically', as he puts it) the legal basis for Murray's recommendation because he could not see where the Act specifically outlawed interracial sex. In his reply, Murray insisted that [. . .] the novel was not worth protecting because it was just 'popular stuff' (McDonald 2009: 50-1).

Dekker was concerned by the fact that the book was dedicated to Sestiger Jan Rabie and his wife, and speaks of the censors' desire to maintain close ties with the Afrikaans intelligentsia. This did not prevent the book from being banned. Nevertheless, this publication attracted many readers curious about the novel, rather than attracted by its literary qualities, as recalled by Chris van Wyk:

It was a clumsy plot and a badly thought story and at the end it had all these case studies: an Indian woman and a white man, a black man and a white woman, and how they met, etc. It was lurid and dirty. And people were just whispering: 'A black man with a white woman in a bed together?' People were reading it for that.[9]

---

9. Van Wyk, interview.

Sensationalism played a role in attracting some readers to this novel, as they read to satisfy a sense of curiosity about an otherwise taboo subject, regardless of their literacy and education level, once again blurring the readers' categorisations imagined by censors.

Readers in the post-1974 censors' reports

Amid increasing political resistance and opposition, the Directorate of Publications, now under the chairpersonship of J.J. Kruger, who succeeded Dekker in 1968, aimed to tighten publications control through an increasingly politicised censorship apparatus. The Directorate's members were selected based on their qualifications and knowledge for such a position, eradicating the literary expertise specifically required in order to be appointed to Dekker's board. Section 6 of the 1963 Act – pertaining to the likely reader – did not appear in the Publications Act No. 42 of 1974. Furthermore, the 1974 introductory provision on the recognition of a Christian view of life set the tone for the legal text spread over six chapters: 'In the application of this Act the constant endeavour of the population of the Republic of South Africa to uphold a Christian view of life shall be recognised.' This shift from a literary to a political, moral and religious approach reveals a desire on the part of censors to focus on the religious and political elite, rather than on the literary elite, in their application of censorship (McDonald 2009: 61).

With this new approach in mind, the likely reader no longer featured in the censors' discourse. The notions of 'average man' or 'man of balance' with a 'Christian view of life' took precedence over literary implications linked to the notion of the likely reader and the 'average man' became the benchmark for undesirability. As Louise Silver (1984: 63) observes: 'The test that was applied was whether a work would have the effect of turning the average, decent-minded man, who embodied the median opinion of the law-abiding citizens in South African society, to revolutionary or lawless conduct.' The 'average man' was understood to be a standard, decent, law-abiding, enlightened citizen with Christian principles. The question at stake here is: 'Who this average member of the South African community was for the censor' (De Lange 1997: 18). The answer not only sheds light on the ways in which censors read submitted publications and drafted their reports, but also indirectly paints a picture of a privileged category of readers whose interests took precedence. This would, generally speaking, be a white reader, but more specifically one rallied around the interests of the Afrikaner *volk* spirit, politically aligned to the NP, of Christian faith and supporting the apartheid regime. It was understood to be an ideal reader moulded on the ideal citizen imagined by censors and could thus be labelled the '*volks* reader' who supported the status quo:

> In the eyes of the Afrikaners, the necessity for strict control resided in their perception that South Africa was a state in transition, working towards the completion of apartheid. Their Afrikaner utopia still seemed an attainable goal in the seventies. Literature was therefore called upon to comply in large measure with the vision of Afrikaner utopian society (De Lange 1997: 29).

The report on *Poets to the People: South African Freedom Poems*, edited by Barry Feinberg, dated November 1975, is divided into two sections, 'Working programme' and 'Directions', developed as guidelines for the reviews. These guidelines seemingly assisted censors in performing their increasingly bureaucratic reading, providing more information on how submitted publications should be read, with the objective of deciding 'whether the publications are undesirable or not within the meaning of Section 47 (2) of the said Act'.[10] The section 'Working Procedure' specifies: 'The chairman of the committee shall hand out the publications to the members of the committee (including himself) and assign them to read the publications and to complete the relevant reader's reports on DP 1E.' As the archival documents reveal, completing an accompanying form represented continuity from the paperwork involved under the Act

---

10. NASA, IDP, Ref: P75/11/119. Objectionable literature. *Poets to the People. South African Freedom Poems.* Edited by Barry Feinberg. 1975.

of 1963. The instructions regarding the ways in which censors had to read the submitted publications were relatively vague, as they did not specify whether a publication had to be read in its entirety or could be read partially or even scanned. However, the 'Assignment' section clearly stated the objective of the exercise, to provide a decision on the undesirability of the publication.

Section 47 (2) of the Act of 1974 outlines the factors against which undesirability was evaluated: (a) morality; (b) religious blasphemy or offensiveness; (c) ridicule or contempt; (d) race relations; and (e) safety of the state. The procedures followed in applying the Act represented a shift from the highly literary considerations of the previous censorship dispensation in favour of an increasingly moralistic and political reading. Censors were reading with a bureaucratic state of mind, in search of damning evidence against a publication under review, as the 1975 report on *Poets to the People* reveals. No references are made to the likely reader or even to the idea of a reader, as vague as it may be. Signed by E.G. Malan, the report reads more as an assessment of the political nature of the collection of poems than with any awareness of the fact that it is a collection of poetry and therefore a work of literature. Throughout the report, poets are merely discussed in relation to their affiliation to the South African Communist Party (SACP) or other banned organisations (such as the ANC) and the poems' titles are discussed in terms of their undesirable nature in relation to key words and topics. Malan recommends a ban on the grounds of the collection's prejudice to public morals, race relations and state security, without further mention of whose morals are under threat.[11]

The controversial banning of Etienne Leroux's *Magersfontein, O Magersfontein!* in the late 1970s proved yet another turning point in the censors' discourse, leading to an eventual amendment to the Act of 1974 (De Lange 1997). Leroux's case clearly illustrates how literary discourse was notably absent from the Publications Act of 1974, leading to discontent

---

11. NASA, IDP, Ref: P75/11/119, Feinberg, 1975.

and contention among the Afrikaner literary elite. As Margreet de Lange recalls, a literary committee had initially passed Leroux's novel on literary grounds when the decision was overturned following the resubmission of the book by a conservative vigilance association:

> According to his own account in the newspaper *Hoofstad* of 24 November 1977, the leader of the AMS [Aksie vir Morele Standaarde], Eddie van Zyl, had read *Magersfontein* three times without understanding what the book was about. While reading Van Zyl made a list of all the words and expressions that he considered immoral or blasphemous. The AMS then sent this list to 2,500 Afrikaners, mostly farmers, housewives and church ministers, with the request to write to the Minister of Home Affairs if the recipient found the list to contain offensive material. On 14 September 1977, Minister Connie Mulder asked the Appeal Board to reconsider *Magersfontein* (De Lange 1997: 39).

The Publications Appeal Board overturned the decision and banned *Magersfontein* on moral and blasphemous grounds, as per section 47 (2) (a) and (b) of the Act of 1974. Afrikaner literary circles and media sided with Leroux, who was shocked to see his work 'dissected in public by people without any literary inclination' (in De Lange 1997: 40). The Supreme Court of South Africa, to which publisher Human & Rousseau appealed, found that the undesirability and morality of the novel should have been evaluated against the 'likely reader' and not the 'average reader'. However, it agreed that the novel could be 'offensive to the religious convictions' of the average South African citizen. The ban remained in effect, but this case reintroduced the notions of the 'likely reader' and 'literary merit' to the censors' discourse. Some works of literary merit that would otherwise be undesirable in terms of the Act could be distributed with restrictions in the light of their 'likely readership'. De Lange (1997: 41) observes that this would inevitably privilege white writers.

With the Publications Amendment Act No. 109 of 1978, so-called serious literature was once again safeguarded and a committee of literary experts could be appointed by the Publications Appeal Board to assess the possibility of a book's conditional release on literary grounds (McDonald 2009: 73). The new procedures were tested in a few cases and it took a change of administration for the amendments to be applied more consistently (74). In 1980, Van Rooyen was appointed chair of the Publications Appeal Board and Abraham Coetzee director of publications. Together they initiated reforms in the censorship system that would be effective in the 1980s, which would also be the last decade of apartheid: 'This period was characterized by an awkward dissonance between the internal reforms of the censorship bureaucracy, which echoed P.W. Botha's wider strategies of political co-optation in the 1980s, and the government's aggressive suppression of political protest in more direct means' (77).

Several mitigating factors could overturn a previous ban or support passing a publication. Literary value was a major factor against a ban, as without it a work could be considered mere propaganda targeting a subversive readership (Silver 1984: 95). Similarly, the academic value of a publication would entail a sophisticated and informed likely readership, which would reduce its undesirability (100). Another mitigating factor that contributed to unbanning was the historical period value, whereby 'a work that was found undesirable at the time of its publication may, on resubmission at a later date, be regarded as a "period piece" because the reader has a sense of perspective based upon insight' (102). Seemingly, the closer a reader was to events depicted in a book, the higher the impact of the book. A limited distribution, the satirical nature of a text and the high price of a publication were also mitigating factors, as they would also limit the size of the prospective readership.

Typical of the patronisingly tolerant approach adopted by the censors in the 1980s and labelled 'repressive tolerance', the board recognised a need for 'South Africans [to] know what blacks think and write' and believed that 'blacks' problems should be understood by whites' (Silver 1984: 109-10). This stance was underpinned by the censors' concern that 'tolerance should be displayed towards black writings as blacks do not have representation in Parliament' (112), revealing an 'awkward dissonance' (McDonald 2009: 77). These mitigating factors were weighed against aggravating factors, including the nature of the publication (as, for instance, a pamphlet could attract a wider and more popular readership), its propagandist character, the sympathy displayed for a banned organisation, the cumulative effect and the possible prescription of a work in schools, affecting vulnerable young minds (Silver 1984: 113-19).

The intricacies of these lines of arguments, and the way these factors intersected with the social construct of the likely reader, can be better understood through an examination of their application in the censors' reports. The cases of Mphahlele's *Down Second Avenue*, several of Brutus's poetry collections and Ravan Press's *Staffrider* and Staffrider series are discussed below. These three case studies exemplify the censors' thought processes as applied to major South African literary publications and authors, who are now recognised as forming part of the South African literary canon.

Case study 1: *Down Second Avenue*

The case of Mphahlele's autobiography *Down Second Avenue* is an interesting one that sheds light on the workings of the censorship system in South Africa, as it was scrutinised by the successive censorship boards. *Down Second Avenue*, now considered a classic of South African literature, was initially published in 1959 by Faber in London, two years after Mphahlele left South Africa for self-imposed exile. The same year, it was allowed through customs as an imported book, legally finding its way to a South African readership. Also published in New York by Macmillan, by the Ministry of Education in Ibadan and by the East African Publishing House in Nairobi, Mphahlele's work began to be published in South Africa by independent publishers Ravan Press and Skotaville once he returned to South Africa in 1977 (McDonald 2009: 245).

In 1966, while in voluntary exile, Mphahlele was banned in terms of the Suppression of Communism Act of 1950, meaning that he was listed as a communist and that all his writings were illegal in South Africa. The censors were, however, ambivalent about how to treat Mphahlele's work after 1966: they banned the short story collection *In Corner B and Other Stories* and his essay *The African Image*, but approved his novels *The Wanderers* and *Chirundu*, the poem and short story collection *The Unbroken Song* and *Down Second Avenue* (McDonald 2009: 245). In 1967, South African Police Commissioner P.J.B. van Wyk wrote a letter to Dekker, who was then the chair of the Publications Control Board, requesting that the status of *Down Second Avenue* be reviewed in terms of section 8 (1) (a) of the Act of 1963, which stipulates that the censorship board may examine and determine the undesirability of any publication 'at the request of any person'. In his letter dated 7 July 1967, headed 'Communist or subversive literature', the commissioner's central line of argument was:

> The contents of the book are calculated to arouse a sense of ill feeling between whites and non-whites. The entire book speaks of hate for the whites and nowhere shows that the author is really expressing his feelings so as to study the hate within himself and to acknowledge his own shortcomings. His prejudices are solely due to his own ignorance and ineptitude yet he blames the whites.[12]

Furthermore, the commissioner suggested that the book should be ruled as indecent, obscene and offensive, and be declared illegal. This letter was the starting point of a lengthy four-month debate within Dekker's board, involving censorship board members Cloete, Dekker, Endemann, Grové, Murray and Van der Merwe Scholtz (McDonald 2009: 250). As illustrated in the first censors' report, dated July 1967, the outcome of their first deliberation was in favour of banning with a vote of four against two.[13] While Murray, an expert on communism, and Endemann, an African language specialist, concluded that there was no propaganda, acrimony

---

12. NASA, IDP, Ref: S14/1/4. Objectionable literature. *Down Second Avenue*. Ezekiel Mphahlele. 1967.
13. NASA, IDP, Ref: 522/67. Objectionable literature. *Down Second Avenue*. Ezekiel Mphahlele. 1967.

or communism in the book and that it was objective and contained nothing not already known to South African readers, Grové, who was a literary censor, expressed concern that it presented a negative portrayal of the police and of everything Afrikaans and therefore recommended that the book should be prohibited among, in the words of the report, 'South African natives' (McDonald 2009: 251). Van der Merwe Scholtz, who was in favour of banning, was preoccupied with the likely impact of the book on the average reader: 'Have we not already decided that it is sometimes not wise to make certain truths available to any and everyone? After all, we have kept some books about, for example, sexuality because we want to protect an immature and youthful reading public' (in McDonald 2009: 251).

On 20 September 1967, Murray wrote to Dekker, requesting that *Down Second Avenue* be retained for further discussion before taking a decision. In his letter, Murray discusses the potential reaction of black and white readerships, pointing out that the book would not incite black readers to subversion and would enable white readers to gain insight into the state of mind of the black population, as the report puts it. Murray opens his argument by stating: 'If we ban this work, it will be almost impossible to pass any work by a native that reflects the prevailing and spontaneous attitude of natives in this country.'[14] He adds that none of the inciting remarks contained in the book are more serious than those made in meetings or in the press and that 'no literary approach to a statement of mind pretends to establish the empirical factual conditions'. Alluding to a white readership, Murray continues: 'The more the white population becomes familiar with and gains an insight into this state of mind, which is brought about by certain factors in the present social and economic situation, the more quickly will healthy race relations be created.' He concludes by noting that 'two of the three persons who voted in favour of a ban expressed reservation about their opinion'.

---

14. NASA, IDP, Ref: 522/67, Mphahlele, 1967.

In response to this request, Dekker initiated a second round of deliberations, pointing out that the question remained as to whether the picture depicted by Mphahlele would have 'an inciting effect on the non-white' (in McDonald 2009: 251).[15] Grové's decision remained unchanged, as for him there was no doubt that the book would have an inciting effect on black readers, as his initial report clearly states: 'And then the image of the police that is created, is that not intended to incite our non-Whites?'[16] In a report dated 28 September 1967, Grové reiterates this view: 'It is still obvious to me that the book – despite truths that it may contain – with its one-sidedness and distortion may have an inflammatory effect and thus should be banned in terms of the Act.'[17] However, Endemann points out that since the events depicted in the book dated from before South Africa was a Republic, the effect on the reader would be limited: 'The reader in this country will immediately realise that conditions are described that would have existed here a considerable time ago. I think even the non-Whites would see it in this light.'[18] Endemann further notes that a ban might actually attract more attention to the book than necessary, as it was freely available, having been passed in 1959: 'Will the banning of the book at this stage not draw attention unnecessarily to a book that would otherwise not have had a substantial market here?' Grové had also raised this issue in his second report, pointing out that the publication had perhaps already 'played its trump card'.[19]

In a letter dated 28 September 1967, Dekker acknowledges the 'considerable difficulties' posed by this publication.[20] He supports Murray's concern that 'it is a matter of principle whether we can deprive non-Whites of their right of expression', as it is a 'question of conscience'. Dekker formulates the bottom-line question in terms of the Act of 1963:

---

15. NASA, IDP, Ref: 522/67, Mphahlele, 1967.
16. NASA, IDP, Ref: 522/67, Mphahlele, 1967.
17. NASA, IDP, Ref: 522/67, Mphahlele, 1967.
18. NASA, IDP, Ref: 522/67, Mphahlele, 1967.
19. NASA, IDP, Ref: 522/67, Mphahlele, 1967.
20. NASA, IDP, Ref: 522/67, Mphahlele, 1967.

'Is the possible effect of this book: "harmful to the relations between any sections of the inhabitants of the Republic (Act 26, Section 5 (2) (d)" and "prejudicial to the safety of the State, the general welfare or the peace and good order (5 (2) (e)"?'

By the same token, he acknowledges that some 'atrocities supposedly perpetrated by the Boers on the Bantu' and some 'actions of the police' did occur, but asks whether 'we can allow the police to be systematically placed in such an unfavourable light', raising a problem of policy.[21] In October 1967, Harvey declares feeling 'very strongly about this matter' and being similarly 'strongly opposed to banning the book', giving great weight to Murray and Endemann's 'expert opinion'.[22] The book was eventually passed with five votes against one, Grové's unchanged vote being in favour of a ban (McDonald 2009: 251).

This was, however, not the end of the matter. On 20 November 1967, the deputy secretary of Customs and Excise, who had been informed of the decision on 15 November 1967, hand-delivered a letter to Dekker, pointing out that in terms of the Suppression of Communism Act No. 44 of 1950:

> The author was named as a person whose utterances etc. may not be published in the Republic. In the circumstances the Board may wish to reconsider its decision, but in any case I should be glad to learn the name and address of the person who submitted the book to the Board, so that I may take the necessary action to prevent its distribution.[23]

A series of correspondence ensued between the Publications Control Board, the Department of Customs and Excise, the South African Police

---

21. NASA, IDP, Ref: 522/67, Mphahlele, 1967.
22. NASA, IDP, Ref: 522/67, Mphahlele, 1967.
23. NASA, IDP, Ref: 522/67, Mphahlele, 1967; NASA, IDP, Ref: 523/67. Objectionable literature. *Down Second Avenue*. Ezekiel Mphahlele. 1967, 1968, 1974.

and the Security Police, which sheds light on the relations between various state departments when applying censorship. On 10 January 1968, the Publications Control Board sent a letter to the commissioner of police, referring to the letter from the deputy secretary of Customs and Excise mentioned above, confirming that Mphahlele was a listed communist, but stating:

> Where a publication cannot be regarded as undesirable on its merits, as in this case, it would still be advisable to warn the person or firm that submitted the publication to the Board that the permission must still be obtained from the Minister of Justice before the publication may circulate.[24]

The letter goes on to point out that it is useless to submit a publication if the author is a listed communist because the onus falls on the minister of justice. A.J. van Wyk, who wrote on behalf of the Publications Control Board's chair, concludes his letter to the police by requesting that he be advised of the 'actual state of affairs' so that he can inform Customs 'whether the order against Mphahlele is applicable or not'.[25] Seemingly, no further action was taken and the book was passed again in 1967.

In 1974, with the Publications Act of 1974 in force, *Down Second Avenue* was once again submitted by the Security Police. In his reply, Kruger, in his capacity as chair of the Publications Control Board, points out that the book was passed in 1959 and again in 1967, despite the fact that the author is a listed person subject to the provisions of the Suppression of Communism Act, but that 'further action against the book, if any, must therefore come from the Department of Justice, irrespective of the decision

---

24. NASA, IDP, Ref: 522/67, Mphahlele, 1967; NASA, IDP, Ref: 523/67, Mphahlele, 1967, 1968, 1974.
25. NASA, IDP, Ref: 522/67, Mphahlele, 1967; NASA, IDP, Ref: 523/67, Mphahlele, 1967, 1968, 1974.

of this board'.²⁶ It seems apparent from the correspondence between the Publications Board and the Security Police and South African Police that a certain ambiguity persisted and that the various Acts simultaneously impacting on censorship at times overlapped and proved to be difficult cases for the censors. In the end, Kruger refused to put the book through the system and the case was seemingly closed, at least until a comic version of *Down Second Avenue* was submitted to the censorship board (McDonald 2009: 252).

The case of *Down Second Avenue: The Comic*, an adaptation of Mphahlele's autobiography by Mzwakhe Nhlabatsi and published by Ravan Press, illustrates how the concept of the likely reader, reintroduced in the Publications Amendment Act of 1978, played a major role in the censors' decision-making process and provides an example of the workings of Van Rooyen's Publications Appeal Board. Upon submission of the publication by the South African Police in 1988, the Publications Board unanimously banned the book in terms of section 47 (2) (e) of the Publications Act of 1974, which pertains to state security. As a letter dated July 1988 from the director of publications to Ravan Press justifying the ban indicates, the initial decision to declare the book undesirable was mainly based on issues of readership and on the popular character of the book.²⁷ The director of publications wrote: 'This book is directed at young scholars who obviously attach great importance to the written word and its presentation', further arguing:

> This publication can be used in a very subtle manner to condition the pupil's questioning thought pattern and to create a sympathy for violence, arson, hate for the police and the state in general; that blacks should be armed, because . . . 'A nation is no nation

---

26. NASA, IDP, Ref: 522/67, Mphahlele, 1967; NASA, IDP, Ref: 523/67, Mphahlele, 1967, 1968, 1974.
27. NASA, IDP, 3/238, Ref: P88/06/162. Objectionable literature. *Down Second Avenue: The Comic.* Ezekiel Mphahlele. 1988.

without arms . . . and . . . Doom to South African white rule and British Imperialism'.²⁸

The effect of the book was therefore considered in the light of the likely readership, which was assumed, according to this quote, to be young, naive, easily influenced and impressed by role models such as their teachers. Noting the alleged subversive nature of the book, the director of publications further denounces the fact that this book will 'create a mental state in the young people that will be conducive to them participating in the violent onslaught against the present order', thus portraying a readership prone to subversion.²⁹ The likely readership was not only defined in relation to the book being published as a textbook, but also in light of its popular nature as a comic, which would inevitably attract a wide and young – read 'easily influenced' – readership: 'With its popular content and its easily readable content, this book will be read by thousands of scholars.' Ravan appealed the board's decision through its lawyers, in a ten-page letter addressed to Van Rooyen's Publications Appeal Board. Ravan claimed, among other things, that the decision was not in accordance with the guidelines of the Publications Appeal Board, it was based on a non-contextual reading of the publication and was vague and unsubstantiated. Ravan's main argument, which underpins the whole appeal, is that the book is unlikely to incite its likely readers, using the kind of rhetoric adopted by the Publications Appeal Board.³⁰

Contextualising its claim, Ravan points out that the twelve-page comic, which is part of the People's College Comics Series, was initially published in 1981 in the magazine *Upbeat*, emphasising the fact that it had already been in circulation in South Africa for the past seven years and that the autobiography the comic is based on had also been freely available in South Africa for several years. Moreover, alluding to questions of authorship,

---

28. NASA, IDP, 3/238, Ref: P88/06/162, Mphahlele, 1988.
29. NASA, IDP, 3/238, Ref: P88/06/162, Mphahlele, 1988.
30. NASA, IDP, 3/238, Ref: P88/06/162, Mphahlele, 1988.

Ravan brings to the attention of the Publications Appeal Board the fact that Mphahlele is 'respected by the black community as a moderate and uncontroversial figure'.[31] The moderate and radical intellectual traditions are highlighted in this argument and formed part of a larger debate in literary and political circles, since colonial missions' literacy programmes.

The function of the text is also touched on in Ravan's appeal and the didactic qualities of the publication are clearly stated, perhaps in the hope it would serve as a mitigating factor as appealing to educational literacy. It is noted that half of the publication contains language and writing exercises 'designed to improve linguistic and literary skills of its readers' and that 'the political content in these pages is merely incidental and is used as a vehicle to stimulate interest in the exercises'.[32] On this point, Ravan seemingly contests the assumed usage the imagined young readers will make of their reading, pointing out that stimulating a 'questioning thought pattern' is something for which the education system should strive. According to Ravan, adults could also be part of the likely readership, as the book could also be used to improve adult English literacy skills.

Intratextual elements are also brought into the argument, for instance, the fact that censors did not consider issues of characterisation in their decision when quoting Zeph's utterances, 'A nation is no nation without arms' and 'Doom to South African white rule and British imperialism'. According to Ravan, Zeph is 'the firebrand of the school' and considerations of the development of his character would have helped in contextualising his statements in an otherwise realistic and balanced depiction of the South African political scene of the 1950s:

> The form of the publication does not permit the development of his character beyond a mere humorous caricature. In addition, he is drawn in a grotesque and exaggerated manner. He is peripheral to the main story line, occupying only two frames of the publication,

---

31. NASA, IDP, 3/238, Ref: P88/06/162, Mphahlele, 1988.
32. NASA, IDP, 3/238, Ref: P88/06/162, Mphahlele, 1988.

and does not exercise any influence on the political development of the main character. The words he utters, being mere political rhetoric, provide an insight into the atmosphere and thoughts of some of the school boys at the time. They are unlike to incite readers to contravene the interests protected in Section 47 (2) (e).[33]

Contesting the censors' one-sided view that the likely young readership will be incited to perpetrate violence, Ravan emphasises the complexities of this readership saying that the youth's political development and political actions are more complex than what is depicted in *Down Second Avenue: The Comic*, quoting from Robert Coles's *The Political Life of Children*: 'One must shun the temptation to leap from the child's political awareness to the adult's political behaviour.'[34] By using this quote, not only does Ravan back up its argument, but also insinuates that the censors projected their own reading as adults onto children, who as Ravan points out, read on a different level. Ravan further argues that the effect of a publication on the likely reader should be measured in terms of the likelihood of violence in relation to the historical context, conveniently quoting Van Rooyen's *Censorship in South Africa*: 'A real threat to the interests in Section 47 (2) (e) will be found to exist only if a substantial number of likely readers are likely to be more pre-disposed to violence than they would have been prior to having read the particular publication.'

The 'light-hearted', 'humorous', 'easy' and 'informal' tone and style of the publication, which for censors represent an aggravating factor as it meant a larger readership and wider diffusion, should be seen, according to Ravan, as an indicator that the publication is 'by no means a serious political piece'.[35] For Ravan, which consciously adopts the censors' vocabulary, the fact that it is easy reading means that the publication is unlikely to pose a threat to state security.

---

33. NASA, IDP, 3/238, Ref: P88/06/162, Mphahlele, 1988.
34. NASA, IDP, 3/238, Ref: P88/06/162, Mphahlele, 1988.
35. NASA, IDP, 3/238, Ref: P88/06/162, Mphahlele, 1988.

In a letter from the director of publications dated 20 December 1988, the decision was overturned and the publication was declared not undesirable, on condition that 'it may only be distributed by bookshops, lending libraries and book distributors'.[36] These conditions and restrictions imposed by censors on 'not undesirable' publications are typical of the post-1978 censorship dispensation. Not undesirable, as opposed to desirable, seemingly implies a pass with conditions related to distribution, points of sale and usage, among other things.

Amid this controversy and the fact that Mphahlele was a listed communist, *Down Second Avenue*, both in its full text and comic forms, was read in South Africa. Probably because of its being a 'difficult case' involving several state departments, readers lost track of whether the book was banned or not. Thinking it was banned, some wondered why that was the case, or what prompted censors to scrutinise the book. Chris van Wyk recalls the relevance he found in *Down Second Avenue*, linking Mphahlele's story to his own personal experience:

> It was a lovely book, an honestly told story about childhood and growing up. And I think in a sense it is the most powerful message in the book: he was not writing out of anger, he was writing quietly [. . .] and the government did not want people to know what was happening, so they banned the book. But that book still kept on selling. It still sells all over the world. It's a classic.[37]

The case of *Down Second Avenue* is a telling example of the censorship apparatus at work. The reports on Mphahlele's autobiography clearly demonstrate the literary considerations at play in Dekker's censorship board. The effect of the publication on a black and a white readership were discussed in the light of literary merit and potentially subversive characters, the censors concluding that white readers would gain insights

---

36. NASA, IDP, 3/238, Ref: P88/06/162, Mphahlele, 1988.
37. Van Wyk, interview.

into the 'black experience', while black readers would not be incited by it, as they were familiar with the reality depicted and Mphahlele's tone was not provocative. Although Mphahlele was a listed communist, his stature and the literariness of his autobiography served as mitigating factors to pass the publication, at least in terms of the censorship board's scope of duties, the censors seemingly aware that banning would attract unwanted publicity for the book. As the reports on the comic version reveal, the censors' discourse returned to a focus on the likely reader after being focused on political content in the mid-1970s, with Van Rooyen's Publications Appeal Board overturning an earlier ban in light of this likely readership. The Appeal Board's reports also illustrate the 'repressive tolerance' in the censors' discourse in the 1980s, in which the 'period value' of a publication was considered in the censors' deliberations.

Case study 2: Dennis Brutus

Another South African poet, educator and political activist who preoccupied the South African authorities during the apartheid years is Dennis Brutus. From 1953, Brutus was the secretary of the South African Non-Racial Olympic Committee and from 1963 its president. Through this organisation, Brutus campaigned against racial discrimination and racism in sports. In 1962, he was one of the 102 anti-apartheid activists silenced by the General Law Amendment Act or Sabotage Act. As McDonald (2009: 33) explains, the Act was invoked to ban Brutus from teaching, publishing and being a member of any organisation: 'Following the terms of the Suppression of Communism Act, this new "gagging clause" banned various writers and journalists as persons, removing their rights of association, among other things, but it also made it illegal for them to be quoted in public.'

Brutus was first arrested in 1963, having contravened the conditions of his ban by attending a meeting, and in 1964 he was given an eighteen-month sentence, which he served on Robben Island. In 1966 he left South Africa on a one-way exit permit for London, where he lived until 1970. He moved to the United States until his return to South Africa in the early

1990s. During his years in exile, Brutus continued to write poetry and pursued his anti-apartheid work while lecturing at various universities.

Brutus's first collection of poetry, *Sirens, Knuckles and Boots*, was published in 1964 by Nigerian Mbari Publications, while he was serving his sentence on Robben Island. Considered a dangerous communist by the apartheid government, Brutus had his work published abroad and it was banned in South Africa during most of the apartheid era, which inevitably limited the size of his South African readership. As McDonald (2009: 288) points out, together with Breyten Breytenbach, Peter Horn, Ingoapele Madingoane, Wopko Jensma, Daniel P. Kunene, Mazisi Kunene and James Matthews, Brutus was one of the 'poets the censors believed posed the greatest threat to the established order'.

Some of Brutus's work was in the possession of the State Library or was intercepted by customs agents, which prompted a series of applications to the censorship board, operating in terms of the Publications Act of 1974 and Publications Amendment Act of 1978. In the 1980s, the Department of Customs and Excise, the State Library and the University of Potchefstroom Library, among other institutions, submitted some of Brutus's poetry collections to the Directorate of Publications for decision or review. A Dutch translation of *Letters to Martha and Other Poems from a South African Prison*, translated as *Aan Martha: Brieven van Robbeneiland*, was also sent to the Publications Board by the State Library in 1980. A.H. Murray drafted the reader's report, in which he points out that like its English original version, this is a collection of 'serious' poetry, 'there are some beautiful poems' and they do not allude to political events or occurrences, but rather to the 'writer's feelings and meditation at the time of his banning and imprisonment and as detainee in the prison'.[38] Murray concludes: 'The book has no propagandistic effect or inciting effect – at least not directly. I think I am in for its being passed but with hesitation.' The likely reader test seemingly worked in favour

---

38. NASA, IDP, 1/52, Ref: P80/2/50. Objectionable literature. *Ann Martha*. Dennis Brutus. 1980.

of the Dutch version of Brutus's poetry collection being passed, as it was assumed that the publication, being serious poetry in Dutch and thus appealing to a Dutch-speaking readership, would have no 'direct' propagandistic or inciting effect on the reader. Without further comment or argument, it was thus considered 'not undesirable' and returned to the director of the State Library.

The original English version of *Letters to Martha*, published in 1968 as part of Heinemann's African Writers Series, was submitted to the Publications Board by the Department of Customs and Excise later in 1980. The censors' report opens with a brief overview of the writer, where it is noted that 'Brutus is known to the committee and on the back cover mention is made of the fact that he is responsible for South Africa's exclusion from the Olympic Games'.[39] The report continues with an analysis of the literariness and political content of the publication. It concludes that 'although most poems have some connection with the prison, there are only some which are problematic and should receive attention' and the book was found to be not undesirable. The report provides the reasons for this conclusion, alluding specifically to these 'problematic' poems. It points out: 'Judging by the remarks on the back cover of the publication, the reader would expect to find a strong political message. However, it is not the case.' It is noted that the word 'apartheid' is used only once with reference to sports and that 'as far as the poem is concerned, it cannot be claimed that its content is subversive or offensive within the meaning of Section (47) (2)'. The censors' analysis continues, singling out the poems 'Blood River' and 'Their Behaviour', both dealing with the celebration of Heroes' Day, and 'On the Island', which deals with life in prison. As the censor observes, in these poems Brutus addresses potentially undesirable issues in a language 'that is not such that the poems can be considered undesirable' and 'to which offence cannot be taken'. Pointing to potential cause for moralistic concern, the report highlights a

---

39. NASA, IDP, 1/52, Ref: P80/2/143. Objectionable literature. *Letters to Martha*. Dennis Brutus. 1980.

'homosexual note' in the poem 'Letters to Martha', but specifies that 'it is too subtle to make the poem offensive'. These arguments mainly touch on aspects of the literary merit of the publication, as it is considered that the tone in which the potentially subversive or immoral issues are dealt with are unlikely to cause incitement, probably in the light of an educated and highly literate readership. Moreover, this report demonstrates how a publication with literary merit could be scrutinised on a literary level, despite the obvious political background of the author, at least since the Publications Amendment Act of 1978.

Stubborn Hope was submitted in 1980 by the Department of Customs and Excise. This collection, also published as part of Heinemann's African Writers Series, was banned, a decision based on readers' reports drafted by R.E. Lighton, who was a signatory of the 1963 anti-censorship petition, and Murray. Lighton argues that the collection has literary merit and that the poems touch on varied subjects, including apartheid and Robben Island. While he points out that in some instances these topics are treated in a way that is not undesirable, some poems 'require close reading'.[40] These poems, at the centre of the undesirability verdict, contain references to conditions in prison, explicitly undesirable allusions to sexuality, attacks on the Security Police and reference to the Sharpeville massacre. Based on these factors, Lighton recommends a ban in terms of section (47) (2) (e) of the Act of 1974, in other words in terms of the poems' possible threat to state security, general welfare and peace and good order. He maintains that the references to 'the Robben Island prison warden "laughing" with his foot on cheek of convict with head under water', 'the sadism of officers', 'the detention without trial for four months by the Secret Police', the events of Sharpeville 'bullet-in-the-back day', which implies that 'they were deliberately shot in the back while retreating', all constitute 'half truths presented as the essential truth'. Brutus was in all likelihood reflecting on

---

40. NASA, IDP, 3/84, Ref: P80/1/147. Objectionable literature. *A Simple Lust*. Dennis Brutus. 1980.

true occurrences that the state wanted to keep secret. This is one of many examples where censors used the guise of 'truth' to hide what was really going on from the general public, censoring and fabricating reality.

Murray reiterates the 'problems' posed by the poems contained in the Robben Island sequence. The director of publications concludes the report and confirms the decision to ban, based on Lighton's and Murray's observations regarding the Robben Island poems, even if consideration is given to the non-vindictive poetic, literary and even contemplative nature of Brutus's poetry, albeit in a condescending and patronising manner:

> In general, they are of good quality, some even of a high standard. On the other hand some other poems are banal and composed in a facile manner. All poems are from his experience: there is no description of episodes or things: all reflect his emotional state regarding the subject matter, concerning his experiences as a banned person, or banning as such, or the political situation in the RSA, there are only about twelve references in passing, mostly of a contemplative nature, although all good natured.[41]

J.P. Jansen's report on *Poems from Algiers*, submitted by the library of the University of Potchefstroom, declares the collection not undesirable, as 'Dennis Brutus is a well-known poet. Some of his poems have been allowed in anthologies. There is no objection to the poems which appear in the booklet, which is not undesirable within the meaning of the Act, Section 47 (2)', a decision endorsed without further comment from the director of publications, M.J. van der Westhuizen.[42] In this case, one can suppose that the literary qualities of the poems and high standard of literary language, when considered against the likely readership – a limited and sophisticated academic one – played a role in the ruling.

---

41. NASA, IDP, 3/84, Ref: P80/1/147, Brutus, 1980.
42. NASA, IDP, 1/58, Ref: P80/9/31. Objectionable literature. *Poems from Algiers* – No. 2. Dennis Brutus. 1980.

The South African Library submitted *A Simple Lust* to Van Rooyen's Publications Appeal Board for review in 1988, as the collection of poems had previously been found undesirable in terms of the Publications and Entertainments Act of 1963. Referring to Brutus's poetry's personal political tone, M. Bosman, one of the readers, points out that given Brutus' political past, 'one could be sceptical about quotations such as "a common hate enriched on love and us"; "victims of a sickly state"; "oppression's power is charred to dust"; "let them die in thousands"'.[43] However, Bosman later emphasises the importance of considering the likely reader and not merely the intention of the author, quoting from Van Rooyen's *Censorship in South Africa*: 'It is the book and its effect on the likely reader that must be judged and not the motives of the readers thereof. The motives of the writer may not be taken into account.' Bosman continues his line of thinking by pointing out, in light of Van Rooyen's advice that 'the expected likely readership is limited since we are dealing with poetry. The subtle nature and degree of suggestion in poetry make it less accessible to the masses (to whom inciting reading material is directed).' The inciting and offensive nature of poetry is then briefly discussed and Bosman concludes that 'the publication will not lead to a situation where "a substantial number of likely readers are likely to be more predisposed to violence than they would have been prior to having read the publication"'. Also sitting on the reader's committee, Van der Merwe Scholtz reiterated Bosman's decision, arguing that the collection of poetry expresses 'sentiments frequently expressed in the media which are mitigated by the vehicle of poetry'. The ban on *Simple Lust* was lifted by unanimous decision of the committee, in a telling example of the application of Van Rooyen's reformist approach in the censorship procedures in the 1980s.

After being banned in terms of the provisions of the Publications Act of 1974, *China Poems* was reviewed upon submission by the South African Library in 1988. The ban was unanimously lifted, as detailed in a report

---

43. NASA, IDP, 3/211, Ref: P87/8/48. Objectionable literature. *A Simple Lust*. Dennis Brutus. 1987–1988.

signed by E.H. van der Merwe Scholtz, then chair of the committee.[44] The report comments that in the preface, 'Brutus does mention that he reported to Oliver Tambo the Chinese support for "your struggle for freedom in South Africa"' and concludes that the book 'no longer qualifies it [as undesirable] in terms of [Section 47 (2)] (d) and (e)'. As Van der Merwe Scholtz notes, 'this remark is not prejudicial to the safety of the State and is not enough for a finding of undesirability'. This decision illustrates some important changes brought about by the Publications Amendment Act of 1978, including the necessity to weigh the potential politically subversive nature of a publication against its literary value and likely readership. Furthermore, the historical context seemingly played a role, as the distance between the events and the report was more than ten years, *China Poems* having been published in 1975.

Zeit-Gedichte, a translation of Brutus's poetry published in Germany, was scrutinised by the security committee as late as 1990, after being submitted by the acquisitions department of the South African Library. The poetry collection is judged not undesirable on the grounds of its limited readership: 'The poems are in German, which already means that it will have a very small readership in South Africa; there must be very few people who speak German and also read poetry. The book's readership will consist, literarily and figuratively, of just a small select group.'[45] Moreover, it is stated that some of these poems are already available in other publications in South Africa and while they are protest poetry in essence, they are not inciting or subversive: 'They are protest poems but are characterised by a remarkable lack of bitterness and vengefulness.'

The censors' reformist and at times even slightly appreciative tone with regard to Brutus's work represents a radical shift from the authorities' non-negotiable condemnation of his work, both literary and politically, which occurred in the 1960s, when seemingly most of his work was banned

---

44. NASA, IDP, 3/227, Ref: P88/3/12. Objectionable literature. *China Poems*. Dennis Brutus. 1988.
45. NASA, IDP, 3/274, Ref: P90/4/69. Objectionable literature. *Zeit-Gedichte*. Dennis Brutus. 1990.

under the Publications and Entertainments Act of 1963 or by virtue of him being a listed communist. The overall approach adopted by censors towards Brutus's poetry is a good illustration of the application of the Publications Amendment Act of 1978. While not being overtly subversive and using a highly poetic language, as pointed out by the various censors' reports discussed above, Brutus's poetry nevertheless included elements of protest poetry, which were tolerated by the censors in the 1980s, seemingly in line with Van Rooyen's advice that 'it is often in the interests of state security to permit the expression of pent-up feelings and grievances' (1987: 16).

As far as unbanning previously banned material is concerned, an examination of Van Rooyen's discussion on 'the question of changing attitudes' provides insight into the changing censorship apparatus and ideology adopted by censors, which at this point is, according to Van Rooyen (1987: 17), in line with the progressive opening of South Africa to the rest of the world through increased access to media and foreign ideas and influences. Rhetorically asking if a decision to overturn a ban signals a change in morality, Van Rooyen answers – perhaps critically – that what changes is not morality or religious precepts, but is in fact 'individual perspective, and this has an influence on tolerance. For example, ten years ago there was little room for political dialogue with blacks, while such dialogue is at present an everyday occurrence.'

Case study 3: *Staffrider* magazine and the Staffrider series

The Johannesburg-based publication *Staffrider*, which enjoyed considerable popularity from when its first issue was published in March 1978 and throughout the 1980s, contributed to the revival of so-called black poetry in South Africa. The first editorial, titled 'About *Staffrider*', set the tone adopted by the magazine and clearly identifies its objective, as well as addressing the censors, with whom *Staffrider* would have regular encounters:

> A skilful entertainer, a bringer of messages, a useful person but ... slightly disreputable. Our censors may not like him, but they

should consider putting up with him. A whole new literature is knocking at the door, and if our society is to change without falling apart it needs all the messages it can get – the bad as well as the good [. . .]

The magazine which bears this name has been established by Ravan Press in an attempt to respond, as publishers, to the great surge of creative activity which has been one of the more hopeful signs of recent times.

The new writing has altered the scope and function of literature in South Africa in ways we have still to discover. The aim of this magazine is not to impose standards but to provide a regular meeting place for the new writers and their readers, a forum which will help to shape the future of our literature.

A feature of much of the new writing is its 'direct line' to the community in which the writer lives. This is a two-way line. The writer is attempting to voice the community's experience ('This is how it is') and his immediate audience is the community ('Am I right?'). Community drama, 'say' poetry, an oral literature backed and often inspired by music: this is the heart of the new writing, and the signs are the prose forms re-emerging in the new mould.

It is for this reason that the work appearing in *Staffrider* flies the flag of its community (in Chapman 2007: 125).

The first issue of *Staffrider* was deemed undesirable in terms of section 47 (2) (a), (d) and (e) of the Act of 1974, after being submitted by Colonel C.J.W. du Plooy of the South African Police in April 1978. The Publications Committee's report states that while some material is of the 'same undesirable nature as that published in *Donga*', a prohibited publication, some material 'has decided literary merit'.[46] According

---

46. NASA, IDP, 3/51, Ref: P78/04/50. Objectionable literature. *Staffrider* Vol. 1, No. 1. 1978.

to the final decision, signed by Lighton, the undesirability is based on the following reading of the publication: 'The undesirable parts of the publication are those in which the authority and image of the police, as the persons entrusted by the State with maintaining law, internal peace order, are undermined'; 'offensive language – such as the use of "fuck" and its derivative, "poes" and "shitty" – is found in the article "Van"'; 'material calculated to harm Black/White relations appears in the poem "Change" and the article "Soweto".' This decision to ban *Staffrider*'s launch issue was published in the *Government Gazette* of 14 April 1978, after the censorship board notified the Ministry of the Interior of the decision. As is observable from the arguments in favour of banning, no consideration was given to the issue of the likely reader, as this case was prior to the adoption of the Publications Amendment Act of 1978, which was effectively implemented from 1980 onwards. Therefore, the tone of political protest alone sufficed to justify a ban. The ban was appealed and overturned in February 1990, based on the fact that:

> The probable reader of this publication will not be offended by most of the description contained therein. The literary nature of most works in the publication makes it seem unlikely that the publication will have a wide circulation or many young impressionable readers. Most works contained in the publication have literary merit.[47]

The tone and issues considered in 1989 contrast with the arguments proposed in the 1978 censors' report and clearly illustrate how a political tone was gradually replaced by considerations revolving around literary merit and likely readership, as can be seen in the subsequent censors' reports on *Staffrider*.

---

47. NASA, IDP, 3/268, Ref: P89/12/05. Objectionable literature. *Staffrider* Vol. 1, No. 1. 1990.

Staffrider's second issue – Volume 1, Number 2 – was also scrutinised by censors in June 1978, after once again being submitted by Colonel du Plooy. This time, the likely readership was taken into account. It was concluded that, given the fact that the educated reader would not be shocked or fazed by the information contained in the publication and that the 'average-black-man-in-the-street' would not grasp the poems and their subtleties, 'the publication was preferable above ground than underground'.[48] These references to the 'educated reader' and the 'average-black-man-in-the-street' would be the beginning of systematic consideration of the likely readership in subsequent censors' reports on *Staffrider*.

An appeal against the banning of *Staffrider* Volume 3, Number 2 of June 1980 was lodged in September 1980 by the Directorate of Publications with the Publications Appeal Board, then chaired by Van Rooyen. This case provides a good example of Van Rooyen's philosophy and rationale applied to a publication that was initially considered undesirable in terms of section 47 (2) (d) and (e) of the Publications Act of 1974. Van Rooyen opens his report with a summary of his main arguments: this is a 'sophisticated publication with derogatory politic comment not undesirable', 'the likely readership is limited', 'it includes items with literary merit or, at least, worthy of literary consideration' and 'the publication is for the literate by the literate and for the converted by the converted'.[49] Van Rooyen considers whether the publication, through its readers, would violate or contribute to the violation of state security:

> Would the likely reader of this publication react in a manner which would violate or contribute to a violation of the interests which are protected in the said paragraph? In regard to Section 47 (2) (d) the same test applied. Would the publication have the effect of leading

---

48. NASA, IDP, 1/31, Ref: P78/6/101. Objectionable literature. *Staffrider* Vol. 1, No. 2. 1978.
49. NASA, IDP, 3/91, Ref: P80/7/31. Objectionable literature. *Staffrider* Vol. 3, No. 1. 1980.

to or contributing to animosity between black and white? Once again the likely readership is of cardinal importance.[50]

In identifying the likely readership, Van Rooyen refers to extra-textual elements of the publication – the editorial quality and price of the publication, which he assesses as high. The likely readership would be 'the more sophisticated black man and the white man who is interested in reading literary material by blacks'. Van Rooyen further points out:

> As may be expected in a review that published whatever can be covered by the umbrella of protest, there is a general derogation of whites and their government, but there are contributions that serve as a corrective to this, for instance John Gambanga's *Orphaned for Birth*, in which a child is orphaned by 'triggerhappy' blacks, and *Chapmans Home Territory*, in which a white man's sense of compassion is the theme.[51]

Van Rooyen argues that these examples 'serve to mitigate the Publications Committee's decision that whites are presented in a bad light'. He also evokes the fact that some potentially subversive passages are already known to an easily influenced black readership and that it is necessary for the probable white readership to 'understand black problems', both considerations serving as mitigating factors:

> The fact is that the black masses, even the illiterate, have heard at gatherings, like funerals, the things that have been re-uttered here, and finding *Staffrider* undesirable on such grounds, would be like locking the stable door after the horse has bolted. Whites are likely to gain more than to lose by being given access to black thinking through this kind of medium.[52]

---

50. NASA, IDP, 3/91, Ref: P80/7/31, *Staffrider*, 1980.
51. NASA, IDP, 3/91, Ref: P80/7/31, *Staffrider*, 1980.
52. NASA, IDP, 3/91, Ref: P80/7/31, *Staffrider*, 1980.

The report goes on to advocate the development of 'black culture', in the kind of rhetoric typical of Van Rooyen's reformist approach, suggesting that 'even though *Staffrider* itself may regard literary standards as "elitist", the fact that it includes items of literary merit and validity serves to advance black culture, and that is, indeed, a mitigating and even commendable consideration'. It is therefore concluded that section 47 (2) (d) and (e) is not contravened by this publication and 'the appeal succeeds and the decision of the Publications Committee that the publication is undesirable is set aside'.[53]

The likely readership imagined by censors contrasts with the image in the editorial and Van Wyk's account of a 'people's magazine', where writers and readers of all levels of literacy and walks of life would interact in the space opened up by the publication, encompassing an inclusive popular readership.[54] However, as illustrated by Van Wyk's view above and Belinda Bozzoli's notion of 'translation' (Bozzoli 2004) discussed in the previous chapter, the readership of a publication such as *Staffrider* went well beyond the select group of intellectuals and literate readers typically associated with poetry. Van Wyk observes that *Staffrider*, which generally published both so-called serious and popular literature, was distributed among writers, intellectuals and readers in trains and on the streets to reach a wider audience.[55] Tom Lodge (1983: 325) reiterates the inclusiveness of the readership rallied around black consciousness publications in urban South Africa in the 1970s and 1980s in these terms: 'If its influence was limited to the urban intelligentsia this would have guaranteed its imprint on almost any African political assertion of the time. Distilled to a basic set of catchphrases, Black Consciousness percolated down to a broader and socially amorphous group than African intellectuals.'

In another report dated December 1980, in which *Staffrider* Volume 3, Number 3, is under review, the Directorate of Publications, which submitted

---

53. NASA, IDP, 3/91, Ref: P80/7/31, *Staffrider*, 1980.
54. Van Wyk, interview.
55. Van Wyk, interview.

the claim for appeal, argues that this issue of *Staffrider*, 'although at times hostile, irritating and provocative, falls within the permissible limits of Black protest literature'.[56] It further points to the fact that 'some articles are not without literary merit' and that 'the probable readership is confined to persons Black and White, who take an interest in Black literature; and that the degree of tolerance shown by the South African community is higher when applied to Black than the other writers'. In its detailed decision, the Publications Appeal Board proposes the same arguments as those raised in report P80/7/31 on Volume 3, Number 2, discussed above: the political tone of the publication is overall not undesirable nor inflammatory and the likely readership is limited and literate. However, the Board goes a step further towards the tolerant approach that came to characterise Van Rooyen's reformist discourse:

> In its well formulated appeal the Directorate submits that *Staffrider* fulfils the need for a publication devoted to the advance of black literature, however uneven the product may at times be. It also favours the growth of black culture and education, in themselves desirable attainments. The Directorate also points out that black literature cannot at all times avoid voicing a protest, justified or not, against allegedly discriminatory actions or conditions. It is common cause between white and black that unnecessary and unfair discrimination should be progressively eliminated. This cause can only be furthered if blacks are given the opportunity of indicating what they regard as unfair treatment, as is done, on more than one occasion in this *Staffrider*.[57]

Based on these premises, the ban on *Staffrider* Volume 3, Number 3 was overturned, 'although the publication is often bitter in its statement of grievances'.

---

56. NASA, IDP, 3/96, Ref: P80/10/146. Objectionable literature. *Staffrider* Vol. 3, No. 3. 1980.
57. NASA, IDP, 3/96, Ref: P80/10/146, *Staffrider*, 1980.

In a report dated 2 March 1981, reader E.H. van der Merwe Scholtz also rules against a ban on the *Staffrider* issue of December/January 1981, arguing: 'The quality is such that it would probably find its public amongst the more discerning and even sophisticated black (and white) readers. This is not a vehicle for blatant and vociferous propaganda, but for sentiments and convictions already channelled into articulate and even aesthetic form.'[58]

The series of reports on *Staffrider* Volume 5, Number 3 also provides an example of the dynamic notion of 'likely readership', which was, in this particular report, conceived of as constantly evolving and changing, in parallel with the socio-political events unfolding in South Africa in the 1980s.[59] This particular issue of *Staffrider* was initially the object of disagreement among censors, but was in the end found to be 'not undesirable' on the grounds of its likely 'sophisticated readership' by a vote of three to two. An appeal of this decision was lodged with the chair of the Board by the director of publications, then Abraham Coetzee, who argued that the publication contravened section 47 (2) (d) and (e) of the Publications Act of 1974. Coetzee's request for appeal, lodged in December 1983, is underpinned by a consideration of mitigating factors used for precedent decisions with regard to the changing South African reality. His line of argument is based on the premise that the readership of *Staffrider* is, as established in previous reports, 'limited' and 'sophisticated', but might have evolved over the years, which shows a thorough reflection on the notion of likely readership: 'The likely readership of the publication would normally have expanded since the 1980 decisions of the Appeal Board. The present circulation is of the order of 3000, of which many copies are sent abroad. This circulation gives a not insignificant readership of more than 10000.'[60]

---

58. NASA, IDP, Ref: P81/2/16. Objectionable literature. *Staffrider* Vol. 3, No. 4. 1981.
59. NASA, IDP, 3/141, Ref: P83/11/122. Objectionable literature. *Staffrider* Vol. 5, No. 3. 1984.
60. NASA, IDP, 3/141, Ref: P83/11/122, *Staffrider*, 1984.

In his request for appeal, Coetzee examines the arguments formulated by Van Rooyen in the two previous Appeal Board cases, emphasising that the 'Appellant's general submission is that the reasoning in those cases, which Appellant accepts, does not always apply, or applies to a lesser extent, to the present third issue of 1983'. Coetzee further argues:

> The likely readership would include sophisticated revolutionary Whites and Blacks who will use some of the content for fuelling and encouraging alleged grievances; for fostering hatred of the system of law and order; for undermining the country's war effort (in extreme cases a treasonable offence) and for praising criminals who had fallen foul of the country's security legislations. The magazine seeks, in part, to convert others for the furthering of the aims mentioned and, insofar as it is by the converted for the converted, the latter will be able to use it as an instrument for furthering those aims and 'convert' others.[61]

The spiralling effect of the publication on its readership is noted and the traditionally mitigating literary factor is now seen as playing against the censors, as can be observed when Coetzee affirms that 'the effect of such literary value can indeed be counter-productive and expand the readership, and strengthen the undesirable impact of dangerous material'. Moreover, Coetzee believes that 'in this issue of *Staffrider* there are, as will be shown, utterances which, in their vileness and hatred, exceed what has been publicly stated by Black agitators'.[62]

In a very detailed analysis of the 'subversive' and 'revolutionary' character of the *Staffrider* issue at stake, the report quotes several passages believed to contribute to the undesirable character of the publication. This is followed by an entire paragraph assessing the potential consequences of

---

61. NASA, IDP, 3/141, Ref: P83/11/122, *Staffrider*, 1984.
62. NASA, IDP, 3/141, Ref: P83/11/122, *Staffrider*, 1984.

the publication on several identified potential readerships. It is pointed out that the publication may incite the likely reader in the light of the fact that:

a) The publication also circulates in Black schools. The vicious poems could be read to *young receptive minds* by teachers themselves influenced by the content;
b) The publication could be used by *banned organisations abroad* to *incite hostility* to South Africa and *seek sympathy* for Communist and allied causes;
c) It could be used as a means of getting funds from *anti-South African organisations abroad*;
d) It could contribute to *student unrest*. It is made readily available at outlets near to universities. On page 49 such outlets as the Campus Bookshop in Braamfontein, Open Books in Mowbray, Logan's University Bookshop in Durban and the University of Zululand Bookshop are mentioned;
e) *Students and other young persons* will be incited to oppose the war effort, to reject military service and to give comfort to the enemy through the contents. It inevitably leads to the death of loyal young South Africans on the border;
f) The attacks on the police *generate contempt for the law, and encourage and incite to criminal acts*, including physical assaults on policemen, resulting in injury and death;
g) The *sympathy shown for communism is calculated to further the aims of that dangerous system*. To do so can make a person guilty of a very serious crime; and
h) An effect not often realised is that scurrilous language of the nature mentioned, if its existence became known, would do lasting damage to the goodwill created in recent years by enlightened Government action. There are *Whites, many Whites, including enlightened ones who will refuse to tolerate such insults to their dignity and culture*. Polarisation will grow, resulting in

> retaliatory action, first in words, later in deeds. Confrontation
> will become inevitable. Is that what *Staffrider* is aiming at?[63]

In the eyes of the director of publications, this issue of *Staffrider* had important consequences for a broad spectrum of potential likely readers, including learners and students in South African institutions, anti-apartheid organisations abroad and political activists inside the country's borders. He states that these arguments warrant a review of the initial decision not to ban the publication.

A committee of readers, chaired by Dr R. Wiehahn, subsequently drafted a report that was received by the Appeal Board in February 1984. According to the report, 'none of the poetry or prose in this particular edition of *Staffrider* can be seriously regarded as being dangerous subversive literature', as 'no new statements about black experience' are made, the type of writing is 'ineffective' and 'airs grievances', and 'the "creative" writing displays no literary merit whatsoever'.[64] Wiehahn seems to hold an elitist notion of poetry, claiming that 'the contributors to this edition of *Staffrider* seem to have a mistaken notion of what constitutes poetry' and later commenting, with reference to particular poems, that 'these strident and formless cries have nothing to do with real poetry'. Because of this lack of literary merit, the committee concluded that this issue of *Staffrider* 'cannot possibly be an effective political weapon in the promotion of revolution in South Africa'. Linking the publication's literary merit to the literary reader, the report concludes that neither a sophisticated nor uneducated readership will show interest in this publication, as Wiehahn emphasises, even using the words 'sophisticated' and 'revolutionary' in the same breath:

> Who is the likely reader of such inferior literature? The sophisticated revolutionary can only reject it as drivel that reduces and

---

63. NASA, IDP, 3/141, Ref: P83/11/122, *Staffrider*, 1984; emphasis added.
64. NASA, IDP, 3/141, Ref: P83/11/122, *Staffrider*, 1984.

trivializes the cause he believes in. And those semi-literates that may be inflamed by emotional outbursts will quite probably reject it too because of the 'literary' guise in which it is cast.[65]

Having received and read the committee of experts' report, Van Rooyen, as chair of the Appeal Board, then proceeds to draft his own report, favouring dismissal of the appeal and thus declaring the publication not undesirable. Addressing Coetzee's concerns regarding the likely readership, Van Rooyen commends Wiehahn's report's references to previous Appeal Board decisions and the extensive development of the argument, quoting from the committee's report:

> Though some poems may be calculated to arouse ill feelings between races, more can be tolerated in such a literary magazine of quality with a sophisticated readership. Nothing new is said which had not appeared in the newspapers over and over. The Appeal Board has stressed the 'sophisticated' reader in the case – *The Classic*, Volume 1 No. 1.[66]

Van Rooyen draws his conclusions regarding the likely readership, before dismissing the appeal:

> A revolutionary will find nothing in this publication that he has not heard before in the line of grievances and complaints and nothing to inspire him to action or to indicate that action, not already suggested, is to be taken. An unsophisticated reader is not likely to acquire the publication, and if he does, he is not likely to find anything in it to hold his interest. Sophisticated readers will recognise the poor quality of much of the writing and find it simply boring and irritating.[67]

---

65. NASA, IDP, 3/141, Ref: P83/11/122, *Staffrider*, 1984.
66. NASA, IDP, 3/141, Ref: P83/11/122, *Staffrider*, 1984.
67. NASA, IDP, 3/141, Ref: P83/11/122, *Staffrider*, 1984.

In reports on subsequent issues of *Staffrider*, appreciation of literary merit seems to have drastically changed, which perhaps coincides with new editorial policies at *Staffrider*, where community editorial groups were replaced with a professional editor, as detailed in the previous chapter. A report signed by A.M. Theron dated February 1987, for instance, points out that 'this is a literary magazine of merit for Black people', adding that 'this magazine is directed at a very limited sophisticated readership. Such a publication should be available to the intelligent reader.'[68] In light of this 'sophisticated' and 'intelligent', 'black' likely readership, the committee of readers unanimously found *Staffrider* Volume 5, Number 3 to be not undesirable, concluding: 'The articles and poems give expression to "black" suffering, frustrations, experiences, ideals and aspirations. All these are expressed without any tendency to incite violence or undermine the safety of the state.'

In a subsequent report, also dated February 1987, Theron examines *Staffrider* Volume 6, Number 1, which was published in 1984. The issue of gaining insight into other racial groups and readerships is raised, for instance, when it is stated that the book review section 'gives good insight of literary works important to this readership'.[69] The likely readership is also discussed, with Theron concluding: 'This magazine is directed at a very limited, sophisticated readership. There is need for a publication devoted to the advancement of black literature and culture, it is essential that the creative section should have a mouthpiece.' These remarks bear witness to the spirit of greater tolerance towards protest literature in particular and so-called black literature in general.

A report on *Staffrider* Volume 6, Number 4, signed by D.M. Morrell, identifies 'a moneyed above average intellectually minded person' as

---

68. NASA, IDP, 3/195, Ref: P87/02/17. Objectionable literature. *Staffrider* Vol. 5, No. 3. 1983.
69. NASA, IDP, 3/195, Ref: P87/02/18. Objectionable literature. *Staffrider* Vol. 6, No. 1. 1987.

the likely readership.⁷⁰ After identifying some passages where 'high level intellectual commentary' and 'distinct literary merit' are observable, the report points out that 'the target market is certainly more than averagely literate'. However, it notes some 'repetitive, wearisome mediocrity of well known situations and viewpoints (reflecting chaos rather than construction) which must jade rather than incite or stimulate the average reasonable reader'. Contrary to some previous decisions, in which a less-educated reader would be assumed to be incited by so-called protest poetry, the censors conclude: 'Overall the effect is unlikely to provoke and for this reason in particular this volume of *Staffrider*, in terms of the Publications Act, cannot be considered undesirable.' This decision is attributable to the sophisticated and therefore limited size of the readership, and to the facts that the publication is, as emphasised by Van der Merwe Scholtz, 'of uneven quality and is not likely to make a marked impact on its readers' and that what could be considered protest is already known to this readership. In its letter to the South African Police, who had submitted the publication, the Directorate of Publications formulates the decision to pass this issue of *Staffrider* in this manner, adopting the rhetoric introduced by Van Rooyen earlier in the 1980s:

> The Committee feels that a revolutionary will find nothing in this publication that he has not heard before in the line of grievances and complaints. An unsophisticated reader is not likely to acquire the publication, and if he does, he is not likely to find anything in it to hold his interest. As has often been stated by the Appeal Board grievances do exist and cannot be ignored [. . .] Publications of this nature serve a useful purpose in that they keep population groups abreast of the feelings and aspirations of others.⁷¹

---

70. NASA, IDP, 3/200, Ref: P87/04/107. Objectionable literature. *Staffrider* Vol. 6, No. 4. 1987.
71. NASA, IDP, 3/200, Ref: P87/04/107, *Staffrider*, 1987.

An even more radical change in discourse is observable in a report dated June 1989 on *Staffrider* Volume 8, Number 1, where the political activist reader, previously considered as a subversive and undesirable one, is elevated to the ranks of 'discerning' and 'progressive': 'The standard of the material is fairly high and obviously intended for the more discerning reader, i.e. the progressive cultural fraternity, all those concerned with establishing a new cultural environment free of ethnic and class prejudices and the abominations of Apartheid.'[72] The reference to the 'abominations of Apartheid' is a considerable shift from the conservative and pro-apartheid discourse embraced by censors in most previous reports and is a reflection of the new discourse emerging in South Africa in the late 1980s and early 1990s. J.M. Els, who drafted the report, justifies his decision to pass this issue of *Staffrider* based on the sophisticated and limited readership, and that 'in these leftist circles a deleterious effect of the publication will be, if any, negligible', as there is 'no call to violence, revolution or Marxism'. Furthermore, Els seemingly guides the reader in reading the poetry section, advocating a 'descriptive' rather than 'emotive' reading of the poems that could otherwise be considered inflammatory if read out of context. The other readers on the committee reiterate Els's analysis of the likely readership, pointing out that 'the density of the text is likely to discourage casual readers' and that 'the likely (regular) readers would find nothing new to provoke them'. This distinction between the 'casual' and 'regular' reader occurs frequently alongside the recognition that the content is already known to literate and seasoned readers. These observations introduce a new categorisation of readers in terms of the likely readership of *Staffrider* magazine.

The ban on *Staffrider* Volume 4, Number 1 was appealed by Ravan Press in December 1989. The committee of readers unanimously signed in favour of overturning the ban, once again raising the fact that 'the stories are to be read in context', since a couple of years have elapsed since their

---

72. NASA, IDP, 3/259, Ref: P89/06/36. Objectionable literature. *Staffrider* Vol. 8, No. 1. 1989.

publication and initial banning in 1981.[73] The report concludes that the likely readership is unlikely to be 'inclined to undesirable activities as a result of reading' the magazine, furthermore arguing that *Staffrider* is 'intended for a more sophisticated readership and in these (leftist) circles, no detrimental effects caused by its reading are likely'.

As is observable from these reports, which are only some of the many on *Staffrider* in the archives, the magazine was well known to censors. Censors initially based their decisions on the undesirable subversive nature of some poems or stories in the late 1970s, but eventually assigned greater importance to its allegedly sophisticated and limited likely readership and literary merit in a spirit of relative tolerance towards 'black writing'. This shift was prompted by the Publications Amendment Act of 1978 that applied to literature by all writers from 1980 onwards, not only in favour of literature by white writers, as was the case between 1978 and 1980.

Besides *Staffrider* magazine, Ravan Press also published books in its Staffrider series. The series was 'conceived as an ambitious publishing experiment intended to bypass the white-controlled book trade, which focused on bookshop sales in the white city and the apartheid education market, by reaching out directly to a mass, black readership in the townships' (McDonald 2009: 323). Since black consciousness ideology underpinned this publishing venture, as it did *Staffrider* magazine, the titles published in the Staffrider series were prone to censorship. Launched in 1979, it was severely affected by censorship in its first four years of existence, before the years of 'repressive tolerance', with 11 of its first 15 titles being submitted by police to the censorship board, and 7 of a total of 28 titles being banned (McDonald 2009: 323).

Miriam Tlali's second novel *Amandla* was published and banned in 1981. The story is set against the immediate aftermath of the June 1976 Soweto youth uprising. In the words of S.S. Steenkamp, who sat on the committee of readers, it 'deals with emotional, very sensitive, even explosive

---

73. NASA, IDP, 3/268, Ref: P89/12/06. Objectionable literature. *Staffrider* Vol. 4, No. 2. 1990.

political and racial issues'.[74] The novel, which adopts a defiant and openly political tone (De Lange 1997: 143), was submitted to the Directorate of Publications by the South African Police in December 1981 and was unanimously found undesirable in terms of section 47 (2) (d) and (e) of the Act of 1974, as it was considered harmful to race relations and state security. It was concluded that ' "this little book" furthers racist and anti-state attitudes. The book will be read in order to promote anti-state action and the revolutionaries', in other words by a subversive readership. The inciting effect of the title ('*Amandla*' means power in isiXhosa and isiZulu and it was often chanted at public demonstrations) was also noted.[75]

The likely readership of the novel was therefore considered as highly subversive and, given the nature and tone of the novel, *Amandla* was declared undesirable. However, in 'black' literary circles, it was considered as a seminal novel on the June 16 Soweto uprising:

> Tlali's *Amandla* was, in [Njabulo Ndebele's] view, [one of] 'the best novels written on the events of June 16' because in recounting the fortunes of two young lovers during the upheavals she was 'not just reporting, she was telling a story'. Questions about the specifically literary status of these stories and novels in the Staffrider Series also arose during the censors' deliberations, though their judgements were unsurprisingly less consistent and less nuanced than Ndebele's. They were also, in some cases, just crudely opportunistic (McDonald 2009: 330).

In 1985, *Amandla* was submitted for review to the Appeal Board and was found not undesirable, which reflects the changes in the censors' discourse brought about by the implementation of the Publications Amendment Act

---

74. NASA, IDP, 3/158, Ref: P85/1/94. Objectionable literature. *Amandla* (*Staffrider* series Number Six). Miriam Tlali. 1985.
75. NASA, IDP, 3/101, Ref: P81/1/108. Objectionable literature. *Amandla* (*Staffrider* series Number Six). Miriam Tlali. 1981.

of 1978. Theron based his decision on Steenkamp's report and essentially cites the historical context, likely readership and tolerance towards protest literature that came to characterise the 1980s' censorship board as justifying the unbanning of the publication: 'The socio-political climate has changed radically. What this publication purports to propagate is well-known to all blacks, young and old. The publication contains nothing that has not appeared in the press on numerous occasions in the past and latitude must be allowed for political criticism.'[76]

The report signed by Steenkamp reads as a literary analysis of the novel's narrative, characters and plot, assessed against its alleged undesirability in terms of section 42 (2) (d) and (e) of the Publications Act. It is considered to be a 'border line case', as *Amandla*, while not undesirable is – confusingly – also 'not desirable'.[77] Alluding to the polysemic and compelling narrative technique, the report notes that 'even the omniscient narrator occasionally overtly interrupts the narrative by directly addressing the reader'. The intrusion of the reader within the narrative and the fine line between the voices of the writer and the narrator are alluded to when the report states that 'everything is explicitly stated; what Tlali is trying to say, is hurled at the reader, hammered into his consciousness'. This notion of the author 'hammering' messages into the readers' conscience depicts an image of a vulnerable reader, passively taking in what is read and easily influenced. This is problematic and the question is thus asked:

> Whether this book in the light of its likely readership and its probable effect on those readers, will contribute to a violation of state security, general welfare, peace and good order by contributing directly or indirectly to an overthrowing of the existing government and the system by extra-constitutional means: subversion, sabotage, public violence, civil disobedience, communist-inspired means and ideals.[78]

---

76. NASA, IDP, 3/158, Ref: P85/1/94, Tlali, 1985.
77. NASA, IDP, 3/158, Ref: P85/1/94, Tlali, 1985.
78. NASA, IDP, 3/158, Ref: P85/1/94, Tlali, 1985.

The impact of the book on its readership was therefore crucial in the deliberation process, which opened the way for the next section of the report, debating the likely readership. The size of the readership is assessed in relation to questions of authorship and special consideration is given to the effect a ban could have in terms of publicity:

> The fact that she is a well-known author, and a banned one at that, will create special attention for this novel. *Amandla* will be a popular novel. Sophisticated, educated black readers and those whites identifying with their cause as well as students of literature will probably be included in the likely readership [. . .] The *Staffrider* series aims at bringing new books at popular prices direct to the readers of the magazine.[79]

In this passage, three likely readerships are identified: 'the educated black reader', 'the white liberal reader' and 'students of literature', which differ greatly from the 'popular mass readership' considered in the initial decision.

Qualifying the novel as propagandistic, the report goes on to enumerate the techniques used by Tlali: 'misrepresentation', 'slanted facts', 'exaggeration' and 'distortion', which, in the opinion of Steenkamp, will be 'decoded' by 'enlightened' and 'erudite' readers familiar with literary conventions. Steenkamp further stipulates that because of the fact that the novel is 'no great, powerful and gripping literary work', the readers will hardly identify with its characters and heroes, and they will therefore not be considered as symbols of a wider context as 'Tlali has not succeeded in making her characterisation "a device for the pointing of vision or meaning"'.[80]

As for the alleged attack on the police in the book, the report once again focuses on 'enlightened readers', seemingly the preferred likely

---

79. NASA, IDP, 3/158, Ref: P85/1/94, Tlali, 1985.
80. NASA, IDP, 3/158, Ref: P85/1/94, Tlali, 1985.

reader with whom the censors identify, who 'will most probably judge the references to police atrocities within their own framework and regard the criticism and accusations as emotionally and politically inspired'. Steenkamp concedes that 'it is granted that the likely readership of *Staffrider* may include revolutionaries and potential revolutionaries. But these people will find their inspiration and incentive in publications of a more direct and inciting nature.'[81] Apart from this 'revolutionary reader', the prospective reaction of an illiterate and immature readership is weighed carefully relative to the clenched fist depicted on the cover of the book, prompting a recommendation in favour of restrictions on circulation:

> The problem is that if this book were to be displayed at cafés, illiterate Blacks, immature Blacks may interpret this sign as a call to violence and a display of their power by means of subversion, sabotage, etc. It is recommended that the display of this book in public spaces be prohibited and that it be sold in bookshops only.[82]

The report also asks whether it is 'practical to suggest a different cover design', interfering with the editorial publishing process. Once again, the alleged reactionary nature of an 'immature' mass readership is highlighted. Steenkamp concludes his report by speculating on the reactions of the various readerships:

> Many readers will probably be upset, annoyed and angered by this book (which sometimes gives the impression of being deliberately challenging and daring) – like I was – but in the light of impending reform of Black Education and the creation of a political forum for Blacks, the need for interracial debate, communication and compromise, as well as of the arguments expounded in the previous pages (likely readership, correctives, etc.), I do not think that it is absolutely necessary that this book

---

81. NASA, IDP, 3/158, Ref: P85/1/94, Tlali, 1985.
82. NASA, IDP, 3/158, Ref: P85/1/94, Tlali, 1985.

should be banned. Although not a desirable book, I consider this book not undesirable in the meaning of section 47 (2) (e) [. . .] This book will most probably be internationally distributed whatever the decision of the Publications Board. The tag: 'Banned in South Africa' will amount to an effective advertisement and free publicity. This, however, is not a relevant factor when the novel's undesirability or not is being considered.[83]

The expected reactions of the likely readership, combined with the qualities of the novel, provided enough justification for overturning the ban on the book. Moreover, the mention of political reforms illustrates the reformist approach adopted by the Appeal Board in the late 1980s, when a somewhat liberal attitude was adopted towards protest literature.

As is apparent from reports on *Staffrider* magazine and the Staffrider series, the recognition of a different set of aesthetics and themes in 'black literature' marks a change in the censors' discourse, where previously the literary was narrowly defined and articulated in terms of elitist standards and conventions. Moreover, the relative latitude granted to black South Africans shows greater complexity and more nuanced understanding of the imagined entity 'black readership'. It recognises that such a readership is diverse and identifies with the issues expressed in literature. The shift from a preoccupation with a mostly white likely readership interested in black literature to a black sophisticated readership – observable, for instance, in the report on the first issue of *Staffrider* and reports from the late 1980s – is also striking and indicates the censors' appreciation of the fact that a black readership is multifaceted and heterogeneous. It also resonates with Van Wyk's account of the heterogeneity of the readerships united around Ravan Press, where intellectuals, authors and readers from all walks of life found common ground in the literary experience of a magazine such as *Staffrider*.[84]

---

83. NASA, IDP, 3/158, Ref: P85/1/94, Tlali, 1985.
84. Van Wyk, interview.

Conclusion

The examples discussed above reveal the general trends adopted by the censorship boards. From a situation where the mere mention of the word 'communism' could warrant a ban, in terms of the Suppression of Communism Act No. 44 of 1950 applied by the Ministry of the Interior, the censorship discourse refined itself with the Publications and Entertainments Act No. 26 of 1963. The 1963 Act provided a space for literary considerations to be articulated against the backdrop of a developing hegemonic apartheid ideology imposed in the social sphere in general and on the literary field in particular. While aiming to protect the interests of those closer to the centres of power, the Act of 1963 was eventually put to the test when dissension on its fundamental principles emerged, leading to a reform of the system with the stricter Publications Act No. 42 of 1974.

Adopting a more direct political approach, the 1974 Act minimised the censors' literary considerations in favour of an increasingly political reading of publications submitted, which once again led to major divisions within the ranks of the Afrikaans intelligentsia. In a bid to appease protests from within, the Publications Amendment Act No. 109 of 1978 proposed a reformist approach, advocating an evaluation of the undesirability of a publication in the light of its likely readership and reintroducing a certain measure of literary reflection to censorship discourse. Although these amendments were passed in 1978, they initially mainly served white writers and were only fully implemented in the 1980s, as the cases above show.

Censors aimed at alienating writers from readers, and readers from one another, but they did not entirely succeed, as their intricate discussions and deliberations on the likely readership, for instance, were for the most part hypothetical and built on suppositions. Readers did not often conform to the likely reader typecast imagined by censors and most certainly did not always support the national project they promoted through their readings (Dick 2006: 10). These alternative reading patterns created a public 'with common visibility and common action', so that an alternative discourse could be articulated (Warner 2002b: 50).

Despite the censors' attempts to regulate reading, some readers seemingly developed their own reading patterns, which were not necessarily aligned to the censors' 'good reading' campaign. Censors tried to create 'book apartheid', in terms of which some books were good for some readers, while other were not, and in so doing tried to limit readers' exposure to allegedly subversive ideas. However, readers inevitably transcended the racial divisions imposed by censors and managed to get hold of books that were thought of as being undesirable for their category of reader. The variety of banned books read by the various alternative readers identified through primary and secondary sources in this book bears testimony to this complexity and shows how readers defied the censors in many ways. Censorship became a space where the links between arts and politics, and the essence of literary and serious literature, were debated. The censors' reports are but one of many spaces where literary discourses were articulated and contested, and tested against debates on similar issues occurring in alternative spaces. These debates influenced the socio-cultural landscape well into post-democratic South Africa, where traces of state censorship and similar debates on the socio-political functions of art and artists are as topical and at times nearly as controversial as they were during the apartheid period.

6 | Conclusion

> The future of literature in our country is inseparable from the
> future of democracy and the difficult task of working towards it.
> — Njabulo Ndebele, *The Rediscovery of the Ordinary*

APARTHEID CENSORSHIP WAS not created overnight. Building on explicit and implicit systems of thought control inherent to Dutch colonialism, British imperialism and Afrikaner nationalism, censorship was used as a political tool in the service of grand apartheid and influenced most aspects of public and private life, including the world of books and reading habits. These successive political regimes used the power of books and reading to enforce their hegemony, actively seeking to regulate the circulation of ideas and texts in South Africa, mainly through control over publishing and reading. With the institutionalisation of censorship in the early years of apartheid, censors imposed their authority as the official gatekeepers of the world of books. The application of censorship was based on imagined categories of readers and on speculation about how they would respond to books, leading to an implicit relationship between censors and readers, and between the workings of censorship and the reading cultures that existed it its shadow. Readers influenced the censors' reading protocols, playing an important role in their reading of books and in the elaboration of notions central to the censorship system, such as literariness, undesirability and likely readership. The literary discourses that developed with regard to censors and censorship in turn influenced broader literary criticism. Censorship inevitably impacted negatively on the provision of library services and the general availability of and access to books, shaping a period of South Africa's literary history that would have long-lasting consequences.

Reading was thus politicised, as was the world of books. While censorship indeed curbed the development of a thriving mainstream reading culture in South Africa, it led to the formation of an alternative reading culture, characterised by political activism and resistance, which coexisted with other marginalised everyday reading (Dick 2013). Through this alternative reading culture, dissident writers, publishers, booksellers, academics and readers created a space where the mainstream literary discourse was challenged. They altered the traditional functioning of the book system to bypass the repressive censorship apparatus, which was backed by a series of stringent laws, such as the Suppression of Communism Act No. 44 of 1950, the Publications and Entertainments Act No. 26 of 1963, the Publications Act No. 42 of 1974 and the Publications Amendment Act No. 109 of 1978. Progressive writers, readers, publishers, librarians and booksellers played an active role in this alternative book system, taking up the baton when the mainstream book industry would not risk dealing with banned books. These readers ensured that alternative books ran the full cycle typically followed by books, albeit in an unconventional and creative manner. Robert Darnton (2002: 10) illustrates this cycle as a communication circuit in which authors, publishers, printers, booksellers, and readers interact in a cyclical manner. In the context of the alternative reading culture discussed in this book, this communication circuit was subverted, remodelled and adapted. Close collaboration between the various actors of the book circuit ensued, creating spaces where culture and politics coincided through a mix of literary discussions and political debates. The cultural space effectively became political.

Reading and literacy were used for political advancement and activism, speaking to the competing usages of literacy. While literacy served the purposes of entertainment and education, in this particular case it was predominantly serving political ends. This reading culture informed broader debates on the function and aesthetics of arts and literature, discussing the relationship between 'art for art's sake' and 'committed art'. In this context, where the world of books was intrinsically political, Amilcar Cabral's observation that opposition and liberation movements find their roots in culture holds true in this case (1994: 56). However, the nature and shape of commitment and opposition were heavily debated in cultural and political circles alike, leading to various strands of resistance and literary activism.

This committed reading culture was closely linked to independent publishers, which often defied censorship. Censorship moderated the relations between readers, publishers and books, but did not succeed in fully alienating alternative publishers from their readers. Through joint struggles in the alternative circuit, the books published, circulated and read were diversified. While the readers imagined by censors did not always exist, alternative publishers catered for real readers, enabling a space where progressive and radical ideas and knowledge flowed. Alternative publishers, which were often breakaways from other publishers, opened up possibilities to respond to the needs of marginalised writers and readerships. Such is the case of Skotaville, for example, which was a publishing house created by and for black writers, and founded by Jaki Seroke when he left Ravan Press and Staffrider. From Skotaville came Seriti sa Sechaba, a black-owned publishing press founded by Dinah Lefakane that catered for black working-class women readers. These initiatives point to the existence of more ordinary reading cultures that would warrant further research – black working-class women readers being among them – whose voices need to be amplified and firmly rooted in the history of reading cultures in South Africa.

The predominance of the white middle-class perspective in the official history of reading in South Africa remains an issue to this day and creates problematic assumptions about contemporary reading cultures. The sparse South African literature on offer in mainstream bookshops and libraries leaves much to be desired and is certainly not a reflection of the wealth of literature produced in this country. Furthermore, book sales and library lending figures are not necessarily indicative of the number of readers, as one copy of a book might well circulate informally among many readers. As the history of alternative reading cultures that developed around banned books suggests, this gap in both bookshops and public library services does not necessarily translate into a lack of reading cultures in South Africa, but might speak to an inherently biased industry, rooted in a deeply divided and controversial literary and publishing history.

Several independent publishers and alternative literary initiatives ceased operation with the end of apartheid, as a result of the withdrawal of international funding and a relative loss of immediate relevance of anti-apartheid literature in a changing society, among other factors. Since the demise of apartheid censorship, independent publishers and bookstores, and progressive literary festivals and book-related events are thriving around the country, indicative of the presence of ordinary readers seeking alternatives to the commercial book industry. This could also indicate the predominance of as yet unchallenged principles and ideas upheld by the mainstream commercial book industry regarding books and reading that survived the democratic transition unchanged. An investigation into the extent and motives of present-day forms of censorship or attempts to curb freedom of speech could also shed light on the politics of the contemporary book industry in South Africa.

The history of the alternative readership of banned literature revisits some key concepts in the disciplines of literary studies and book history. Orality and literacy are entangled through the reading practices of ordinary readers in alternative spaces, where books are circulated in oral forms as well as photocopies, for instance, thus creating a wider readership. Far from upholding the contentious myth that African cultures rely on oral culture, the case of readers discussed in this book reveals that oral and written cultures can coexist, as can public and private reading habits (Dick 2013: 6). Some fundamental concepts inherent to book history, including definitions of reading, readers, books, literature, publishers, literacy and orality are questioned and redefined in this book. What is the relationship between the various actors in the world of books? What are the everyday reading practices of ordinary readers? Can a book transcend its materiality? Can a reader exist without a book, and conversely can a book exist without a reader? What is the future of the book, as we know it? These are important questions addressed by book history scholarship and through the study of alternative readerships for banned literature during apartheid.

This book suggests that readers of banned books during apartheid unsettled some fundamental principles upheld by the book industry and its guardians, the censors. Uncovering this alternative reading culture suggests that alternative conceptions of readers and books are possible. A book is multidimensional, being a technology, a carrier of ideology and discourse, and produced and consumed in specific social contexts. It can be read differently based on the material form and social context in which it is disseminated and reaches readers. Furthermore, innovative ways of studying reading can shed light on reading cultures and practices marginalised by dominant narratives of literary history. Archie Dick (2013: 4, 5) speaks of the surprising dissonance between South African ordinary readers' reading preferences and official book and library services designed for them, and the reading struggles led by such ordinary readers to assert their positions in these spaces of contradiction and influence. The case of politicised alternative reading practices under apartheid highlights this gap, which real readers were partly able to fill through their resourcefulness, claiming their own identity against what censors had imagined them to be.

Select Bibliography

Badat, Saleem. 1999. *Black Student Politics, Higher Education and Apartheid: From SASO to SANSCO, 1968–1990*. Pretoria: Human Sciences Research Council.

Barthes, Roland. 2002 [1967]. 'The Death of the Author'. In *The Book History Reader*, edited by David Finkelstein and Alistair McCleery, 221–4. London: Routledge.

Berger, Guy. 2000. 'Publishing for the People: The Alternative Press 1980–1999'. In *The Politics of Publishing in South Africa*, edited by Nicholas Evans and Monica Seeber, 73–106. Pietermaritzburg: University of Natal Press.

Biko, Steve. 1970. 'Editorial'. *SASO Newsletter* (August): 1. http://disa.ukzn.ac.za/sites/default/files/pdf_files/saaug70.pdf.

———. 1978. *I Write What I Like*. London: Heinemann.

———, ed. 1972. *Black Viewpoint*. Johannesburg: SPRO-CAS.

Bourdieu, Pierre. 1994 [1984]. 'Mais qui a créé les créateurs?' In *Littérature et société*, edited by Jacques Pelletier, 277–91. Montreal: VLB.

Bozzoli, Belinda. 2004. 'The Taming of the Illicit: Bounded Rebellion in South Africa, 1986'. *Comparative Studies in Society and History* 46, no. 1: 326–53.

Brink, André. 1983. 'Censorship and Literature'. In *Censorship: A Study of Censorship in South Africa by Five Distinguished Authors*, edited by Theo Coggin, 37–54. Johannesburg: South African Institute of Race Relations.

Brutus, Dennis. 2006. *Poetry and Protest*. Pietermaritzburg: University of KwaZulu-Natal Press.

Cabral, Amilcar. 1994 [1973]. 'National Liberation and Culture'. In *Colonial Discourse and Post-colonial Theory*, edited by Patrick Williams and Laura Chrisman, 53–65. London: Harvester Wheatsheaf.

Chapman, Michael. 2003. *Southern African Literatures*. Pietermaritzburg: University of Natal Press.

———. 2007. *Soweto Poetry: Literary Perspectives*. Pietermaritzburg: University of KwaZulu-Natal Press.

Chartier, Roger. 1989. 'Texts, Printing, Readings'. In *The New Cultural History*, edited by Lynn Hunt, 15-175. Berkeley: University of California Press.

———. 2002a [1992]. 'Labourers and Voyagers: From the Text to the Reader'. In *The Book History Reader*, edited by David Finkelstein and Alistair McCleery, 47-58. London: Routledge.

———. 2002b [1989]. 'The Practical Impact of Writing'. In *The Book History Reader*, edited by David Finkelstein and Alistair McCleery, 118-42. London: Routledge.

Clayton, Cherry. 1993. 'Women's Writing: What's New in South Africa?' *Southern Africa Report* 9, no. 1: 30.

Cloete, Dick. 2000. 'Alternative Publishing in South Africa in the 1970s and 1980s'. In *The Politics of Publishing in South Africa*, edited by Nicholas Evans and Monica Seeber, 43-72. Pietermaritzburg: University of Natal Press.

Cobley, Alan. 1997. 'Literacy, Libraries and Consciousness: The Provision of Library Services for Blacks in South Africa in the Pre-apartheid Era'. *Libraries and Culture* 32, no. 1: 57-80.

Coetzee, J.M. 1996. *Giving Offense: Essays on Censorship*. Chicago: University of Chicago Press.

Coggin, Theo, ed. 1983. *Censorship: A Study of Censorship in South Africa by Five Distinguished Authors*. Johannesburg: South African Institute of Race Relations.

Darnton, Robert. 1982. *The Literary Underground of the Old Regime*. Cambridge: Harvard University Press.

———. 2002. 'What is the History of the Book?' In *The Book History Reader*, edited by David Finkelstein and Alistair McCleery, 9-26. London: Routledge.

Davis, Caroline. 2005. 'The Politics of Postcolonial Publishing: Oxford University Press's Three Crown Series 1962-1976'. *Book History* 8: 227-44.

———. 2011. 'Histories of Publishing under Apartheid: Oxford University Press in South Africa'. *Journal of Southern African Studies* 37, no. 1: 79-98.

Davis, Caroline and David Johnson, eds. 2015. *The Book in Africa: Critical Debates*. London: Palgrave Macmillan.

De Certeau, Michel. 1984. *The Practice of Everyday Life*. Berkeley: University of California Press.

De Kok, Ingrid and Karen Press, eds. 1990. *Spring is Rebellious: Arguments about Cultural Freedom by Albie Sachs and Respondents*. Cape Town: Buchu Books.

De Lange, Margreet. 1997. *The Muzzled Muse: Literature and Censorship in South Africa*. Amsterdam: John Benjamins.

Dick, Archie. 2004a. 'Book Burning and the Complicity of South African Librarians'. *Innovation* 28 (June): 31-40.

———. 2004b. 'Building a Nation of Readers? Women's Organizations and the Politics of Reading in South Africa, 1900-1914'. *Historia* 49, no. 2: 23-44.

———. 2006. 'Book History, Library History and South Africa's Reading Culture'. *South African Historical Journal* 55: 33-45.

———. 2007a. 'Censorship and the Reading Practices of Political Prisoners in South Africa, 1960-1990'. *Innovation* 35 (December): 24-55.

———. 2007b. 'The Development of South African Libraries in the 19th and 20th Centuries: Cultural and Political Influences'. In *Libraries for the Future: Progress and Development of South African Libraries*, edited by T.J.D. Bothma, P. Underwood and P. Ngulube, 13-24. Pretoria: LIASA.

———. 2013. *The Hidden History of South Africa's Book and Reading Cultures*. Toronto: University of Toronto Press.

Du Toit, André. 1983. 'The Rationale of Controlling Political Publications'. In *Censorship: A Study of Censorship in South Africa by Five Distinguished Authors*, edited by Theo Coggin, 81-129. Johannesburg: South African Institute of Race Relations.

Escarpit, Robert. 1971. *Sociology of Literature*. Translated by Ernest Pick. London: Frank Cass.

Everts, R. Alain. 1993. 'The Pioneers: Herbert Isaac Ernest Dhlomo and the Development of Library Service for the African in South Africa'. *World Libraries* 3, no. 2: n.p.

Fanon, Frantz. 1994 [1961]. 'On National Culture'. In *Colonial Discourse and Post-colonial Theory*, edited by Patrick Williams and Laura Chrisman, 36-52. London: Harvester Wheatsheaf.

Fiske, John. 1987. *Television Culture*. London: Routledge.

Gee, James Paul. 1996. *Social Linguistics and Literacies: Ideology in Discourses*. London: Taylor and Francis.

Gordimer, Nadine. 1973. *New Black Poetry*. Johannesburg: SPRO-CAS and Ravan Press.

———. 1988. 'Censorship and the Artist'. *Staffrider* 7, no. 2: 11-16.

Gray, Stephen. 2005. *Indaba: Interviews with African Writers*. Pretoria: Protea Book House.

Hachten, William A. and C. Anthony Giffard. 1984. *The Press and Apartheid: Repression and Propaganda in South Africa*. Madison: University of Wisconsin Press.

Heywood, Christopher. 2004. *A History of South African Literature*. Cambridge: Cambridge University Press.

Hofmeyr, Isabel. 1985. 'Setting Free the Books: The David Philip AfricaSouth Paperback'. *English in Africa* 12, no. 1: 83-94.

———. 1993. *'We Spend Our Years Like a Tale That is Told': Oral Historical Narrative in a South African Chiefdom*. Johannesburg: Wits University Press.

———. 1996. 'Response to Burn and Taylor'. In *Transgressing Boundaries: New Directions in the Study of Culture in Africa*, edited by Brenda Cooper and Andrew Steyn, 114–15. Cape Town: University of Cape Town Press.

———. 2001. 'Metaphorical Books'. *Current Writing* 13, no. 2: 100–8.

———. 2004. 'Popular Literature in Africa: Post-resistance Perspectives'. *Social Dynamics* 30, no. 2: 128–40.

———. 2005. 'The Globe in the Text: Towards a Transnational History of the Book'. *African Studies* 64, no. 1: 87–103.

Hofmeyr, Isabel and Lize Kriel. 2006. 'Book History in Southern Africa: What is it and Why Should it Interest Historians?' *South African History Journal* 55: 1–19.

Horrell, Muriel. 1963. *Action, Reaction and Counteraction: A Companion Booklet to 'Legislation and Race Relations'*. Johannesburg: South African Institute of Race Relations.

———. 1966. *A Survey of Race Relations in South Africa of 1965*. Johannesburg: South African Institute of Race Relations.

Jacobsen's Index of Objectionable Literature: Customs and Excise Act No. 55 of 1955 and Publication Act 42 of 1974 – Containing a Complete List of All Publications in Alphabetical Order, Together with Authors, Prohibited from Importation into the Republic of South Africa [. . .]. 1974. Pretoria: Jacobsen's Publishers.

Johns, Adrian. 2002. 'The Book of Nature and the Nature of the Book'. In *The Book History Reader*, edited by David Finkelstein and Alistair McCleery, 59–76. London: Routledge.

Johns, Sheridan and R. Hunt Davis. 1991. *Mandela, Tambo, and the African National Congress*. Oxford: Oxford University Press.

Kagan, Alfred. 2015. 'Library and Information Workers Organisation (LIWO)'. In *Progressive Library Organisations: A Worldwide History*, 7–52. Jefferson: McFarland.

Leach, A., J.A. Verbeek and C.S. Stilwell. 1994. 'The Reading of Black South Africans: A Historical Overview'. *African Journal of Libraries, Archives and Information Science* 4, no. 1: 1–13.

Le Roux, Elizabeth. 2012. 'The University as Publisher: Towards a History of South African University Presses'. In *Print, Text and Book Cultures in South Africa*, edited by Andrew van der Vlies, 437–48. Johannesburg: Wits University Press.

Lodge, Tom. 1983. *Black Politics in South Africa since 1945*. Johannesburg: Ravan Press.

Lyons, Martyn and Lucy Taksa. 1992. *Australian Readers Remember: An Oral History of Reading 1890–1930*. Melbourne: Oxford University Press.

Mackay, Hugh. 1997. 'Introduction'. In *Consumption and Everyday Life*, 1–12. London: Sage and Open University Press.

Magaziner, Daniel R. 2010. *The Law and the Prophets: Black Consciousness in South Africa, 1968–1977*. Ohio: Ohio University Press.

Mandela, Nelson. 1995. *Long Walk to Freedom*. London: Lancaster-Abacus.

Mashishi, Thapelo. 2000. 'The Storage Place of Tradition: The Reading Experience of Black Adults in African Languages'. *Reading Africa* 83: 75–84.

McDonald, Peter D. 2004. 'The Writer, the Critic, and the Censors'. *Book History* 7: 285–302.

———. 2009. *The Literature Police: Apartheid and its Cultural Consequences*. London: Oxford University Press.

Merrett, Christopher. 1994. *A Culture of Censorship: Secrecy and Intellectual Repression in South Africa*. Cape Town: David Philip.

Modisane, Bloke. 1998 [1963]. *Blame Me on History*. Johannesburg: Ad Donker.

Moss, Glenn. 1987. 'Ten Years of *Work in Progress*'. *Work in Progress* 50/51 (October/November): 37–46.

Motlhabi, Mokgethi. 1984. *The Theory and Practice of Black Resistance to Apartheid: A Social-Ethical Analysis*. Johannesburg: Skotaville.

Mpe, Phaswane and Monica Seeber. 2000. 'The Politics of Book Publishing in South Africa: A Critical Overview'. In *The Politics of Publishing in South Africa*, edited by Nicholas Evans and Monica Seeber, 15–42. Pietermaritzburg: University of Natal Press.

Mzamane, Mbulelo Vizikhungo. 1991. 'The Impact of Black Consciousness on Culture'. In *Bounds of Possibility: The Legacy of Steve Biko and Black Consciousness*, edited by N. Barney Pityana, M. Ramphele, M. Mpumlwana and L. Wilson, 179–93. Cape Town: David Philip.

Naidoo, Beverley, ed. 1984. *Censoring Reality: An Examination of Books on South Africa*. Proceedings of a conference on racism in educational media. London: ILEA Centre for Anti-racism Education and the British Defence and Aid Fund for Southern Africa.

Ndebele, Njabulo. 1991. *The Rediscovery of the Ordinary*. Johannesburg: COSAW.

———. 1992. 'South African Literature and the Construction of Nationhood'. *Staffrider* 10, no. 4: 23–5.

———. 2007. *Fine Lines from the Box: Further Thoughts about Our Country*. Johannesburg: Umuzi.

Newell, Stephanie. 2002a. *Literary Culture in Colonial Ghana: 'How to Play the Game of Life'*. Manchester: Manchester University Press.

———, ed. 2002b. *Readings in African Popular Fiction*. Bloomington: Indiana University Press.
Newell, Stephanie, T. Barringer, I. Hofmeyr and P. Mpe. 2000. 'Introduction'. *Reading Africa* 83: 3-10.
Ngũgĩ wa Thiong'o. 1997 [1981]. *Writers in Politics: Essays*. Oxford: James Currey.
Nkosi, Lewis. 1983 [1965]. *Home and Exile and Other Selections*. London: Longman.
———. 2016a [1990]. 'Bloke Modisane: *Blame Me on History*'. In *Writing Home: Lewis Nkosi on South African Writing*, edited by Lindy Stiebel and Michael Chapman, 247-63. Pietermaritzburg: University of KwaZulu-Natal Press.
———. 2016b [1965]. 'Fiction by Black South Africans'. In *Writing Home: Lewis Nkosi on South African Writing*, edited by Lindy Stiebel and Michael Chapman, 49-61. Pietermaritzburg: University of KwaZulu-Natal Press.
———. 2016c [1986]. 'South African Fiction: Writers at the Barricade'. In *Writing Home: Lewis Nkosi on South African Writing*, edited by Lindy Stiebel and Michael Chapman, 231-7. Pietermaritzburg: University of KwaZulu-Natal Press.
———. 2016d [1981]. 'Southern Africa: Protest and Commitment'. In *Writing Home: Lewis Nkosi on South African Writing*, edited by Lindy Stiebel and Michael Chapman, 63-108. Pietermaritzburg: University of KwaZulu-Natal Press.
Okri, Ben. 1997. *A Way of Being Free*. London: Phoenix House.
Oliphant, Andries. 2000. 'From Colonialism to Democracy: Writers and Publishing in South Africa'. In *The Politics of Publishing in South Africa*, edited by Nicholas Evans and Monica Seeber, 107-26. Pietermaritzburg: University of Natal Press.
Ong, Walter. 1982. *Orality and Literacy: The Technologizing of the Word*. New York: Methuen.
Peterson, Bhekizizwe. 1991. 'The Black Bulls of H.I.E. Dhlomo: Ordering History out of Nonsense'. *English in Africa* 18: 25-49.
Philip, David. 1990. 'Book Publishing under and after Apartheid'. In *Book Publishing in South Africa for the 1990s: Proceedings of a Symposium Held at the South African Library, Cape Town, 22-25 November, 1989*, 9-21. Cape Town: South African Library.
Radway, Janice. 1984. *Reading the Romance: Women, Patriarchy, and Popular Literature*. Chapel Hill: University of North Carolina Press.
Ramphele, Mamphela. 1995. *A Life*. Cape Town: David Philip.
Rose, Jonathan. 2001. *The Intellectual Life of the British Working Classes*. New Haven: Yale University Press.
Sachs, Albie. 1990. 'Preparing Ourselves for Freedom'. In *Spring is Rebellious: Arguments about Cultural Freedom by Albie Sachs and Respondents*, edited by Ingrid de Kok and Karen Press, 19-29. Cape Town: Buchu Books.

Sandwith, Corinne. 2014. *World of Letters: Reading Communities and Cultural Debates in Early Apartheid South Africa*. Pietermaritzburg: University of KwaZulu-Natal Press.

Silver, Louise. 1984. *A Guide to Political Censorship in South Africa*. Johannesburg: University of the Witwatersrand Press.

Stadler, Alf. 1975. 'Anxious Radicals: SPRO-CAS and the Apartheid Society'. *Journal of Southern African Studies* 2, no. 1 (October): 102-8.

Stilwell, Christine. 1993. 'More Than Mere Novel Reading: An Examination of Proactive South African Librianship'. In *Proceedings of the Info Africa Nova Conference 1993*, 91-118. Pretoria: Info Africa Nova.

———. 1994. 'Towards Transformation? An Update on the Resource Centre Fora of South Africa'. *International Information and Library Review* 26: 303-13.

Street, Brian. 1996. 'Preface'. In *The Social Uses of Literacy: Theory and Practice in Contemporary South Africa*, edited by Mastin Prinsloo and Mignonne Breier, 1-10. Cape Town: John Benjamins Publishing.

Stubbs, Aelred. 2004 [1978]. 'Martyr of Hope: A Personal Memoir'. In *Steve Biko, I Write What I Like*, 175-244. Johannesburg: Picador Africa.

Thale, Mary. 1995. 'Women in London Debating Societies in 1780'. *Gender & History* 7, no. 1: 5-24.

Thompson, Leonard. 2000. *A History of South Africa*. Johannesburg: Jonathan Ball.

Van der Vlies, Andrew, ed. 2012. *Print, Text and Book Cultures in South Africa*. Johannesburg: Wits University Press.

Van Rooyen, J.C.W. 1987. *Censorship in South Africa*. Cape Town: Juta.

Warner, Michael. 2002a. *Public and Counterpublics*. New York: MIT Press.

———. 2002b. 'Publics and Counterpublics'. *Public Culture* 14, no. 1: 49-90.

Wilson, Lindy. 1991. 'Bantu Steve Biko: A Life'. In *Bounds of Possibility: The Legacy of Steve Biko and Black Consciousness*, edited by N. Barney Pityana, M. Ramphele, M. Mpumlwana and L. Wilson, 15-77. Cape Town: David Philip.

Index

Aan Martha: Brieven van Robbeneiland
  (Dennis Brutus) *see Letters to*
  Martha and Other Poems from a South
  African Prison
Abrahams, Lionel 76
Abrahams, Peter 79, 103
Achebe, Chinua 80
An Act of Immorality (Des Troye) 28,
  105, 159-61
Acts of Parliament
  Bantu Education (47 of 1953) 14, 84,
    93
  Customs Management (9 of 1913) 11,
    14, 24, 147-8
  Entertainments Censorship (28 of
    1931) 11-12, 147, 148
  Film and Publications (65 of 1996)
    47
  General Law Amendment (Sabotage,
    76 of 1962) 24, 30, 177
  General Law Amendment (101 of
    1969) 30
  Internal Security (74 of 1982) 43
  Obscene Publications (31 of 1892)
    11, 147
  Post Office (44 of 1958) 14
  Publications (42 of 1974) 10, 37, 38,
    41, 43-4, 46, 47, 88, 93, 107, 112,
    146, 161-4, 171, 172, 175, 178, 179,
    180, 182, 183, 187-8, 189, 191,
    200, 201, 205, 208
  Publications Amendment (109 of
    1978) 39, 41, 46, 146, 164-5,
    172, 178, 180, 183, 184, 186, 199,
    200-1, 205, 208
  Publications Amendment (90 of
    1992) 46-7
  Publications and Entertainments (26
    of 1963) 21, 23-6, 27, 29-30, 35,
    38, 41, 49, 90, 93, 105, 107, 108,
    146, 147, 150, 151-60, 161, 167,
    169-70, 182, 184, 205, 208
  Reservation of Separate Amenities
    (49 of 1953) 84-5
  Suppression of Communism (44 of
    1950) 12-14, 15, 18, 24, 30, 31, 33,
    48, 93, 107, 108, 110, 111, 112-13,
    134, 147, 148, 149, 166, 171-2, 177,
    205, 208
  Suppression of Communism
    Amendment (97 of 1965) 64
  Terrorism (83 of 1967) 30

Ad Donker (publisher) 76
Africa My Beginning (Ingoapele Madingoane) 70
Africa South 109
African-American literature 103, 130
African Bookman (publisher) 64
The African Image (Es'kia Mphahlele) 167
African language books 56
African Library Association of South Africa 85
African National Congress 129, 163
African Writers' Association 73
African Writers Series (Heinemann) 79, 80, 110, 115, 179, 180
AfricaSouth Paperbacks series 66
Afrikaans literary avant-garde and intellegentsia 21-2, 27, 35-6, 39, 56-7, 60, 74-5, 150, 152, 205
Afrikaans literature 20, 27, 35, 41, 49-50, 56-7, 150, *see also* publishers and publications, Afrikaans
Afrikaans Writers' Circle 22, 27, 37, 152
Afrikaanse Pers-Boekhandel (APB) 57
Afrikaanse Skrywersgilde (Afrikaans Writers' Guild) 36, 75
Afrikaanse Studentebond 66
Afrikaner nation 19 n.2, 20, 21-2, 54, 150
Aksie vir Morele Standaarde (Action for Moral Values) 39
Alan Paton Centre (Pietermaritzburg) 119
Alexandra (Johannesburg) 129, 131

Alienation and the Body in Racist Society (Noel Chabani Manganyi) 102
Amandla (Miriam Tlali) 93, 199-204
autobiographies 7, 102, 110
The Autobiography of Kwame Nkrumah 109

banned and listed persons 13, 14, 29, 30-1, 33, 48, 66, 79, 148, 166, 171, 176
banned organisations 14, 29, 43
banned publications, *see also* specific titles
  academic exemptions 18, 86-7
  Afrikaans 34-5, 39, 40, 60
  ambiguities in law 171-2, 176
  appeals 35, 36, 37-8, 40-1, 42, 46-7, 66, 151, 158, 164, 173-6, 178-9, 181-2, 186, 189, 191-5, 198-9, 200-4, *see also* unbanning of
  covers of 203
  distribution and dissemination 77-80, 88, 94-5, 114, 117-18, 120-1, 125, 126, 189
  effect on academic research 86-7
  hiding places for 118-19, 128
  in libraries 116, 127-8
  mutilation of 92
  photocopying of 121-2, 127, 144
  possession prohibited 18, 38, 113
  statistics 13-14, 27, 30, 32, 107-8, 112, 118
  and trials 111
  unbanning of 45-6, 47, 165, 176, 182-3, 184

Bantu Education 55
Bantu Men's Social Centre (Johannesburg) 81, 82, 83, 101
Barnard, Chris 22, 57
Bateleur Press 76
Bible 136
bibliocide *see* book burning
bibliodiversity 53-4
Biko, Steve Bantu 33, 66, 67, 68, 79, 80, 88, 102, 104, 105, 124, 135, 136-7
Bills (parliamentary)
  Film and Publications 47
  South African Languages 56
  Undesirable Publications (1960) 19, 21
BLAC Publishing 76
Black Community Programmes (BCP) 67, 68-9
Black Consciousness Movement (BCM) 32-3, 34, 67, 68, 70, 124, 130, 131, 135, 141, 143, 189
Black Review 67
Black Viewpoint 67-8
black writers *see* writers, black
Blame Me on History (Bloke Modisane) 14, 108-9, 123, 154-6
'Blood River' (Dennis Brutus) 179
Bloom, J.J. 28
Board of Censors *see* Publications Control Board
book burning 89-90
booksellers and bookshops 90-2, 94, 96, 113-15, 144, 209-10, *see also* specific names

Bosman, M. 182
Botha, P.W. 19, 41, 165
Braamfontein (Johannesburg) 135
Breytenbach, Breyten 22, 35, 51, 57-8, 60, 76, 157, 178
Brink, André 22, 23, 35-6, 48, 57-8, 78
Brown, Susan 105
Bruin, John *see* Brutus, Dennis
Brutus, Dennis 14, 31, 103, 104, 110, 111, 121, 122-3, 133-4, 177-8, 179, 183-4
Bunting, Brian 30
Buren Publishers 60, 76
Burger's Daughter (Nadine Gordimer) 46
Buthelezi, Mangosuthu 47

Call Me Not a Man (Mtutuzeli Matshoba) 46, 70, 72, 110
Cannon, Fred 92
Cape Coloured Carnegie Library Services 82
Cape Library Assistants Section 88
Cape Library Association 88
Cape Town Library Services 90
Carnegie Non-European Travelling Library and Library Services 82, 83, 101
Carnegie report on libraries (1929) *see* libraries, Carnegie report
Castro, Fidel 110
censors and censorship
  apartheid 2-3, 5, 6-7, 8, 9, 12, 14, 17-18, 20, 22, 23, 24, 27-30, 35, 37-9, 40-6, 48-52, 54-5, 60, 61,

62, 71, 74, 93-4, 96, 98, 107, 139, 140, 141, 145, 146, 147, 148-206, 207-8
  colonial 11-12, 24, 49, 51, 146, 147-8, 207
  post-apartheid 46-7, 206
  self- *see* self-censorship
  writing on 9-11
Central News Agency (CNA) 30, 91
Césaire, Aimé 88, 104, 134, 137, 140
China Poems (Dennis Brutus) 182-3
Chirundu (Es'kia Mphahlele) 167
Chocolates for my Wife (Todd Matshikiza) 109
Christian Institute 67, 69
Civil Liberty in South Africa (Edgar Brookes) 65
The Classic 73
Cloete, T.T. 152, 167
CNA Literary award 39
Coalition of the Free Book 56-7
Coetzee, Abraham 42, 46, 146, 165, 191-2, 195
Coetzee, Ampie 75
Coetzee, J.M. 124
Commission of Enquiry in Regard to Undesirable Publications (Cronjé, 1954-7) 17-19, 20, 21, 23, 37, 150-1
The Communist Manifesto 57
Communist Party of South Africa 12, 100, 163
The Companion to South Africa English Literature 76
Cone, James 104

Congress of South African Trade Unions 143-4
Congress of South African Writers (COSAW) 72
Contact 91
Conyngham, John 76
Council of Unions of South Africa 144
Cronjé, Geoffrey 17, 19-20
Cronjé Commission *see* Commission of Enquiry in Regard to Undesirable Publications
Cry Freedom (film) 43
Cry Rage (edited by James Matthews and Gladys Thomas) 32, 67
Cullinan, Patrick 76
Currey, James 80
customs officials 92, 113, 117-18, 147-8, 170, 171, 179

Dadoo, Yusuf 111
Darkness at Noon (Arthur Koestler) 103
David Philip Publishers 62, 65, 66, 76, 77-8, 79, 94
De Jager-Haum (publisher) 56
De Jong (Johannesburg bookshop) 113
Dekker, Gerrit 26-7, 28, 32, 88, 146, 151-2, 160, 161, 167, 169-70, 177
Department of Bantu Education 84
Detention and Torture in South Africa (edited by Don Foster and Dennis Davis) 77-8
detention without trial 13, 29, 43, 77
Dhlomo, H.I.E. 82-4, 101, 102
Dhlomo, R.R.R. 83
Directorate of Publications 37, 38, 47

District Six (Cape Town) 99
Donga 185
Down Second Avenue (Es'kia Mphahlele) 80, 103, 108, 110, 123, 128, 166, 167-72, 176-7
Down Second Avenue: The Comic (adapted by Mzwakhe Nhlabati) 172-6, 177
Drum 108, 109
A Dry White Season (André Brink) 46, 78
Du Bois, W.E.B. 102. 106, 110
Du Plessis, I.D. 57
Du Plooy, C.J.W. 185, 187
Du Toit, André 86

East African Literature Bureau 79
East African Publishing House 166
Eiselen Commission on Native Education (1951) 84
Eisenstein, Raymond 29
Els, J.M. 198
Endemann, T.M.H. 152, 167-8, 169, 170
exile 13, 31, 51, 117, 131
The Eye of the Needle (Rick Turner) 67

Faber & Faber (publisher) 80, 166
Fanon, Frantz 88, 102, 104, 137, 140, 143
Federasie van Afrikaanse Kultuurvereniginge (Federation of Afrikaans Cultural Associations) 36
Fifteen Group 132
Film and Publications Board 47

Film and Publications Review Board 47
films 148
First, Ruth 29, 30
Fischer, Bram 92
Fools and Other Stories (Njabulo Ndebele) 134
Forced Landing (Mothobi Mutloatse) 44
Fort Hare University Press 62
Frank Talk *see* Biko, Steve Bantu
Freedom Charter 43
freedom of speech, ideas and knowledge 3, 22, 23
Fugard, Athol 23, 76

Garvey, Marcus 110
Go Well, Stay Well (Hannah Stanton) 109
The Godfather (Mario Puzzo) 111
Gone with the Wind (Margaret Mitchell) 111, 133
Gordimer, Nadine 23-4, 31, 41-2, 43, 46, 48, 51, 52, 80
Government Gazette 30, 38, 113
Gramsci, Antonio 110
Great Gap (silent decade of the 1960s) 6, 10, 31-2, 33, 65
Grové, A.P. 152, 167, 168, 169, 170
Gwala, Mafika Pascal 76

Handbook of Black Organisations 67
Harvey, C.J.D. 32, 152, 156-7, 158, 170
Head, Bessie 76, 79
Heinemann (publisher) 58, 59, 79, 80
Hepple, Alexander 19

Hertzog Prize 39, 40
Higher than Hope (Fatima Meer) 73
Hodder & Stoughton (publisher) 58, 72
Hope, Christopher 123
Hope and Suffering (Desmond Tutu) 73
Horn, Peter 178
house arrest 13
Human & Rousseau (publisher) 40, 56, 57, 75, 164
Human Sciences Research Council 86
Hutchinson, Alfred 31

I Write What I Like (Steve Biko) 80, 109, 121, 127
imported and smuggled books 11, 12, 14, 17, 18, 50, 60, 113, 117, 132
In Corner B and Other Stories (Es'kia Mphahlele) 167
Inanda Seminary 81
Inkululeko 117
Innovation: Journal of Appropriate Librarianship and Information Work in South Africa 85
Inside (Jeremy Cronin) 134
International Club (Durban) 84

Jacobsen's Index of Objectionable Literature 107, 113
Jansen, J.P. 32, 181
Jazz (Rex Harris) 103
Jensma, Wopko 178
J.L. van Schaik (publisher) 55
Jol'iinkomo (Mafika Gwala) 38
Jonker, Abraham 21, 151

Jonker, Ingrid 22, 57, 74-5
Joubert, W.A. 154, 155-6
journalists 15, 16, 177
Juta & Company (publisher) 56

Kathrada, Ahmed 136
Kennis van die aand (*Looking on Darkness*, André Brink) 34-5
Khoapa, Bennie 67
'Die kind wat doodgeskiet is deur soldate by Nyanga' (Ingrid Jonker) 74-5
King, Martin Luther 135
Kirkwood, Mike 70, 71, 72
Kol 58
Kolbe, Vincent 116
Krige, Uys 57
Kruger, J.J. 146, 161, 171-2
Kruger, J.T. 37
Kruger, Jannie 32
Kruger Commission (1973) 34
Kunene, Daniel P. 178
Kunene, Mazisi 31, 178
Kuper, Leo 92-3

La Guma, Alex 31, 80, 102, 110, 115, 122-3, 148-9
Lady Chatterley's Lover (D.H. Lawrence) 45
Langa, Mandla 102, 114-15
Lefakane, Dinah 74, 209
Leighton, J.M. 32
Lenin Club 82, 99
Leroux, Etienne 23, 39, 40, 57, 164
Let my People Go (Albert Luthuli) 109

Letters to Martha and Other Poems from a South African Prison (Dennis Brutus) 178-80
Lewin, Hugh 29
Liberal Party 119
liberation theology 69
librarians 28, 82, 85, 88-90, 96, 113, 116
libraries
  academic 86-7, 94, 116
  alternative *see* resource centres
  for blacks 80-3, 84-5
  Carnegie report on (1929) 82
  post-liberation 95
  public 89-90, 91, 132, 208, 209-10
  segregation of 82, 84-5
Library and Information Workers' Organisation (LIWO) 85
Liebenberg, Ernst 75
Lighton, R.E. 32, 180, 181, 186
literacy 3-4, 81, 101-2, 142, 208-9
Longman Green (publisher) 56, 58
Looking on Darkness (André Brink) *see Kennis van die aand*
Louw, Eric 15
Lovedale Institution 81
Lovedale Press 55
Luthuli, Albert 23

Macmillan (publisher) 58, 166
Madingoane, Ingoapele 178
Magersfontein, O Magersfontein! (Etienne Leroux) 39, 40-1, 45, 163-4
Malan, E.G. 163
Malan, Jacques 57

Malcolm X 104, 110, 135
Mandela, Nelson 46, 92, 111
Mao Tse-tung 106, 110
Maré, Gerhard 105, 134
Marquard, Leo 65, 92
Matshikiza, Todd 31
Mattera, Don 136
Matthews, James 76, 178
Mbari Publications 79, 80, 122
Mbeki, Govan 30, 64
McGraw-Hill (publisher) 58, 59
Mgxashe, Mxolisi 106
Mhudi (Sol T. Plaatje) 55
Miles, John 75
Millin, Sarah Gertrude 22
missions 11, 49, 55, 81, 99, 100
Modisane, Bloke 31, 155
Mokhele, Tsoeu 117
Mokoena, Papi 122
Moment of Truth: A Collection of Poems (Portia Rankoane) 74
Morija Training Institution 81
Morrell, D.M. 196-7
Moss, Glenn 69, 71, 105, 125-6
Mphahlele, Es'kia 31, 45, 50, 64, 73, 115, 166-7, 171, 174, 176
Mtshali, Oswald 76
Mulder, Connie 164
Muriel at Metropolitan (Miriam Tlali) 45-6, 93
Murray, A.H. 152, 160, 167-8, 170, 178-9, 180, 181
Mutloatse, Mothobi 70, 73
Mzamane, Mbulelo Vizikhungo 72

Nakasa, Nat 115
Nasionale Pers (Naspers) 55, 56, 57
Natal Provincial Library 90
National Party (NP) 50, 54, 56, 59, 148, 152
National Union of South African Students (NUSAS) 66
Naudé, Beyers 67, 69
Naught for your Comfort (Trevor Huddleston) 109
Ndebele, Njabulo 108-9, 123
New Era Fellowship 99
Newspaper Press Union (NPU) 16, 17
Nienaber, G.S. 32
Nkosi, Lewis 31, 79, 102, 115, 156
Nkrumah, Kwame 106, 109, 110
Nolwazi Publishers 74
Non-European Public Library (Johannesburg) 83
Non-European United Front (NEUF) 99, 100
Non-European Unity Movement (NEUM) 99, 100

Observer 92
The Ochre People (Noni Jabavu) 109
O'Connor, T.P. 148
Oliphant, Andries 72
On Liberty (John Locke) 103
'On the Island' (Dennis Brutus) 179
Oomblik in die wind (André Brink) 75-6, 77
Open Books (Cape Town bookshop) 113-14, 193
Opperman, D.J. 21, 36

orality 4, 138, 210
Oxford History of South Africa (edited by Monica Wilson and Leonard Thompson) 92-3
Oxford University Press (OUP) Southern Africa 56, 58-9, 65, 92-3

PEN South Africa (PEN SA) 21, 22, 27-8, 37, 73, 151
Penguin (publisher) 58, 80
Penguin African Library series 30
People and Policies of South Africa (Leo Marquard) 65
People's College Comics Series 173
Perskorporasie van Suid-Afrika (Perskor) 55, 56, 57
Peterson, S.P. 22
Philip, David 31, 61, 65, 92
Philip, Marie 65
Phillips, Ray 83
Pienaar, Louis 46
Pieterse, Cosmo 31
Pityana, Barney 33, 66, 67, 79, 102
Poems from Algiers (Dennis Brutus) 181
poetry 32-3, 34, 38, 76, 130-1, 134, 136, 138, 156-7, 162, 163, 178-84, 185, 187, 189, 194, 198
Poets to the People: South African Freedom Poems (edited by Barry Feinberg) 162, 163
political trials 29, 111
Post 16
Press Code 27
Press Commission (1950-64) 15-16, 17

Press Council 16, 17
Pretorius, J.L. 37, 40
Prog (publisher) 76
pseudonyms 104–5
Publications Appeal Board (PAB) 18, 37–8, 39, 40–1, 42, 44, 47, 71, 164, 165, 173, 174, 177, 190
Publications Control Board 18, 26–7, 32, 87, 92, 151, 170–1
publishers and publication 97–8
  Afrikaans 56–7, 60
  alternative 5–6, 53–4, 59–60, 61, 62–77, 80, 94, 96, 107, 114, 121, 143, 144, 209, 210
  British 58, 60
  independent *see* alternative
  mainstream 51, 54, 56, 59, 63, 96, 119
  mission 55–6, 64
  university 61–2

Rabie, Jan 23, 57, 160
Rabkin, Lily 57
Radio Bantu 30
Ramphele, Mamphela 67, 135
Randall, Peter 67, 69, 70, 71
Ravan Press 62, 69–70, 71–2, 73, 94, 115, 116, 117, 134, 166, 172, 173–5, 185, 198, 199, 204
readers and readerships 1–4, 97, 100–2, 210–11
  academic 87–8
  alternative 2–3, 5–6, 8, 19–20, 52, 76–8, 79, 94–5, 96–7, 98–100, 102–4, 105–7, 108–11, 112, 114–17, 119–30, 132–6, 137–43, 144–5, 154, 189, 204, 205–6, 208–9, 210, 211
  average 29, 38–9, 43, 46, 48, 49, 52, 146, 161–2, 164, 168
  black 33, 67–8, 69, 70–1, 80–3, 85, 99, 102–3, 137, 209
  ideal *see volks*
  liberal 20
  likely 25, 41, 42, 43–5, 46, 48, 49, 146, 153, 164, 172, 173, 175, 177, 178–9, 181, 182, 183, 186, 187–8, 189, 191, 192, 193, 194–5, 196–7, 198, 199, 201–3, 205
  volks 18–19, 20, 29, 36, 154, 162
Renoster Books (publisher) 76
resource centres 84, 86, 132
Rex Collings (publisher) 59, 79
A Ride on the Whirlwind (Sipho Sepamla) 44–5
Riverlea (Johannesburg) 122
Rivonia Treason Trial (1963–4) 111
Road to Ghana (Alfred Hutchinson) 108
The Road to Sharpeville (Bernard Sachs) 15
Robben Island 136, 180, 181
Rogers, Joel 102
Rollnick, Julian 64
Rook en Oker (Ingrid Jonker) 75
The Roots of Segregation (David Welsh) 65
Roux, Eddie 64

Sartre, Jean-Paul 102, 115
Sechaba 47

security police 171, 172
Segal, Ronald 30, 92
self-censorship 16, 88, 92-3, 94
Sensuur, literatuur en die leser (Charles Malan and Martjie Bosman) 149
Sepamla, Sipho 73
Seriti sa Sechaba Publishers 74, 209
Seroke, Jaki 42, 70, 73-4, 209
Serote, Mongani Wally 34, 76
Sestigers 22-3, 57-8
Seven Seas Books (publishers) 79, 80
Sharpeville massacre (1960) 24, 180
Shooting at Sharpeville (Ambrose Reeves) 14-15
Shuter & Shooter (publisher) 56
A Simple Lust (Dennis Brutus) 182
Sirens, Knuckles and Boots (Dennis Brutus) 178
Skotaville (publisher) 62, 73-4, 166, 209
Small, Adam 22, 57-8
Smit, Bartho 23, 57
Smith, Margaret 29
smuggled books *see* imported and smuggled books
Snyman, J.H. 37-8, 40
Sophiatown 154
The Soul of Black Folks (W.E.B. Du Bois) 103
South Africa: The Peasants' Revolt (Govan Mbeki) 110
South Africa: The Struggle for a Birthright (Mary Benson) 109
South African Broadcasting Corporation (SABC) 30
South African Communist Party (SACP) 148, 163
South African Council of Churches (SACC) 67
South African Institute of Race Relations (SAIRR) 64-5, 81
South African Library (Cape Town) 86, 106, 182, 183
South African Library Association (SALA) 85, 88
South African Library Conference (Bloemfontein, 1928) 82
South African literature 50-1
South African Public Library (Cape) 81
South African Students' Organisation (SASO) 33, 34, 66, 103, 104
Soweto Uprising (16 June 1976) 200
Sowing the Seeds of Revolution (Samora Machel) 109
Splendid Sunday (James Ambrose Brown) 109
Staffrider 70-1, 72, 99, 115-16, 184-99, 204
Staffrider series (Ravan Press) 70, 72, 199, 200, 202, 203, 204
Standpunte 57, 150
State Library (Pretoria) 86, 178
states of emergency (1960, 1985, 1986) 24, 43
statutes *see* Acts of Parliament
Steenkamp, S.S. 199-200, 201-4
The Stone Country (Alex La Guma) 148
Store up the Anger (Wessel Ebersohn) 46
street vendors (of publications) 115, 116

The Struggle is My Life (Nelson Mandela) 106
Stubborn Hope (Dennis Brutus) 180-1
Student Perspectives on South Africa (edited by H.W. van der Merwe and David Welsh) 65-6, 79
Study Project on Christianity in Apartheid Society (SPROCAS) 67, 69
Survey of Race Relations in South Africa (SAIRR) 64-5

Taurus (publisher) 36-7, 60, 75-6, 77, 78, 94
Teachers' League of South Africa 103
television 30
Tell Freedom (Peter Abrahams) 109
textbooks 55-6, 58, 59
'Their Behaviour' (Dennis Brutus) 179
Thema, R.V. Selope 82
Themba, Can 31, 115
Theron, A.M. 196, 201
Three Crowns series 59
Tiger Kloof Native Institution 81
The Times 92
Times Literary Supplement 92
Timol, Ahmed Essop 117
Tlali, Miriam 32, 73, 93
torture 13, 77
Traditional Market Agreement (1947) 60
Transvaal Episode (Harry Bloom) 109
Trewhela, Paul 29

The Unbroken Song (Es'kia Mphahlele) 167
United Nations Declaration of Human Rights 111
United States Consulate 114, 136
universities 85-6
University College of Fort Hare 81
University of Cape Town Press 62
University of Natal Press 62
University of South Africa Press 62
Upbeat 173

Die Vaderland 30
Van der Merwe Scholtz, E.H. 36, 152, 159, 167, 168, 182, 183, 191, 197
Van der Westhuizen, M.J. 181
Van Niekerk, A.J. 32
Van Rhyn, A.J.R. 15
Van Rooyen, J.C.W. 42, 46, 71, 146, 165, 184, 187-9, 190, 192, 195, 197
Van Schaik (Johannesburg bookshop) 113, 114
Van Wyk, A.J. 171
Van Wyk, Chris 71, 103, 110, 114, 117, 118-19, 122, 128, 134, 136
Van Wyk, J.T. 35
Van Wyk, P.J.B. 167
Van Wyk Louw, N.P. 21-2, 26, 56, 57, 75, 150, 151-2
Van Zyl, Danie 69
Van Zyl, Eddie 39-40, 164
Verwoerd, H.F. 57
The Voice 70
Vorster, John 16-17, 30, 41

A Walk in the Night (Alex La Guma) 14
Wallace, Marjorie 160
The Wanderers (Es'kia Mphahlele) 167
Welsh, David 87
Westra, Piet 89-90
When the Lion Feeds (Wilbur Smith) 158-9
Wiehahn, R. 194-5
Winifred Holtby Memorial Library (Soweto) 83
Witwatersrand University Press 62
Women in South Africa: From the Heart, an Anthology of Stories (Dinah Lefakane and Seageng Tsikang) 74
Work in Progress 105, 125-6

writers
   alternative 102
   black 31, 32-3, 34, 45, 51, 62, 72-4, 76, 79, 80, 143, 156, 199, 209, *see also* specific names and book titles
   feminist 74

Xuma, A.B. 81-2

Die ysterkoei moet sweet (Breyten Breytenbach) 156-7

Zeit-Gedichte (Dennis Brutus) 183
Zeph (character in *Down Second Avenue*) 174-5